NEXT YEAR
IN JERUSALEM

The author with her father, 1959.

NEXT YEAR
IN JERUSALEM

Everyday Life in
a Divided Land

DAPHNA GOLAN-AGNON

Translated by Janine Woolfson

THE NEW PRESS

NEW YORK
LONDON

Originally published as *Eifo Ani Bassipur Haze* by Keter Books
Published in the United States by The New Press, New York, 2005
Distributed by W. W. Norton & Company, Inc., New York

LIBRARY OF CONGRESS CATALOGING-IN-PUBLICATION DATA

Golan-Agnon, Daphna.
   [Eifo ani bassipur haze? English]
   Next year in Jerusalem: everyday life in a divided land / Daphna Golan-Agnon.
     p. cm.
   Includes bibliographical references.
   ISBN 1-56584-930-2 (hc.)
    1. Golan-Agnon, Daphna—Diaries. 2. Human rights workers—Jerusalem.
   3. Human rights movements—Israel. 4. Palestinian Arabs—Civil rights. 5. Peace
   movements—Israel. 6. Arab-Israeli conflict—1993— I. Title.

JC599.I68.G6413 2005
956.9405'4—dc22   2004060953

The New Press was established in 1990 as a not-for-profit alternative to the large,
commercial publishing houses currently dominating the book publishing industry.
The New Press operates in the public interest rather than for private gain, and is
committed to publishing, in innovative ways, works of educational, cultural, and
community value that are often deemed insufficiently profitable.

www.thenewpress.com

Composition by Westchester Book Composition

Printed in the United States of America

10 9 8 7 6 5 4 3 2 1

For Amotz, Gali, and Uri

CONTENTS

ACKNOWLEDGMENTS

I thank the many friends, students, and activists who helped me write this book, not all of whom are mentioned here by name.

I thank the interviewees, human rights activists who spent hours telling me about their concerns, questions, dilemmas, and actions. Not all of them are quoted in the book, but each and every one helped me better understand the society in which I live: Roni Talmor, Yuval Ginbar, Shirli Eran, Eitan Felner, Yael Stein, and Zehava Galon, who told me about their work in B'Tselem; Neta Ziv, Amos Gil, Bilhah Berg, and Tamar Peleg for their work in the Association of Civil Rights; Naama Carmi from Open Doors; Jeremy Milgrom from Rabbis for Human Rights; Hassan Jabareen and Orna Cohen from Adalah; Bassem Eid from the Palestinian Human Rights Monitoring Group; Yvonne Deutsch from Kol Haisha; Hanna Zohar from the Workers' Hotline; Hedva Radovanich from Physicians for Human Rights; Michael Warschawski (Mikado) from the Alternative Information Center; Leah Tzemel and Allegra Pacheco from the Public Committee Against Torture in Israel; Rela Mazali from New Profile; Sumaya Fahat-Nasser from the Jerusalem Center for Women; Andre Rosenthal and Dalya Kirstein from the

Hotline for the Defense of Individuals; Jeff Halper from the Israeli Committee Against House Demolition; and Danny Zeidman of Ir Shalem, who gave me an enormous amount of information about Jerusalem.

I also thank all the members of the organizations working to further human rights and peace. These organizations are described individually at the end of this book in order to enable readers to volunteer and make donations.

Thanks to my friends for bearing with me despite the ongoing confusion between writing and life. To Dafna Galya, whose weekly nighttime visits and conversations about the salads we should make were the most fruitful breaks I took during the writing. To Rachel Talshir for hundreds of hours spent talking—from girlhood discussions, when we were promised that things would be better here, to the times when it just got worse. Thank you, Andrea and Steve Peskoff, for friendship, food, music, and love. To Naama Zifroni and Micha Odenheimer, for nights of blessing the new moon. To Suad Amiry and Salim Tamari for friendship despite distances and checkpoints, and for reminding me that there is still a world outside of politics. Thank you, Rema Hammami, for trying to write and organize, and for having smoky visions with me—even if many of our efforts do not materialize in the difficult situation we all live in. Special thanks to Richard Johnson, who taught me about generosity and friendship beyond time and place. And many thanks to Shula Marks, who taught me much of what I know about research and teaching.

Thank you, Aaron Back, for friendship and dozens of conversations about human rights and what we can do here to effect change. The financial support of the Ford Foundation enabled me the time to research, think, and write; your friendship and belief in me helped me to continue searching for my voice, and made the writing of this book possible.

Thanks to the Minerva Center for Human Rights and the Harry S. Truman Institute for the Advancement of Peace for funding and support, and to Lisa Perlman and all the good people in these dual homes of mine at the Hebrew University of Jerusalem.

Thanks to the groups of researchers at the Institute for Research on Women and Gender at Stanford University, for a year of shared inquiry into questions and theories of feminist writing, and for suggesting that I write the book the way I talk.

I thank Eyal Erlich, Rana Nashashibi, Ziad Abbas, Adina and Uri Solomonowitz, Jabir Asaqla, and the late Hagar Rublev for shards of conversations about the "situation" that found their way into the book.

Thank you, Jack Persekian, for support throughout the long, agonizing process of thinking about the genre and format of the book: from diary through collection of letters to the present shape. Jack's optimism and determination to continue exhibiting contemporary art in Jerusalem, his dream of a city with a vibrant cultural and creative life, enables me to dream—even in these difficult times—of a different life in this city, where we live together in worlds so different.

Special thanks to Janine Woolfson, who translated the book with care, wit, love, and much enthusiasm.

Thanks to all the men and women—peace activists, human rights activists, feminists, social justice activists—who shared their thoughts with me and were my partners in activism, working to make this a better place.

I thank the students and especially the fellows of my

internship program at the Minerva Center for Human Rights, who shared their experiences of volunteering at human rights organizations with me—including fears, joys, disappointments, and the excitement of acting for change. I thank the organizations that train and supervise the human rights fellows, including those organizations that are not directly addressed in this book. They gave me strength through their commitment to making Israeli society more just and egalitarian.

I thank Devorah Manekin, Keren Segal, Pazit Fleisher, and Sarit Shmuel, my wonderful research assistants, who worked long hours, always gladly and in good spirits. They searched, asked, took an interest, and shared many happy moments through all the years of working together on the book.

My thanks to Stanley Cohen, for years of friendship, writing, and shared visions. We asked many of the questions that are raised in this book together, in the course of writing reports on torture in prisons, and in the years after. Together we wondered not why people are so busy seeing and feeling so much of the evil around them but why so many people around us don't.

I thank my late father, Meir Golan, who taught me not to believe everything I was taught. I thank my mother, Ofra Golan, who taught me that acting for social change begins with the question "Is this what I want for my children?"

Thank you, Amotz, Gali, and Uri—for your love and support during so many years of writing and documenting our lives.

Jerusalem, May 2004

INTRODUCTION:
ONLY YESTERDAY

As we sat around the table on New Year's Eve eating the traditional chicken soup, Hemdat, my father-in-law, read us excerpts from *Only Yesterday,* a story written by his father, Shai Agnon, the most influential figure in modern Hebrew literature.

Usually the serving of chicken soup is accompanied by proclamations—who wants theirs without noodles, or who especially loves onion, carrots, or zucchini. This time there was silence: we sat mesmerized by Hemdat's voice and the story of Isaac Kumer, who spent long years in the Diaspora longing for the Land of Israel. Hemdat paused to explain phrases to my children and their cousins and smiled in all the places where we, the adults, were not certain of the author's intentions. I listened to the old-fashioned language and watched Hemdat's smile, and I could feel Isaac Kumer's yearning for the Land of Israel. I remembered the stories told by my grandmother, who spent most of her childhood making the journey from Russia to the Land of Israel on foot. This is how Agnon begins:

Like all our brethren of the Second Aliya, the bearers of our Salvation, Isaac Kumer left his country and his homeland and his city and ascended to the Land of Israel to build it from its destruction and to be rebuilt by it. From the day our comrade Isaac knew his mind, not a day went by that he didn't think about it. A blessed dwelling place was his image of the whole Land of Israel and its inhabitants blessed by God. Its villages hidden in the shades of vineyards and olive groves, the fields enveloped in grains and the orchard trees crowned with fruit, the valleys yielding flowers and the forest trees swaying: the whole firmament is sky blue and all the houses are filled with rejoicing. By day they plow and sow and plant and reap and gather and pick, threatening and pressing wine, and at eventide they sit every man under his vines and under his fig trees, his wife and his sons and daughters sitting with him, happy at their work and rejoicing in their sitting. And they reminisce about the days of yore Outside the Land, like people who in happy times recall days of woe and enjoy the good twice over. A man of imagination was Isaac, what his heart desired, his imagination would conjure up for him.[1]

During the salad course, Hemdat read the parts of the story that describe Isaac Kumer's hardships once he reached the Land of Israel after years of anticipation, only to find himself facing poverty and starvation. I considered when to take the tofu casserole out of the oven and the carrots from the microwave and tried to remember who eats hot meat, who cold meat, and who no meat. I know that throughout the book, no matter what hardships he has to endure, Isaac Kumer is glad he came to the Land of Israel. I know too how much I love Israel, where I was born, where I live and raise my children. I tried, for just one night, to forget the fear, and to hope that this land will run with milk and honey one day, in reality and not just in our imaginations.

Agnon could not have dreamed that his great-grandchildren would not be allowed to take a bus for fear of being killed by a suicide bomber. I am scared. I am scared every morning when I send my children to school. I am scared when I go to work, trying to guess the safest way—driving through areas where there have been many suicide attacks, or through areas where no attacks have taken place. I ask myself where the next one will be.

Each year, on the new year, we wish with our family and friends that the next year will be better, and know that it will probably be worse. What future will we give our children? What hope?

Is this the Israel we have dreamed about? When you say "next year in Jerusalem" at the Passover Seder, is this the Jerusalem you yearn for? Can you help us begin to build our tomorrow? Can we hope for a better future here in Jerusalem?

NEXT YEAR
IN JERUSALEM

ONE

THE LAST CLASS AT
SUMMER SCHOOL

July 13, 1999

One especially hot summer day I took my summer school
students to see Zechariah and Jerash, two Palestinian villages that were destroyed in 1948, and the Deheishe refugee
camp, outside Bethlehem, where most of the inhabitants of
those two destroyed villages now live. We began at Mount
Scopus, taking the breathtaking tunnel road that enables settlers in the Hebron and Bethlehem region to reach Jerusalem
easily without having to go through Palestinian areas. We
passed Beit Sahur, near Bethlehem, a sleepy-looking, mostly
Christian town. In the early days of the First Intifada, Beit
Sahur became famous for a tax insurrection. The merchants
organized themselves and refused to pay Israeli taxes because, as Palestinians, they had no rights, and this gave them
a few moments of world renown. It sounded wonderful on
CNN: no taxation without representation. In reality, the
pharmacy that led the insurrection had all its drugs confiscated, and the pharmacist and other rebels spent months in
jail until they paid their tax under duress. The villagers of
Beit Sahur have been engaged in dialogue with the Israelis

for many years. Every year, before Christmas, this tradition culminates in hundreds of Israelis and Palestinians marching through the decorated streets of Beit Sahur.

After the second roadblock, inside Area A, our guide, Ziad Abass, was waiting for us. Two minutes later we passed through Area B, then through Area C and back into Israel, behind the Green Line—the 1967 border before Israel occupied the West Bank and Gaza Strip. All these lines and borders are imaginary and unmarked, both on the maps available in stores and in the field. Only the roadblocks and soldiers mark the transition from the West Bank into Israel. But Ziad, in his journey into his parents' past, before 1948, took us beyond these imaginary borders.

I was reminded of my own journey through KwaZulu in South Africa during the mid-1980s. The roads connecting parts of KwaZulu to white South Africa were also unmarked. There were no signs indicating the entrance to or exit from the Bantustan. All the water sources, factories, and well-paved roads were in white South Africa; the poverty, hunger, and anger were in KwaZulu, a state composed of forty-nine units and dozens more separated pieces of land. These areas of the West Bank—A, B, and C—were defined by the Oslo accords to grant incremental autonomy to the Palestinians. Area A is completely controlled by the Palestinian Authority, while Area B is ostensibly administered by Palestinians and controlled militarily by Israelis. Area C is controlled by Israel alone. Area C, which comprises more than 60 percent of the West Bank, is home to the Jewish settlers, some 250,000 of whom live scattered among more than two million Palestinians. This draft map, which was agreed upon in the Oslo negotiations, is very much like the map of the South African

Bantustans. The Palestinians call it the Swiss cheese map: "we got the holes," they say.

Ziad didn't appear troubled by the physical borders or those marked on the map. He held in his hand *All That Remains*, Walid Khalidi's book about the Palestinian villages occupied and depopulated by Israel in 1948, and, without opening it, pointed out the window at places that used to be Palestinian villages. The names sounded familiar, not because I'd heard them before, but because after 1948 the Jewish settlements established in their wake have retained similar names.

We passed Beitar, an ultra-Orthodox city built on land that was once Batir, and Netiv Halamed Hey, the kibbutz where my uncle Israel and his extended family live. I told Ziad the version that I know of the story behind the kibbutz's name, which in Hebrew means "the way of the thirty-five," in memory of the thirty-five Israeli soldiers who were killed near the Palestinian village of Dir Hassan on January 16, 1948. Many stories have been written about the thirty-five people who went to deliver weapons and medical supplies to four Jewish settlements that were under siege in a region populated mainly with Arab villages. Because all thirty-five were killed, their account has never been heard. Nevertheless, the story commonly accepted in Israel is that they met an old Arab shepherd and decided not to harm him. This shepherd (or, in another version, two elderly Arab women) alerted the Arab villagers, who killed the thirty-five young men. This became one of the best-known stories of heroism in Israeli mythology, and it is still part of the battle legacy passed down in the IDF. Several days after the incident, in January 1948, Yitzhak Sadeh, the commander of the elite Palmach fighting unit, wrote:

There is no doubt that an armed Arab force would not have done the same if it met a Jew along the way. It is well known how military people behave in similar circumstances. However, our soldiers not only have a fighting spirit, but also delicate souls and are extremely humane. This is because their war is for life and against death.[1]

I did not tell Ziad or the students about the pleasant Saturdays we spent at the kibbutz with Uncle Israel and Aunt Margalit, or about the blue swimming pool there that we still seek out on weekends and free days in the summer.

Instead we talked about the water shortage in the territories.

"The sound Palestinians miss most is the sound of a toilet flushing," Ziad told us. There's no water for plants, no water for a shower; there's enough water to drink, but not to flush the toilet. In 1999 the drought was particularly severe. Almost no rain fell during the winter. We Israelis talk about the water shortage, especially about the red line below which the level of the Sea of Galilee has dropped, but we barely feel the consequences. Our taps run freely. Hundreds of thousands of Palestinians, however, have no running water throughout the entire summer. There are approximately 180 villages in the West Bank that are not connected to the water system. Israel controls the water sources and divides them inequitably. The statistics don't show how many kilometers Palestinians in the Hebron region have to walk in order to get drinking water, and they don't show how green the grass is at nearby settlements. What they do indicate is that Israel's per capita water consumption is almost four times that of the Palestinians.[2]

Our first stop is at a small moshav (agricultural cooperative), Zechariah, a Jewish village established by immigrants from Yemen in 1951. Interspersed with the Jewish Agency houses that were built in the 1950s are large renovated houses of the second generation and the new houses of young couples who moved here from Jerusalem to breathe the fresh air and find respite from the crowded city. Only one house remains from pre-1948 Palestinian Zechariah, a kind of reminder of the village that was but is no longer. Next to it is the mosque: large, well built, but neglected and reeking. We all went inside the derelict mosque, littered with building debris, garbage, and a lot of dog feces. As we watched the two brave souls who decided to try out the steep stairs leading to the roof, Ziad said, "I'm not a religious person, but this place is sacred to Muslims." His eyes filled with longing for a world that no longer exists, and he told us about the dances that were held outside the mosque in the clearing where our bus was waiting, and about the people who came home from work in those days and shared their food with one another. "That was before the catastrophe," he says. Before *al naqba*—the expression Palestinians use to refer to the war leading up to Israeli statehood. I'd never heard this word used so many times. Every time he repeated it something contracted within me. *The catastrophe. The catastrophe. The catastrophe.* In my home, the 1948 war was the War of Independence. There was no catastrophe involved except for the six thousand people, 1 percent of the Jewish population, who were killed. I've never heard how many Palestinians were killed in that war. In the 1980s, Israeli "new historians," to much controversy, began to revise the Israeli myths and the official history of the state's founding, and to document Israel's role in expelling, frightening, or encouraging Palestinians to leave their homes, not allowing them to return, destroying their villages, and causing them to live as refugees in camps in the West Bank and the Gaza Strip or in other communities. In my own family, the day the State of Israel was declared is remembered as the most joyful of days, and my mother described that evening, with everyone out dancing in the streets, to me many times over.

"My father was born in this village, in Zechariah," Ziad said. His house had been over where the kindergarten is now. His mother grew up in the village of Jerash, a few kilometers from here. Ziad's father worked in the fields of the Italian mission station at Beit Jamal two days a week. It was there he met Ziad's mother, who rode over on a horse to grind wheat at the mission's mill.

After the visit to Zechariah we continued on to Beit Jamal. An elderly monk told us the history of the church, which was built in the fifteenth century, about the education and medical services that the mission offered to the region's inhabitants, the renovation in the 1930s, and the beautiful stained-glass windows. Nothing in his story recalled the political transitions in the region: the change of sovereignty, the establishment of the State of Israel, the eviction of thousands of Palestinians from the surrounding villages, and the establishment of the nearby Israeli town of Beit Shemesh.

At noon the bus driver dropped us off by the roadside, and we started to climb the hill to the village of Jerash. It was terribly hot, the oppressive heat of a midday in July. The scenery around us was yellower than usual because of the recent drought. I thought about the name of nearby Beit Shemesh (House of the Sun), as if this entire valley was indeed home to the powerful sun. The ascent was hard for the students and for me. Every few minutes I asked them to stop and drink some water, afraid they would dehydrate. The sparse signage along the way told us, in Hebrew, that we were in an area protected by the Nature Reserves Authority.

When we reached the top of the hill one of the students asked, "Where's the village?" Ziad pointed to the cairns of stones surrounding us. "This is my mother's village, Jerash. Breathe the wonderful air, look at the view," he said as we sat down under a large almond tree. "When I open the window of my house in the refugee camp the only thing I can see is the wall of my neighbor's house." Ziad pointed to a pile of rocks between a fig tree and a carob tree and told us it was where his mother's house had stood. In the valley below us, between the pine trees planted by the Jewish National Fund, lay Beit Shemesh.

On the way back to the bus the students began to complain. They had come to a summer course at the Hebrew University to enjoy themselves. Most of them were American Jews who had already visited Israel several times before. In the two weeks of this intensive course they had heard all about the demolition of homes and the torture and administrative detention of Palestinians. Our previous trip had been to the settlements around Jerusalem, and we had traveled on the wide roads built for the settlers—roads built to bypass Palestinians. They had also taken the winding and difficult road that Palestinians must use to get from the northern West Bank to the southern West Bank, from Ramallah to Bethlehem, a road that bypasses Jerusalem because Palestinians do not have permits to enter the city. This was the last day of the summer course, and they were incapable of hearing any more.

It was hot, terribly hot, and they did not understand the point of going to see a village that no longer existed.

Later, as we sat in the community center of the Deheishe refugee camp, one of the students burst out: "You only show us one side of the story!"

"This is not reality," added another student.

Neither of them was angry with Ziad. They didn't question him about his memories, his pain, or his hopes. They were angry with me. I had made them meet him, hear his parents' story, see the refugee camp where he grew up and still lives. They were angry because I had not helped them to digest all this new information, this reality that they had not known about before, which they did not necessarily want to know.

The room we were in was decorated with embroidered fabrics. Fifteen new computers, wrapped in plastic, waited on tables against the wall. The voices of the young people in the room upstairs seemed to indicate that they were having a good time at this community center in the refugee camp.

Ziad gave us a short lecture about the camp: eleven thousand people in one square kilometer, with 30 percent unemployment. One school for girls and one for boys, run by UNRWA, the United Nations Relief and Works Agency for Palestinian Refugees. One part-time doctor for the entire camp. Most of those who fled from Zechariah and Jerash in 1948 still live in the Deheishe refugee camp. Many others live in Jordan.[3]

The students did not ask Ziad many questions. It was hot, it was late, and we were all tired. They liked him, though: his sense of humor, the way he told his parents' story, and how he took care of them in the restaurant we stopped at for lunch.

Because this was the end of the course it was, in effect,

our farewell party. But a happy party it was not. "Why didn't you show us the other side?" Rebecca asked accusingly.

"Why didn't you invite an Israeli officer to explain why the refugee camp was put under curfew? Why were the Palestinian universities and schools closed for years during the Intifada? You didn't explain. And why are these people living in a refugee camp at all?" asked David. "Why do they insist on living here? Why don't they go and live in one of the seventeen Arab states?"

Ziad had just finished telling them about his childhood in the refugee camp surrounded by a high fence, guarded by two posts of soldiers. When he was a boy, Ziad told us, he and his friends would throw stones at the Israeli cars that drove by. "We were in a cage," he said, "and we saw the Israeli cars driving so freely down the road. The schools were closed, there were no playgrounds in Deheishe, and we wanted to hurt them. But it was also a children's game."

One of the moments that most moved me was when Ziad told us how his mother would wrap "forbidden" books in plastic and hide them under the bed.

In the final discussion one of the students angrily argued, "If Israelis forbid Palestinians to read certain books, there must be a good reason. What is that reason?"

Exhausted by the long day, the heat, two weeks of intensive and frustrating teaching, and the anger directed toward me, I rose to answer.

"I don't care about the reason for burning books, or detaining those who read them. There are things that should not be done. There are things that you don't do, no matter what the reason. You don't burn books and you don't detain people just for reading books. That's what I believe as a Jew."

The title of the course was "The International Language of Human Rights and Its Implementation in the Israeli-Palestinian Conflict." I had presented them with the international norms of human rights by studying the Universal Declaration of 1948, the International Covenant on Civil and Political Rights, the International Covenant on Social, Economic, and Cultural Rights, and the international laws of human rights in wartime. I had spoken with them about the shared universal values of human dignity. But when I could no longer bear the anger and pain, I spoke with them about how we, as Jews, cannot burn books.

I made no reference to the Fourth Geneva Convention, which we had studied thoroughly in class. I did not examine the rights of "protected people" according to international humanitarian law. I just repeated, in a voice that cracked a little, that as Jews we are supposed to know that burning books is illegitimate.

If human rights are universal and the moral source of our behavior, why did I speak to them about the Jewish people and our commitment to justice? Why, after a protracted course in universal human rights values, did I need to invoke our historical memory as Jews in order to say that there are some things that are unacceptable?

During the course we'd read the Geneva Convention together and been shown a film by the International Committee of the Red Cross (ICRC) about how it tries to protect human dignity during wartime. The ICRC gave us white books containing the Geneva Convention that specified, among other things, the rights of people living under occupation. The International Red Cross distributes these books just as missionaries once distributed the New Testament. "This is our bible," they mean to say, as they show films and give lectures accompanied by perfectly organized slides. "This is the new covenant between the nations: these are the laws we have agreed upon that will ensure basic dignity for every human being even in the terrible days of war. Even in these times we have to protect the human image."

But the students did not see Ziad and his mother with her plastic-wrapped books in the formulations of the Geneva Convention. The ICRC people and I taught them a wealth of laws pertaining to protection of people during wartime, but here there was no war under way. In comparison with what their televisions showed them was going on in Bosnia, the refugee camp seemed a fine place to these students, and Ziad did not appear to be a victim.

I had not managed to connect—either for the students or for myself—the principles with the reality; I had not managed to connect the international conventions of human rights with the sight of the neglected mosque, the refugee camp, and the pain in my gut every time Ziad said the word *catastrophe*.

January 2001

Prime Minister Ehud Barak looked straight at me from the television screen and said that we would never recognize the Palestinian Right of Return. With festive decor behind him, and with his gaze, which just avoided being caught, he seemed serious but perhaps also a little comical. After all, less than two years earlier he had said with the same deep seriousness that united Jerusalem would remain the capital of Israel for all time. Before elections you could say anything, people told me, and I couldn't understand if he really thought we'd never recognize the Right of Return of the Palestinian refugees or whether it was just until after the elections.

What is the issue with the Right of Return? Why is it so obvious, according to Israeli conventional wisdom, that "we can't live with the Right of Return"? After we've already understood that the Palestinians' dreams of Jerusalem cannot be ignored, perhaps it's time to stop talking this way, refusing to recognize the Right to Return?

Have you noticed that there is a Law of Return for Jews only, while any mention of the Palestinian Right of Return is taboo? Even the words we use are different. The Law of Return stipulates that any Jew in the world can immigrate to Israel and become a citizen with preferential rights. The word used for return in this case, *shvut*, sounds biblical, and is closer in meaning to "resettle," to remind us that Israel is the land of the Jewish people. For the Palestinian return, we say *shiva* ("return")—that is, if we talk about it. Most Israelis, when asked, will say, "There is nothing to talk about. We don't want four million Palestinians coming back to live here."

The evening after Barak looked at me from his election campaign broadcast I called Suad Amiry to see how she was doing. It had been a long time since we'd spoken and even longer since we'd met, because somehow Ramallah—only ten miles from Jerusalem—had seemed beyond the pale to me recently. I wanted to ask how she was and how things were with the new intifada.

"Let's meet," she said to me. "Let's try to understand what's going on here. I have a feeling that we don't understand what they're agreeing to in all their talks, and I want to hear what you think." After we agreed to meet on Friday at Rema Hammami's house, Suad added, "I know how sometimes one has to be alone and sometimes together. You called just on time. Rema and I want to meet and talk; we worry that perhaps we're so insistent about the Right of Return that we're conceding the presence of too many settlements."

Suad had lost eight kilograms since we last saw each other, and she was beautiful, as always. I decided for the thousandth time to go on a diet. Dr. Rema Hammami teaches at Birzeit University near Ramallah but lives in Jerusalem in a big arched house with a giant library of books and DVDs. The hours we've spent there eating haven't helped anyone's figure.

Suad told me about an Israeli-Palestinian encounter that she participated in many years ago in the United States. One of the work groups had discussed the Right of Return. Suddenly, after days of tranquil sessions, she had become irritable; she had begun to cry and could not speak. Telling me this, sitting on the beautiful white sofa, the blue walls lined with books behind her, she laughed and cried at the same time. "I don't know what's wrong with me," she said, and got up to get a tissue. "I can't talk about this without my eyes filling with tears."

Calmer, she resumed. "At the same session, one of the Israelis asked me, 'What do you want, Suad? What do you want? Do you want us to say that Israel was born in sin?'"

"So?" she said to me. "Does a child born in sin not deserve love?" and she clenched her beautiful long fingers as she continued to talk about the love that even a child born in sin deserves. "Don't you send him to school? Take care of him? Doesn't he deserve to have happiness? What do you think, Daphna, can Israelis not say, 'We're sorry, we did you wrong,' because they're afraid that five million Palestinians will come to Israel? And if they knew that not everyone would come back, if they knew that only half a million would come back, would they then be able to say 'We're sorry'?"

"I think so. I'm not sure, but I think it would be possible to persuade most Israelis to recognize the wrong done to the Palestinians if they were not afraid of the return of millions of Palestinians. It could be formulated so that everyone is satisfied. Israel could say, 'We had no choice, but we're sorry for causing you so much pain when we established the state and expelled hundreds of thousands of people from their homes and lands,' and then an international court could decide who among the Palestinian refugees is eligible to return to their own homes and lands, who returns to the future independent Palestinian state, who gets compensation, and who receives help settling in another country."

I decided to talk with Israeli friends in order to obtain a deeper understanding of why it's so hard for us to apologize, and in the meantime Suad, Rema, and I resolved to study the subject of the settlements together and visit those near Jerusalem in order to better understand which of them Israel might conceivably agree to forgo. When I came back from the car with my map of the city—with the smiling face of our right-wing mayor, Ehud Olmert, who had himself done so much to build settlements in Jerusalem, on its cover—Rema made more coffee and took out her book of the agreement maps, and Suad asked us to consider the demographic argument. "It's an argument that Meron Benvenisti presented in *Ha'aretz* a few weeks ago," she said, and I was struck yet again by how many Palestinians avidly read the English version of the Israeli *Ha'aretz*. "In any case," she said, trying to reconstruct Benvenisti's argument, "today there are more than one million Palestinians who are citizens of Israel because they remained within the boundaries of the state after its founding in 1948. They are 20 percent of Israelis, and we all know that in ten years that proportion of the population will grow." Suad calculated how quickly the return of tens of thousands of Palestinians would accelerate this demographic process, and I asked myself what will happen here in another fifty years, and what will we be leaving to our children.

I remember the first time I met Suad. It was in Belgium in 1992, at a time when it was illegal for Israelis to be in contact with Palestinians who were identified with the Palestine Liberation Organization (PLO), and because all Palestinians who wanted a peace agreement were identified with the PLO, it was impossible to meet. The law, however, permitted interactions at academic conferences, and thus our meetings took place under the aegis of an American or European university abroad.

In the evening, after we'd finished an exhausting discussion of one or another question relating to the occupation, we all went out to eat gelato—some forty Israelis and Palestinians. I remember her sitting there with the big brightly lit window of the ice cream store behind her, her large green eyes laughing as she told me that every three months she needed to leave the West Bank and travel to Jordan to request an entry permit in order to return home to be with her husband in Ramallah. This was, of course, not the first time I had heard that Palestinian women from Jordan who had married residents of the West Bank were not granted residence permits. At the beginning of the 1990s, the army used to appear in the night, collect the men in the center of the village, and go through the houses checking the women's residence permits. Women who had not extended their residence permits and children who were not registered as residents of the Occupied Territories were loaded onto a vehicle and transported to the bridge, where they were deported into Jordan.

Suad told her story not with anger but instead with a great deal of humor. I could imagine her as a student, and later a married woman, standing in line waiting for a permit to return to her husband. Dr. Suad Amiry is an architect who specializes in the preservation and restoration of buildings. She manages RIWAQ, the Centre for Architectural Conservation, which is located in Ramallah. Their goal is to preserve Palestinian houses and neighborhoods of historical and architectural value. Years after that first meeting, after the signing of the Oslo accords, when we could finally meet in Jerusalem, we sat in the courtyard of the American Colony Hotel and drank freshly squeezed orange juice. Suad was excited. She had just returned from a visit to a nearby house, which she had been asked to assess for renovation and preservation.

"This house is now the consulate of one of the European countries, and when I was invited, they warned me to ignore an old crazy neighbor who lives next door. When I went into the yard," Suad said, "the old woman asked me, 'Are you Siham's daughter?'

" 'Yes,' I answered.

" 'Poor thing, she only had daughters and no sons. Did Allah give Siham a son in the end?'

" 'Yes,' I reassured her, 'Allah gave her a son, and today he is fifty-something years old.'

" 'Thank God,' she said with relief.

"That," Suad explained, "used to be my parents' house."

That meeting at the American Colony seems so far away now. Suad, like other Palestinians who do not live in Jerusalem, does not have a permit to enter the city. This is why our meetings at Rema's in Jerusalem—which Suad came to anyway, without a permit—were so rare. I used to visit her in Ramallah; now I'm afraid.[4]

I told Rema and Suad about my work at the Ministry of Education and thought out loud about how the argument over the Right of Return is related to what I'm learning there about the attitude to Palestinian citizens of Israel. I thought about the attacks against the Ministry and the subsequent prohibition of a textbook that dared to challenge the conventional narrative of twentieth-century Jewish history, presenting not just the Jewish people's tortured journey to an empty land (as I learned as a child) but a story with a little more complexity. When I was a high school student the 1948 war had no other side, there were no Palestinian refugees, and there was certainly no public debate over the history books. I tried to see the very existence of this discussion—of a topic that has for years been completely erased from the public memory—as a positive development.

Several months earlier, I had been invited by Zvulun Orlev, the chair of the Knesset Education Committee, to discuss a position paper I had written for the Ministry of Education on the subject of education toward peace. He was angry at what I had written, and I asked him what exactly was troubling him. In one of the lessons, the position paper proposed holding educational tours of the "uprooted" localities for teachers. The word *uprooted* bothered him. "It's one thing," he told me "if you're referring to those who were removed from Ikrit and Baram," two Christian Palestinian villages whose residents were evacuated from their homes in 1948. "The court has already ruled that they were uprooted. But I don't want that word to be used in reference to people who live in other villages."

"What would you like them to be called?" I asked him. "If you change the word, will it change the fact that they were uprooted? If we change the words, will the problem disappear?"

Rema, Suad, and I talked about attempts to prohibit the use of history books and the public condemnation of the new historians, while I tried to convince myself that these were signs that the struggle for memory had not been silenced.

I told them about my childhood memories of trips to the beach, with suntan lotion and lots of fruit. The beach was called Tantura then, and we could see the remains of some Palestinian houses that used to be part of the village of that name, which was destroyed and depopulated. Now the beach is called Dor, like the kibbutz that was established on the ruins of Tantura. One recent summer—on holiday with my family and those of my brother and sister—we sat on the beach as our children played in the water, and I asked them when we had stopped calling this beach Tantura. They gave me a look that said, *She's going to ruin our holiday with her politics again,* and did not answer.

The landscape of my childhood and adolescence still had many Arabic names, which are slowly disappearing. When I was a soldier, I used to hitchhike to my home in Beer Sheva from the Masmiyya and Qastina junctions. Both now have new Hebrew names.

The erasure of the past also influences the attitude toward Palestinian Israelis or Arab Israelis in the present. In my work at the Ministry of Education I feel their present absence all the time. Not only are we educated to forget that Palestinians lived here and were deported when the state was established, but those Palestinians who did stay and became a minority among us are seen mainly as a threat to the Jewishness of the state. Although the education systems for Hebrew-speaking and Arabic-speaking children are separate, in towns with mixed Jewish-Palestinian populations, such as Jaffa, Ramle, and Lod, there are kindergartens with a high proportion of Palestinian Israeli students, although the teachers are Jewish and the schools classified as Jewish. We held an in-service training course in order to enable the Jewish teachers to get to know the Muslim and Christian festivals, which they would then teach in the kindergartens. "And what will happen to *our* children?" one of the teachers, whose kindergarten has ten Arab students and ten Jewish students, asked.

"Are the Arab children in the kindergarten not our children?" the facilitator replied.

I wonder every day whether the education system within which I work considers Israeli-Palestinian children "our children." Almost a quarter of elementary school children in Israel are Palestinians—24 percent, to be precise. They are discriminated against in various ways: their classes are more crowded, the equipment older, the budgetary investment smaller, curricula more out of date. The daily encounter with this exasperating discrimination makes it difficult for me to believe that the Israeli establishment would be willing to absorb tens or hundreds of thousands more Palestinians and treat them as equals.

Before the Second Intifada began and before we all talked about the Right of Return, and not long after I returned with my students from visiting villages that are no longer there, I interviewed Dr. Salim Tamari about the refugees. Salim is Suad's husband, and during the negotiations in Madrid in 1991 and 1992, he was the head of the refugee delegation. To-day he is the director of the Institute for Jerusalem Studies. He recently edited a book on Jerusalem in 1948 in which, among other things, he discusses the refugees who were chased or who fled from the city. In contrast to places such as Jaffa, where Salim was born, the refugees from Jerusalem remained in the region. In 1967 Palestinians were evacuated from the Jewish quarter in Jerusalem, and an entire residential area was razed in order to make space for the Western Wall plaza.

Salim's office in the East Jerusalem neighborhood of Sheikh Jarrah is a five-minute walk from my office at the Hebrew University. Still, when I visit him I feel that I have entered another world. When I invited him for lunch at the Meirsdorff Faculty Club on Mount Scopus, in the two minutes we spent together in the car we talked about the crossing of borders and the vast distance between our worlds. I asked him about the Palestinian boycott of Israeli universities, and he laughed and asked if I minded being seen with him on my campus. In the cafeteria on Mount Scopus, I asked what would happen with the refugees and how he envisioned the solution.

SALIM: Are you asking what the best outcome from my point of view is, or what I think will almost certainly happen?

DAPHNA: What will happen is my second question. First tell me what you'd like to see happen.

SALIM: I think the ideal solution is one in which the refugees have the right to express their wishes: where they want to live; whether they want their houses back, or to stay where they are and receive compensation, or to receive Palestinian citizenship and do whatever they want with it. That would be the ideal solution.

DAPHNA: And then let's say they want to come.

SALIM: And then everyone lives happily ever after.

DAPHNA: And let's say everyone wants to return to their houses in Jerusalem.

SALIM: Some will, but it's not at all likely that everyone will.

DAPHNA: But what will happen to those who want to return to their houses?

SALIM: There are two options: either they will be compensated for the value of the houses, and then they can build wherever they live or in other parts of Jerusalem, where possible, or they can buy their houses back with the compensation money. The second option would be like what was done in the Jewish quarter, namely, asking people to

leave and paying the Jewish residents compensation for
their houses.

DAPHNA: What was done in the Jewish quarter?

SALIM: The Arab residents were evicted from the city.

DAPHNA: That happened everywhere, in Jaffa too.

SALIM: No, the Jewish quarter was evacuated in peacetime,
not during war. They offered the people compensation,
very low sums. The residents refused, and almost no one
accepted the compensation. Some people refused to
leave; then they were removed by force. Jews lived in the
Jewish quarter before 1948, but ownership was not entirely Jewish.

DAPHNA: The owners of the houses weren't Jewish?

SALIM: Not all of them. Sixty percent of the houses in the
Jewish quarter belonged to Christians and Muslims.
And in any case the people who entered these houses are
not the original owners, except for one family. Mostly
poor people lived there. Most of the people who live in
the Jewish quarter today are rich.

Before 1948, Salim continued, Jerusalem was a much
more heterogeneous city. Muslims even lived in the Jewish
Orthodox neighborhood of Mea Shearim. I asked him
whether the negotiations in Madrid addressed compensation
for houses that no longer exist. I told Salim that my father
also became a refugee in 1948, when Jordan confiscated the
houses at Kalya, next to the Dead Sea. Salim laughed and
promised me that when all the refugees are compensated he
would not forget me. However, he went on, unlike the refugees
from Jerusalem who remained in the area, the refugees from

other regions are scattered all over the world and will doubt-
less find it harder to return.

SALIM: I think that compensation with symbolic recognition
would be the solution. There will be a certain number of
people—a hundred thousand, fifty thousand, seventy
thousand—who will return to Israel itself, and the rest
will be compensated for their property.

DAPHNA: How will it be decided who will return?

SALIM: One way to do it is to find out who wants to return.
You'd be surprised by the number of Palestinians who
won't want to return. And then add a quota or lottery for
those who do want to.

DAPHNA: And when they return?

SALIM: They'll become Israeli citizens and in any event be
subject to the law of the state. They'll live in the Negev,
the Galilee, in mixed cities. We're not talking about the
people who left in 1948. We're talking about their rela-
tives, their descendants.

DAPHNA: But why would they want to live in other places in
Israel—in the Negev?

SALIM: Because they live in miserable camps in Lebanon and
the Lebanese don't want them there. Look at Lebanon, a
once serene country, swamped with refugees. Why should
they pay the price of the refugee problem? Today there are
350,000 refugees in Lebanon. The Lebanese already gave
citizenship to 100,000, Israel will take another 100,000,
and the rest will go to the West Bank or Gaza or a third
country. Israel has to recognize its responsibility.

DAPHNA: Do you think this could happen?

SALIM: What do you think?

DAPHNA: I don't know. What about your house in Jaffa? Have you been there?

SALIM: Of course. A third of it belongs to me.

DAPHNA: And if you could move there?

SALIM: I'd be glad to live there in the winter, but I couldn't bear to spend the hot summer there.

TWO

THE DANCE FOR JERUSALEM

The Eve of Passover, March 1999

Last week we went to see Gali, my daughter, dance in an annual performance staged by youth dance troupes in Jerusalem. The Gerard Bachar Theater was filled with hundreds of parents and children. They watched hip-hop, Spanish, and Moroccan dances, but the dance that got the most applause was called "The Conquest of Jerusalem." Ten-year-old children dressed in olive vests danced to the strains of the song "Ammunition Hill," throwing imaginary grenades in a simulated gun battle. As a child, I loved this famous song, which tells the story of the heroic soldiers who fought to conquer East Jerusalem. When the audience applauded enthusiastically the music changed and the young dancers took a bow to a peace song in Hebrew and Arabic: "Shalom—Salaam." The audience was still applauding when my son, Uri, and I went to look for Gali in the dancers' gallery. "Who would think up such a dance?" I asked on the way out, and Gali said to me sadly: "Why do you have to take your politics with you everywhere you go?"

Every year on Jerusalem Day my children are asked to

wear white shirts. The schools are filled with pictures of the Old City and the Western Wall, and the children go on tours of the city to celebrate its reunification. Jerusalem has celebrated this imaginary unification every year since 1967. Millions of people have yearned for Jerusalem for hundreds of years, and we have added this celebration of conquest and victory. All the applause and parade songs are accompanied by words about peace. All of us Israelis talk about peace. But we celebrate in a poor city, a city where ten thousand inhabitants don't have the right to see a doctor, a city where you can order pizza in the west but not in the east, a city closed to almost all Palestinians, a city where the municipal parking lot has no signs in Arabic, the language spoken by 30 percent of its inhabitants. Imagine if all the roads in the city you live in were guarded by armed soldiers, and everyone who entered was required to show an identity card. If you have a blue identity card, you're allowed in. If your ID is orange, you're stopped. If your license plate is yellow, the soldiers at the checkpoints let you through. Cars with blue license plates are turned back. Now imagine you work in the city and live in one of the suburbs; let's say you're a doctor at a large hospital in the city. In order to get to work you have to wait in line at a military base to receive an entry permit. Sometimes, after hours of anticipation spent in line, you receive a three-month permit. This permit enables you to pass through the checkpoints, but not in your own car. Your car doesn't have a yellow license plate, because you're a Palestinian.

I know this is not how we think of Jerusalem, but this is the city I live in. This is the city where I am raising my children. Like other Israelis, my life is unaffected by the closures, the checkpoints, the lines at nearby military bases. Soldiers at checkpoints never stop me.

Since 1991, on regular days, the closure prevents 96 percent of Palestinians from entering Jerusalem, which is also their cultural, political, and economic center. The severity of the closure depends on political circumstances, or sometimes on our festival calendar. This closure, I am told, is meant to protect me.

Before the 1967 war Israeli Jerusalem was a small town. After the war, Israel annexed 70 square kilometers to the area of West Jerusalem. In addition to East Jerusalem (some 6 square kilometers) Israel annexed twenty-eight Palestinian villages and parts of Bethlehem and Beit Jallah. Jerusalem tripled its size and became the biggest city in Israel. More than two hundred thousand Jews moved into the new "neighborhoods," as we Israelis call them—the new settlements built in the areas annexed after the war.

Close to 30 percent of Jerusalem's residents, some 210,000 Palestinians, are perceived mainly as a "demographic problem" that threatens the Jewish majority in the city. The closure is just one of the "bureaucratic measures" we take in order to "protect the city." Other measures include the expropriation of Palestinian land for Jewish-only building and the inadequate provision of services.[1] Palestinian residents of Jerusalem were given the choice to declare their loyalty to Israel and hence become Israeli citizens with full rights. Very few of them did. The majority of Palestinians receive "temporary residence" status. This means that they hold blue identity cards, as Israelis do, and they can move in and out of Jerusalem, but their identity cards can be revoked. Since

1996, it has been state policy to withhold identity documents from Palestinian residents of Jerusalem when possible. This means that Palestinians who travel out of Jerusalem for study or work, or those who have another passport, lose their right to live in Jerusalem. All these measures are meant to encourage Palestinians to leave. Like the blacks in South Africa during apartheid, the Arab inhabitants of Jerusalem live as foreigners in their own city.

I was ten in 1967. I remember sitting beside the big radio that told us that "Jerusalem is in our hands" and "Jerusalem has been liberated." I had never seen my father so happy. That was the only time in my life I saw him cry. He went up to an overhead storage space and pulled down all sorts of things I knew were connected with the fight for Jerusalem in 1948, items from prison that my father had kept all those years.

My father had been one of the leading commanders in the Jewish underground movement that fought to end the British mandate in Palestine. In the years before the 1948 war, there were three main Jewish underground groups fighting the British. My father's group, the Lehi (the Hebrew acronym for Freedom Fighters of Israel), also known as the Stern Gang, after Avraham "Yair" Stern, their leader, was the most radical of the groups, choosing to use arms against British soldiers and bureaucrats. In 1947 the British sentenced my father to ten years in prison for attempting to blow up a British munitions train. The prison where he was held, from which he and twelve other underground fighters escaped, still stands as a museum in the center of Jerusalem. The tale of his escape from prison was my favorite story as a child. He would tell it over and over, even though he was not much of a talker. But he believed all his life that Jerusalem is ours, just as "Greater Israel"—from the Nile in Egypt to the Hiddekel (Tigris) on the border of Iraq—is the promised land of the Jewish people. His views were of the extreme right, and he supported Meir Kahane's line that Arabs have no room in this Jewish land. I remember wondering, as a child, why my gentle father read the bulletins that arrived in the mail from Kahane's Kach movement, which was later declared to be a terrorist organization by the Israeli cabinet.

When I was a child I loved going with my father to Yair Stern's memorial service every year. This memorial service for Stern, who was murdered by the British in 1943, became an annual meeting of people who had lost their dream. We would meet his friends from the Lehi, and the ceremony would end with the singing of their anthem: *Unknown soldiers, we come without uniforms, with terror and darkness around us. Recruits for life we all are, from our ranks only death can dismiss us.* Some of the Lehi people were radical leftists; others were radical right-wingers. They all saw themselves as fighting against colonialism, but the difference between the two sides became clearer with the years. While some saw their struggle as that of the natives, both Arabs and Jews, against foreign domination, the right wing was concerned only for the rights of the Jews.

A few months after the 1967 war, my father took me to Jerusalem. We went up on the roof of the Notre Dame Hotel, and he showed me where he had fought in 1948. The Notre Dame, opposite the New Gate in the walls of the Old City, was the tallest building in the area; from the roof it was possible to see the entire city and control two of the gates leading through the old walls. He told me about his friends who had been killed or wounded on this roof. Down the road, he showed me where Haganah forces—the first Jewish militia—attempted to blow a hole in the ancient walls and enter the city; their bomb, however, did not explode.

As we stood on the roof of the Notre Dame a few months after the 1967 "liberation," or conquest, of East Jerusalem, strands of the barbed wire that had separated the eastern and western sides of the city for nineteen years were still clearly visible. It seemed to me that the barbed wire fences of the border had been moved so that my father's dream of a liberated and unified Jerusalem could come true.

I remember the excitement of first visiting the Old City that day in 1967. Everything was new, full, and so colorful. The Arab stalls sold nice pens that looked like umbrellas, but I was told it wasn't safe to buy them, that they exploded when you wrote with them. My father was filled with joy. I hadn't known that he spoke Arabic until he bought us *tamarindi*—and he was so happy to be reacquainted with that taste from his youth that I drank every last drop even though the juice was too sweet.

On our next visit to Jerusalem, we went to visit friends in Beit Hashiva. Seven Jewish families had settled in the heart of the Palestinian Shuafat neighborhood in East Jerusalem, far removed from any Jewish neighborhood. Since then hundreds of Jewish families have moved into houses in the heart of Palestinian neighborhoods, houses that used to be Jewish-owned, or Palestinian houses whose inhabitants had agreed to sell. Some bought the houses; others just occupied them, expelling the Palestinian inhabitants or making their lives so miserable that they had no choice but to leave. The windows on these houses were always protected with bars or barbed wire, and soldiers guarded the area. An Israeli flag would be raised right there in the middle of a Palestinian neighborhood.

Beit Hashiva (the House of Seven) was a large house with enormous windows and decorated floors. It seemed amazingly beautiful to me. Its walls were filled with books. I remember sitting in the big bathroom and looking at a bidet for the first time in my life. My parents tried to explain what it was used for. "Rich Arabs import bidets from France," they told me, and I never asked myself who they were, these rich Arabs who brought bidets from France, whether their children used the bidet, and where they had gone. I remember the admiration I felt for these heroic families living in the middle of an Arab neighborhood, and how they said they couldn't even buy bread nearby.

It has been more than twenty years since my father died, and my Jerusalem will always be tied to him. The Jerusalem of my childhood in Beer Sheva, the Jerusalem of gold, was the Jerusalem of heroic stories. As a child, my strongest image of Jerusalem was of a besieged city, a city without water.

My mother and I would spend hours in the kitchen over stories of days gone by. I would sit beside the table as my mother washed dishes. She'd rinse a plate and turn off the faucet, rinse another and turn off the faucet again. Her hands moved fast, and she never stopped opening and closing the faucet as she talked to me at the same time. The saving of water was never connected in my mind with the aridity of the Beer Sheva area, but rather with Jerusalem. My mother had not been in Jerusalem during the siege, but she told me dozens of stories about the ways that people had saved water in Jerusalem during the 1948 war on the city.

My mother always told these stories with a bit of a wink, as if to say, *Look how good we have it now, and how hard it was then.* My mother is always optimistic: she was born in Tel Aviv. Trips to Tel Aviv with her were a celebration of family and food—lots of family, and lots of food, and long, long talks. I still wash dishes like she does, and love Tel Aviv like she does—but I live in Jerusalem.

Several weeks after my father died, in October 1978, I moved to Jerusalem to begin studying at the Hebrew University. My new Jerusalemite friends at the university were much wealthier and knew a lot of words that I didn't. My new boyfriend made a "tentative" date with me, for the next day, and I asked him where "tentative" was. The articles I was supposed to read for my classes were all written in English, and I didn't understand a single complete sentence. In the garden of my rented student house there were grapevines and cherry trees, plums, olives, and a giant fig tree. For me Jerusalem was rich, cold, complicated, and wonderful. The Old City was the place where we ate hummus and bought cigarettes on Shabbat when everything in the western part of the city was closed. Since 1978, I have left Jerusalem a few times to study, but I have always come back.

In 1988, when my husband and I returned from studying in the United States, the First Intifada, or Palestinian uprising, was at its peak. We moved into an apartment near the promenade of Armon Hanatziv, close to where the northern border of Jerusalem used to be. From our windows, we heard the distant sounds of giant loudspeakers, smelled burning tires, and saw helicopters hovering over the nearby Palestinian village.

Our grass was very green, but the view through our lovely windows was very hard to bear. From the balcony we could see our soldiers who had been sent to restore order . . . as if there had ever been order here.

While studying in the United States, I had been active in the anti-apartheid movement, and I was also involved in establishing an American chapter of Yesh Gvul, which in Hebrew means both "there is a limit" and "there is a border," to support Israeli soldiers who refuse to serve in the Occupied Territories. But what truly changed my life, after I returned to Israel, was just one meeting.

I was invited by Dr. Edit Doron, a linguist, to go with a group of women to meet Amal Aruri, a Palestinian woman about my own age, whose husband, a physicist, was in jail and about to be deported. I had just returned from the United States with a fifteen-month-old baby and a new Ph.D.; Amotz, my husband, was still in California finishing his own doctoral thesis. My first six weeks in the country, waiting for Amotz to return, seemed like the longest in my life, but Edit kept calling me, asking me to come with them, to see for myself the reality of the occupation.

We sat on Amal's balcony, talking and looking at the beautiful mountains surrounding Ramallah, and I was never the same. I felt that I had to tell every Israeli; I wanted Israelis to know that this beautiful woman, Amal, was going to be alone with her three children because her husband, Taysir, was in jail and about to be deported—though he had not been charged with a crime. He was being held under administrative order, because the authorities viewed him as a political figure who might commit a crime. A few days earlier, he had participated in a rally organized by Peace Now—one of the first Israeli peace groups—in Tel Aviv and signed a petition; now he would be deported.[2]

I knew nothing then about human rights. I had a Ph.D. in sociology but no clue about human rights law; I just wanted Israelis to know what was happening. After our visit to Amal, I could not stop thinking about her and talking about her. I told my friends and my family; I asked them, "Do you know what is happening there?" I invited one friend, the editor of a weekly newspaper, to come with me to meet Amal; he said he did not think his readers would be interested in such a story, but after I nagged him, he sent me with a photographer back to Ramallah to write the story myself.

I continued to visit Amal after my article was published, through the long weeks when her husband appealed his deportation order to the High Court. She told me about her efforts to establish nurseries in Ramallah so that women could work. She told me about her first meeting with Taysir at the university, after he was released from jail the first time, after four years in prison without a trial. She would go over the file of documents that she kept, among them a petition by 180 American scientists, including many Jews, who called for the Israeli government to release her husband. She looked for the court documents—which were all in Hebrew, a language she could not read—and once she found the court decision not to accept his appeal I read it for her. "We have no doubt," it read, "that the appellant will become a leader even within jail. We are afraid that even outside the area he will continue to be active in the Communist Party, and without the control of the security services, might even be more active in pursuing his goals." There was, needless to say, no mention of what these goals might be, no mention of violence or any attempt at violence.[3]

Taysir appealed the decision to the High Court of Justice, but Amal knew all along that nothing would help and that he would be deported. She explained that the Communist Party—the party Taysir was accused of leading—had been consistent, since 1947, in calling for peace and the establishment of two states side by side. She told me that she taught her children that there were many good Israelis but that they were scared of the soldiers; they could not believe there were any good soldiers.

Taysir Aruri was deported. The last time I saw him was in the courtroom before the High Court of Justice, which, without allowing him or his lawyer to see the "evidence" against him, approved his deportation.

The women who first took me to meet Amal were involved with a larger group, the 21st Year Against the Occupation, a movement that called on Israelis to refuse to participate in the oppression of Palestinians.[4] (Although the movement consisted almost entirely of women, it was run by men.) We declared our refusal to cooperate in the continuing occupation of Palestinian territories and lives. We announced that we would not buy any products made by Jewish settlers in the Occupied Territories, that we would not take trips to the Occupied Territories, or let our children visit them. The group was founded in 1988, and we declared that that year, the occupation's twenty-first, should be its last. That year was a turning point in the history of the state: from that point on, the length of the occupation would exceed the years, between the founding of the state and the 1967 war, that Israel had existed without it.

Together with Shifra Itertur, Zehava Galon, Ilana Hammerman, and many new friends, we set up a protest tent in the Negev desert, near the Ansar III prison camp at Ketziot, where hundreds of Palestinian administrative detainees were imprisoned for long months without charge or being brought to trial.

The first night in that protest tent was the first time I spent a night apart from Gali. She was eighteen months old, and although it was only one night, that particular cold night in January 1989 seemed terribly long. We pitched our camp outside the high barbed wire fences of the prison where thousands of Palestinians had been detained without trial. We did this because we wanted Israelis to know that Palestinians were being arrested in their homes at night, on the streets, or at work and taken to the Negev to this giant tent prison, where they were held without knowing why or for how long. We believed that if more Israelis knew what was going on in the Occupied Territories in their name, what their children and friends were doing there, they would call for an end to the occupation. Amotz brought Gali on the second day, on the bus that carried supporters to the demonstration. An exhibition by the finest Israeli artists was set up in the Ketziot tent camp, in the heart of the Negev desert.

Ghassan Abdallah, the head of the Palestinian teachers' union, who was under administrative arrest, told me years later that in their tents, they had spoken of our tent outside with hope. We went home after three days and kept talking about resistance to the occupation, while he and his friends remained there for months.

During the First Intifada, several Israeli peace movements were formed, of which the 21st Year Against the Occupation was only one; they all organized protests, demonstrations, and vigils to motivate the Israeli public to call for our government to begin negotiations with the Palestinians. Within a few months of returning to Jerusalem, I also helped to establish a new human rights organization; the peace movement and the human rights movement were natural allies, but they followed very separate routes.

In February 1989, we formed B'Tselem, the Israeli Information Center for Human Rights in the Occupied Territories, an Israeli monitoring organization. B'Tselem, we wrote, had "taken upon itself the goal of documenting and bringing human rights violations in the Occupied Territories to the attention of the general public and policy and opinion makers and of fighting the repression and denial which have been spread through Israeli society." In Hebrew, the name B'Tselem means "in the image of" (Genesis 1:271:27: "So God created humankind in his image, in the image of God he created them; male and female he created them"). We formed B'Tselem using the model of American and international human rights monitoring groups such as Amnesty International, the Lawyers Committee for Human Rights, and Human Rights Watch. We adopted very technical, objective language, documenting violations in very detailed "neutral" reports. I was one of the founders of B'Tselem and its first research director. We were careful not to exaggerate, not to adopt any political stand, and not to use adjectives in our reports.

A number of professional, established human rights organizations emerged around the same time in Israel. In addition to documenting rights violations, some groups, such as the

Association for Civil Rights in Israel, appealed cases to the High Court of Justice, while others, such as the Hotline for the Defense of the Individual, devoted themselves to assisting individual Palestinian victims.

At B'Tselem, we went to great lengths to remain apolitical, sometimes to the point of near absurdity. In 1989, twenty-seven activists in the 21st Year, including myself, were arrested in the West Bank Palestinian city of Qalqilya after demonstrating against house demolitions. Nineteen women had been arrested, and three of us worked at B-'Tselem—half of the organization's staff. Some on the board felt we should resign for having mixed political action with human rights work. But Zehava Galon, who was both the director of B'Tselem and one of the leaders of the 21st Year, insisted against it: we had been arrested, she argued, not as B'Tselem staffers but as activists with the 21st Year. Zehava is a unique leader with a great sense of humor, and she always found ways to articulate the distinctions between human rights work and political advocacy. But the truth is that on many occasions in the years after she left B'Tselem, I felt the lines between such groups were drawn very inexactly; the main distinction, I think, is in the tools each group uses to realize its aims.

Yom Ha'shoah (Holocaust Remembrance Day), April 13, 1999

I was alone at home when the siren sounded. I stood for a minute of silence while the siren was on, as we all do every year in memory of the six million Jews murdered by the

Nazis, watching the children at the kindergarten across the way standing in silence. Earlier that morning Gali and Uri had gone to school dressed in white shirts and black pants. The children at the kindergarten were still too young, and they were dressed colorfully. The next week, on Yom Ha'zikaron, the memorial day for Israel's fallen soldiers, everyone would wear blue and white.[5]

I remembered my childhood fear of Holocaust Remembrance Day films and the many long sleepless nights I spent thinking about Anne Frank hiding and writing her diary. I remembered the annual school ceremonies mourning the victims, and my fear and respect for the parents of some of my best friends, who came from "there," as we called it then; I remembered the numbers on their arms, and the way their faces hid secrets and pain from horrible days they never talked about.

In 1991, in the course of my work with B'Tselem, I was given permission to go inside Ansar III prison at Ketziot in the Negev, where three years earlier I had protested with the 21st Year Against the Occupation. The giant camp was divided into blocks of tents, surrounded by barbed wire fences. It was terribly hot, and the only shade to be found was inside the tents. Each tent housed twenty-eight prisoners, who ate, slept, read, prayed, played, and lived inside. Each prisoner had a bed and a small cupboard. Part of the camp was fenced over, like a giant metal cage, and the terrible sound of loudspeakers ruled the entire camp. The prison commander wanted to show us—representatives of a human rights organization—that no torture happened in his prison and that he had introduced many innovations for the inmates' benefit. He was especially proud of the fact that since taking the position he had allowed the prisoners to wear watches. Most of the prisoners had never been brought to trial. They were administrative detainees: they had been imprisoned not as punishment for a crime but ostensibly in order to prevent them from committing illegal acts. Attorney Tamar Peleg was supposed to guide Bassem Eid and me on our visit to the camp, but when we arrived, dozens of prisoners were already waiting for her, eager to appeal their arrest before the military judge or request shortened terms. So she left Bassem and me to wander around the prisoners' tents alone.

Bassem, today the director of the Palestinian Human Rights Monitoring Group, was a researcher at B'Tselem for many years. He would go to the territories every day and gather testimonies about what was happening to the Palestinians there. Bassem lives in the Shuafat refugee camp in North Jerusalem and is maltreated not only by the Israelis but also by Palestinians who object to his work in Israel and his criticism of human rights violations on the Palestinian side.

Israel issued more than twenty thousand administrative detention warrants between 1987—the beginning of the First Intifada—and 1999. Thousands of people were arrested on their way to work, at home, or in the street, tortured, and then locked up for months in jail. It was terribly hot at Ketziot, and after eight hours of wandering with Bassem from tent to tent talking with prisoners about the conditions of their arrest, I wanted to run away.

Some of the prisoners asked us to call their families and tell them they were all right. Visits were not permitted at Ketziot, and there were those who had not seen their families for many months. Bassem wrote down who was ill and needed medical attention that had not been provided, and how many kilograms of food reached the prisoners' kitchen each day. I asked myself, *What if one of the dozens of soldiers wandering around the prison with guns is an acquaintance of mine?* We asked detainees to keep diaries and send them to us once they were released.

In order to understand more about what life as a detainee without trial meant, I interviewed Nahman Shulman, a seventy-year-old Jewish professor who was detained without trial by the British in the 1940s. He told me:

> The worst thing in prison is time—the amount of time you're there, and not how you're kept. If there is basic food and hygiene (and the British were very careful about hygiene), you can stay for 10 years. The problem is time. It is difficult for people to understand this—they ask, "How was the food, how were the beds," but the important thing is that they took away six years of my life.

Sami Kilani, a poet who was imprisoned for months at Ansar III, wrote:

> The path I took the first time from Jeneid Prison, near Nablus, to the Negev, which was, in a sense, the writing on the wall, cannot be erased from memory. In those same moments, in the morning hours which I love, I reflected on the visit that was supposed to take place the following day, I thought about my son who had been born just a few days before, and whom I would see tomorrow for the first time. The officer

entered with a few guards and they began calling off a list of names. We understood the matter: we were to be transferred to the Negev. The soldiers on guard wanted us to pay careful attention: before leaving the internal prison gate, they instructed us to cover our eyes with a strip of cloth from our clothing and they checked that the cover was tight and that no light seeped through. The buses remained in the prison courtyard from 11:00 am until 4:00 pm, with us inside them, blindfolded and tied two by two. When we would ask them to decrease the pressure of the metal handcuffs, one of the soldiers would answer with a string of curses, strike the iron part of the seats with his club in order to instill fear, or strike the nearest prisoner. Five hours in a tin box, in the August heat, when you are tied and blindfolded, is not something that can be forgotten. An additional picture is etched in my mind: shouts were heard from the second bus. I lifted my blindfold very slightly and looked out the window: a soldier bearing a club burst into the bus as if he were storming a military stronghold. Another soldier kicked Jamal, who was seated on the ground in the scorching sun, with his eyes tied. Things one sees in a stolen glance are etched in the mind, just as a photographed picture is etched in the camera's sensitive film.

And a friend of mine—a physicist who was a lieutenant in the reserves and served at Ketziot—gave me excerpts from his diary, which I published anonymously:

The worst is to guard during a count (and the name count takes a long time) and look at the people standing there, [it's better to look] at the stars, or at anything, but just not into the eyes of this large group of some 300 people who you see are the fathers of children whom they have not been able to see for a long time, [or lovers of] wives or girlfriends — the worst is to see that they are people. Even though during the day you see them playing ping-pong or volleyball, talking, reading, or playing backgammon, now, when they're all sitting in front of you across from the barrels of guns, an armed jeep in the background, they look like encaged animals.[6]

In the B'Tselem report that was published after the visit I noted that Israel was violating international law: arresting thousands of people without trial and jailing them outside the occupied zone in contravention of the Geneva Convention, which the country had signed. We reported the harsh conditions of imprisonment, the prohibition of family visits, and the medical neglect. But I never, not once, wrote about the pain, the fear, the confusion — and those seconds, just flashes, when I repressed visual memories from other places.

"You have to be really careful with this. You have to say it with a thousand caveats. That's only right, because we're not Nazis. But we are certainly an invading force — and that's awful too," Yuval Ginbar, an activist in B'Tselem, told me. "Look, I've had opposite experiences: when I was at a conference in Portugal once I was approached by an Egyptian who started to tell me that he'd visited Dachau and seen how bad it was and been really shocked. He said: 'Why are you doing the same thing at Ketziot?' So I got up and said: 'Look, my father was in Dachau. I really object to having to defend Ketziot because of what you say. It's not a concentration camp. People don't die there. It's a terrible place, and in Israel I try to speak out all the time against what they are doing there. So leave it alone . . . stop saying that Dachau is Ketziot.' We have to be really careful of this wild inflation."

The report, entitled "Detained Without Trial," was the last one that I wrote at B'Tselem. I don't know if it had any influence, but as Tamar Peleg told me repeatedly—in the many hours she spent teaching me, showing me her case files, and telling me about the bizarre nature of appellate proceedings on administrative detention, with all the evidence closed to her—you have to document, you have to write it down, so that people can know.

Yom Ha'zikaron (Memorial Day), April 20, 1999

I gave Gali and Uri the prettiest of the flowers from my little rooftop garden to take with them to school. Together with the flowers their classmates brought, they wove big round wreaths to remember the fallen. Uri told me with pride that his class had made the biggest wreath of all. The day before, they took their wreaths to the military cemetery on Mount Herzl. I don't like it that they went there lined up in pairs; I don't want them to grow up to go to the army, to go to war. When I was small, my mother told me that by the time I was big there would be peace.

When the Six-Day War happened I was ten. In the 1973 war I was sixteen. At Soroka Hospital, where I volunteered, I fell in love with a boy in my class as we took the injured up to the X-ray room together. In 1982, during the Lebanon war, I was a student, and a year later, when the war had ostensibly ended and the occupation of southern Lebanon continued, I met Amotz. In 1991, during the first Gulf War, Gali was three and a half and Uri was a six-month-old baby who hated his sealed gas tent.

Now Uri is almost nine, and he asked me which day is sadder—Yom Ha'shoah or Yom Ha'zikaron. He learned to sing the national anthem, "Ha'tikva," at school. Gali is almost twelve, and she read us the passage she was going to recite in the Yom Ha'zikaron ceremony at school: a poem by the mother of a boy who was killed in the 1973 war.

How can you raise happy children in Jerusalem amid so many annual ceremonies of war and bereavement?

In October 1996 Rana Nashashibi called me and asked me to go to Hadassah Hospital in Jerusalem with her to visit some injured people she had not been permitted to see the day before. It was already four in the afternoon, and I knew I wouldn't be back in time to pick Gali up from her dance lesson at the community center. I went by the center and asked Gali to wait for me upstairs in the library, then went on to Hadassah.

Rana is a child psychologist and the director of the Palestinian Counseling Center in East Jerusalem. Her center treats children who have dropped out of the education system and children with special needs. I've known Rana for many years through meetings between Israeli and Palestinian women. Rana has a blue identity card, which means that although she is not an Israeli citizen, she is a resident of Jerusalem and can move around in the city. Prior to 1948, Rana's family lived in West Jerusalem and owned large houses and property close to where the Jerusalem Theater currently stands.

On the seventh floor, in the surgery ward, first room on the left, an Israeli soldier with a rifle sat between two beds hidden by curtains. He was eighteen or nineteen and looked like a good kid. "No one is allowed in," he said to us, closing the curtains that we'd opened. "So shoot me," I said to him when I saw two children chained to the beds by their hands and feet. The younger one was fourteen but looked small for his age. He couldn't speak and was unresponsive. The soldier kept yelling and closing the curtain as Rana spoke in Arabic with the bigger child.

"You want me to take a photo of you and show your mother what you're doing in the army?" I asked the soldier.

"That's not fair," he answered. "You think I enjoy sitting here? These are prisoners, and no one is allowed to talk to them."

After I finished arguing with the soldier and Rana had heard from Jabar what happened and what state Muataz was in, we went downstairs in the elevator, too shocked to speak. When the elevator reached the ground floor, one of us said aloud that this could not be allowed to happen, and we went back up to the seventh floor. We approached the nurses' station to inquire as to who the attending doctor was. "I can't tell you that," the nurse said.

"What do you mean? This is a hospital, not a military base," I said to her. "Why is the doctor's name confidential? I can always look for the department director's name at information!"

"I can't tell you who the department head is," she said. "We have instructions from the army representative here."

The argument continued, and more nurses joined in and gathered around us. "Security is not our concern," one said. "We give them the best medical care possible."

"Go to their hospitals," said another nurse. "They won't treat you at all there. They'll kill you."

On the way home from the hospital Rana and I discussed what we should do. Rana told me how she had heard that the injured boys were at the hospital in the first place. Two days earlier she had gone to visit friends in Ramallah with her sister. On the way they had seen an old man who seemed lost on the road. Rana asked him if he needed help, and when he said no, they carried on. On the way back he was still there, and they stopped to find out if there was something they could do to help all the same. It turned out that the family decided to send the eighty-year-old grandfather to try to visit Muataz, as none of them had entry permits to Israel. They thought the old grandfather was less likely to be arrested. The shared taxi he had taken from Hebron was not allowed to enter Jerusalem and, via a mountainous bypass road, had reached Ramallah. The old grandfather did not know how to get home. Rana took him home and promised to try to visit Muataz.

On the way home from the hospital we stopped to pick up Gali from the library. I told Gali that Rana was a relative of ours. When Rana left, Gali wanted to know how she could be a relative if she didn't even speak Hebrew. I told Gali that many years ago her father's aunt married Rana's uncle. Jerusalem was different then, I told her; Jews and Arabs were friends. But it seems to me that even then, the marriage between a woman from the Agnon family and a man from the Nashashibi family of the Palestinian mayor had been somewhat extraordinary.

Eventually I got the name of the doctor, Professor Avi Rivkind, who appears frequently on television. When I called him that evening he had no idea what I wanted from him and what the problem was with the handcuffs. "They're not letting the children's families talk with them," I said, "not even on the phone. Perhaps someone should talk to the patients, someone from the hospital who speaks Arabic—a psychologist or social worker, or a nurse."

"They have each other," Rivkind said to me, "and anyway, there's lots of Arabs in the hospital."

It's a good thing there are Palestinian maintenance workers at Hadassah. On the night of the demonstration at which Jabar and Muataz were injured, Palestinian radio announced that the two had been killed. People began to gather at the homes of the two families in mourning. At three in the morning one of the maintenance workers, who came from the same village, called the one family that has a telephone with the news that Jabar and Muataz were alive.

Later that evening, after I had called the Israel Defense Forces (IDF) spokesperson and a few reporters and human rights organizations, the soldier and the handcuffs disappeared, and the dangerous prisoners became injured children.

Gali eventually heard the full story of the visit to the

hospital. She accompanied Rana and me to a women's conference in Belgium where we presented Palestinian and Israeli women's shared vision of real partnership in Jerusalem. I told the story of the visit to Hadassah Hospital in my lecture.

I don't know why I told this story again and again, everywhere I lectured. At every meeting I would tell the audience about those two Palestinian boys shackled to their beds, seriously injured, on the way to surgery. As if talk would change the sights, the reality. As if talk could make me forget the sentence that Rana uttered as we left the hospital together: "They're drawing a curtain between us. They don't see us as human beings."

The Eve of Yom Ha'atzmaut (Independence Day), April 20, 1999

The day before, I'd come home from a New Profile meeting with a few blue and white flags. We had met in order to do a mailing: some of us sticking stamps, others stuffing envelopes. Our blue and white flags had "Save the Peace" printed across them. Personally, I'm not mad about them. I don't like flags in general, but I knew that Uri would be really pleased with them. He wouldn't care what they said, as long as he could play with them.

Of all the political groups that I have known, New Profile is the most welcoming and encouraging. We're all mothers who don't want our children to serve in the army—and the meetings are always pleasant and funny. We seek the abolition of the compulsory draft and the recognition of the right to refuse military service on grounds of conscience; we believe that Israel, as a whole, needs to become a civil rather than a military society—that the military outlook that dominates our lives and generates war after war must be replaced. Some in the group focus their efforts on the state education system and work to change it so that our children will not be taught to be soldiers and to believe that generals know best what is good for our country. We refuse to raise children for war. We refuse to deny the pain, suffering, and injustice in the continuation of the occupation. We call on all mothers who don't want their children to serve in the Occupied Territories, all the women who want to end the occupation and want peace with mutual recognition and respect, to join us.

I'm the only Jerusalemite in the group and therefore attend less often, but I always come home happy. Rela Mazali and Hagit Gor Ziv, my good friends and the mothers of New Profile, walked me to the car. We kept talking although it was already after one in the morning. Hagit gave me a bag of sunflower seeds with a bag for the shells so that I would stay awake, and I drove off back to Jerusalem with my blue and white flags.

On the next day, eve of Independence Day, when Gali was at the community center and Uri and his friends were playing, pretending the flags were swords, I went with Amotz to the alternative Yom Ha'atzmaut ceremony opposite the prime minister's office. It was a twenty-minute walk from our house to the demonstration—the whole way overflowing with flowers. We walked through the Hebrew University campus at Givat Ram and were glad to encounter again the grass where we had spent our student days. On the way up to the Bank of Israel, with the Science Museum behind us, we heard the sounds of the official Independence Day ceremony from Mount Herzl. We were walking in an area occupied by a lot of important buildings—the Bank of Israel, the government ministries, the Knesset, the High Court, and the museums. Most of the buildings that make Jerusalem the capital are here, near the entrance to the city, opposite my home in Beit Hakerem. When they were built, nobody was using big empty words about unified Jerusalem. Far from the sacred sites and the Temple Mount lie the government quarters and the Knesset, all the buildings whose occupants could make Jerusalem a sane place.

Behind us, at the official ceremony near the military cemetery on Mount Herzl, where dignitaries such as Yitzhak Rabin are buried, twelve people (nearly all men each year) had the honor of lighting torches to celebrate the glory of Israel's independence. The alternative ceremony that we were attending had been organized by Yesh Gvul and others, like us, who believe that we cannot fully celebrate our own independence so long as we repress millions of Palestinians, millions who do not have the chance to celebrate any independence day in their own state.

On the way to the ceremony we passed dozens of bored policemen. About 250 Israelis, most of whom we knew, came in solidarity to support the twelve activists who are lighting torches for a better Israel. Neta Amar lit one torch and spoke about discrimination against the Mizrahim (Jews from Eastern countries, also known as Sephardim) in Israel. Reserve General Dov Yirmiyahu spoke about the 1948 war, in which he fought, and about the expulsion of thousands of Palestinians. We were among friends; many of us had become active around the time of the First Intifada, when many peace groups were formed, though some were organized during the Lebanon war in the early 1980s, such as Yesh Gvul, founded by reservists who refused to participate in the terrible and unnecessary invasion and occupation of Lebanon into which we were led by Ariel Sharon, then minister of defense. The ceremony included feminist groups such as Bat Shalom (Daughter of Peace) and Kol Haisha (A Woman's Voice), a coalition that works to improve the status of women, who are marginalized in Israeli society by religion and militarism: Other groups were composed of soldiers who refuse to enforce the occupation, and young people who refuse to be drafted into the army, which has become a force of repression rather than defense. All of them are Israelis who love Israel and aim therefore to make it more free, more just, more egalitarian.

Michael "Mikado" Warschawski, the director of the Alternative Information Center, which provides information that the mainstream media are not brave enough to report, lit a torch as a beacon of hope for the millions of Palestinian refugees; as a sign of solidarity with the one million Palestinian citizens of Israel; as a sign of identification with the foreign workers, the hundreds of thousands of unemployed, homeless, and welfare-dependent; and in honor of the thousands of men and women, Jews and Arabs, who devote days and nights to the struggle against discrimination, "to the glory of the democratic state that we will establish in this beautiful country."

We left the ceremony early to go home and take the kids to the neighborhood Yom Ha'atzmaut celebrations at the community center. Gali appeared onstage in a hip-hop dance that we had already seen, and she was lovelier than ever. Uri was happy to meet the boys from his class. We ate hot corn together and watched the fireworks. It was fun. The fifty-first Independence Day of the State of Israel.

THREE

COMPASSION AND THE LANGUAGE OF HUMAN RIGHTS

In 1994 I was invited to Tunis to teach a course called "Human Rights: Theory and Practice." The course was part of a three-month program for leaders of nongovernmental organizations from the Third World. The international campus of El Tayer is located in a beautiful hotel in a suburb of Tunis, right beside the sea.

I was very excited to be one of the first Israelis invited to Tunis, and surprised at the warmth of everyone I encountered: from the people at the airport to the hotel manager and taxi drivers. During the week I spent in Tunis dozens of people told me with longing about Jewish childhood friends who had left in 1967, after some violent attacks against Jews took place. I was born in a country whose borders—the borders of enemy Arab countries—could not be crossed. Following the 1979 peace treaty with Egypt, Israelis could travel there, but all the other Arab states remained off-limits, and this visit to Tunis marked my first time in an Arab country. After the signing of the Oslo accords in 1993, a slow process of normalization began with other Arab states, but Tunisia was especially unwelcoming to Israelis: Israel had launched air raids in Tunisia against the PLO, which was headquartered there after being driven from Lebanon in 1983.

The first lesson I prepared was on torture. Big mistake. This is how I began the course:

> I was born and raised in Israel. Like all eighteen-year-old Israelis, I served in the army. I am married to an Israeli who still does several weeks of reserve duty every year. I grew up in a nationalistic family that did not think that Palestinians had the right to their own state.

> My father used to say that if he were an Arab, he would fight for his country, but he was a Jew, and so he fought for his country. I didn't tell them that, especially not the second part. I also didn't mention that as a child I would count the hundreds, perhaps thousands, of postcards depicting the greater Land of Israel, from the Nile to the Euphrates, that my father had at home. *I have given this land to your seed*, the postcards said, quoting Genesis 15:18, though my father was not a religious man. I did tell them, however, that when I was a girl, most people didn't think there were Palestinians. We called them Arabs, and we refused to recognize that there were Palestinians who also thought this land belonged to them.

> In 1987 the First Intifada broke out. More than two million Palestinians said they could no longer bear it, that they wanted to be free, that they wanted their own state. We called it a popular uprising and on

television showed children throwing stones at armed Israeli soldiers. In 1989, after we'd heard stories about soldiers who had shot at children, after reports about prisons bursting with Palestinians were published in the press, we established an Israeli organization called B'Tselem, the Israeli Information Center for Human Rights in the Occupied Territories. We wanted to know more about what was going on in the territories that were so close to us and yet so far. Are my friends shooting at children? What is going on over on the other side of the city in which I live? What is going on in the police station and detention facility opposite the pub where we have a drink at night?

We wanted Israelis to know. We wanted more and more people to hear about what our army was doing over there. In the words we used then, we wanted Israelis to know the price of the occupation. The price of our imperialist dreams, and those of our leaders, is that more than two million people are living lives of misery. We wanted Israelis to cry out: "Enough!" We wanted them to call the soldiers home, to implore them to take off their uniforms.

I did not describe to them, in that classroom in Tunis, what the little organization we established on the fourth floor of an apartment building looked like. I did not describe the neighbors who refused to let us put a sign at the building's entrance, or our spirit of excitement—our belief that by means of the reports we wrote, the press conferences, the faxes, we would be able to stop the tanks, the torture, and the occupation.

I did not tell them about the big house we moved to after two years, with large Arab windows and decorative floors. Zehava Galon, the first director of the organization and its living spirit, promised us that the house had been British and not Arab. I don't know why, but at the time I thought, *Good, then it's okay.*

I did not tell them about the reports, the press conferences, the daily routine in which Bassem Eid would return with another terrible story and five or six of us would sit down and think about what we could do, how to get it in the media. I certainly didn't tell them about the question Zehava asked at the end of every meeting: "Is there something sweet to eat? Some chocolate?" I did not tell them how we were awarded the Carter-Menil Human Rights Foundation prize in our first year or about Shirley Eran, who sat for years counting fatalities, comparing her lists with those of the IDF spokesperson, with Palestinian human rights organizations, with the testimonies of families. I meant to tell them about the report we wrote about the torture of Palestinians in Israeli jails, without describing the crazy atmosphere in which it was written: sitting in the office with our Gulf War gas masks, waiting for the daily siren.

I suppose I began the course this way in order to say: *Hey, I'm an Israeli, but I'm all right. We speak the same language, the language of human rights — a language that should be spoken throughout the world. In this language torture is not permitted, period. There's no reason in the world that can justify torture. The International Declaration of Human Rights prohibits torture under all circumstances, always. The Geneva Convention, which delineates the boundaries of the use of force during wartime — a convention that was written by generals and is honored throughout the world—also prohibits torture.*

But before I could even open my mouth to say any of this, a beautiful young woman dressed in a miniskirt, with makeup and shiny painted nails, got up and left the room in protest.

I didn't really understand what had happened or why she had left, and I continued with my lesson. Later, after long hours of trying to talk to her and after committing to teach the course in French especially for her, she told me that she was the director of an organization that evacuates the dead and cares for the wounded in southern Lebanon. "I take care of them after your army has bombed them," she said.

That morning in class, with the orderly notes that I had prepared for my lecture on the prohibition against torture in international law and what nongovernmental organizations can do to report torture and to try to stop it, I did not really grasp that she had left in protest. I did not see how bizarre the situation was—an Israeli in Tunis teaching a course on human rights to a group of leaders from South America, Asia, and Arab countries.

I had two friends in Tunis besides the director of the course who had invited me. Salawa Mustafa is a Tunisian married to a Palestinian. She and her husband worked for the PLO in Tunis for many years. Mayada Abassi is a Palestinian who has also lived in Tunis for many years; she is one of the leaders of the International Women's Organization. She was born in Jaffa. In 1948, when she was one year old, her family was exiled. I had met the two women through encounters between Israeli and Palestinian women and through my work at Bat Shalom. When they asked to join me, it seemed a little inappropriate at first, a mixing of stories. That morning, however, they came and sat on each side of the large square table in the classroom like two queens. Mayada is a large woman with a strong presence; Salawa is beautiful and impressive. Only in the middle of the lecture did I understand that they had come to protect me.

The lesson on torture did not go as I had planned. I knew that there were countries where torture was more terrible than in Israel. I knew that not even a fraction of the horrendous methods that are used elsewhere are employed in Israel. Nevertheless, I was not prepared for what happened next.

A Colombian woman began by describing how she had witnessed the torture of her father. Others from Senegal, India, and Morocco joined in and spoke of torture they had experienced, the disappearance of family members and friends. The stories were translated into English, French, Spanish, and Arabic. I was not prepared for the pain, the tears. At the end of the lesson we were all crying, even the translators. Were we speaking one language? Were we speaking different languages?

In 1991, when Stanley Cohen and I wrote the B'Tselem report entitled "Interrogation of Palestinians During the Intifada: Ill-treatment, 'Moderate Physical Pressure,' or Torture?" we thought nobody would believe us. Professor Stanley Cohen is one of the most important sociologists in the world, and he taught me how to verify, examine, and check each testimony. We were still afraid, however, that people would say we were unreliable, that there was no torture in Israel. I was pregnant when I began writing the report, and when Uri was three

weeks old we met again—Stan, G., and I—to continue working on it. Stan and I did not meet prisoners. There were good
methodological reasons for this: we do not speak Arabic, and
Palestinians would not want to talk to Israelis about torture
in the Israelis' language. But I think we were also afraid. My
nights were already filled with nightmares. Once someone
asked me how I knew the stories were true. I told him about
the man and the hard-boiled egg. After days without food
and water, the man told us, they sat him down beside a toilet
and gave him the yolk of a hard-boiled egg to eat. Without
water. For long weeks I could taste that hard-boiled yolk in
my mouth.

I'm not sorry we did not meet with prisoners, but I am
sorry about how Stan and I treated G. He was the one who
went to the West Bank to meet Palestinians who had been
arrested, held in Israeli jails, and interrogated and tortured
by our internal security force, the General Security Service
(GSS), known in Hebrew as the Shabak. Many of the detainees were released after severe torture without even being indicted. G. went to them and interviewed them, writing
the atrocities down in close handwriting on yellow pages. In
the margins of the pages G. would sketch stick figures. These
stick figures were contorted into different positions, and G.
would explain to us how their hands were tied behind them
or how high the stool was. He drew a stick figure inside a
closet: it was a small space and the stick figure could neither
stand nor sit.

G. is of course not his real name. He was so afraid that
the GSS would harass him that he asked to remain anony-
mous. His fear turned out to be justified. The GSS maltreated
at least two of the interviewees after the report was published.

And we, the human rights organizations, what help did we give them? What can we really do to help someone who is taken to an interrogation room in the middle of the night? We did not even give G. enough support. In retrospect, I ask myself what his nights were like.[1]

We thought it would be worthwhile including G.'s illustrations in the report. They were schematic, like the dry wording of the report. It seemed appropriate. Then I looked for someone who could turn the tiny stick figure illustrations into something that could be published in the report. When Dudu Gerstein gave me the illustrations—which have since accompanied every B'Tselem report on torture and so many newspaper articles—they seemed at first glance too real, almost unfit for publication in a human rights report that was supposed to be objective, reliable, and not manipulative. B'Tselem's line, which I had participated in formulating, was "Don't be emotive." I had often said, *Don't use adjectives—not terrible, not cruel. Only describe the facts. Measure the height of the cell, describe the differences between the closet and the lock-up called the "fridge," verify with as many interviewees as possible what the temperature was, document the most minute details of the horror.* But the more I looked at the figures tied up in inhuman positions, the more I became convinced that they conveyed what we were unable to put into words.

When we wrote the first report, in 1991, we were thinking mainly about the dissemination of information. We wanted to overcome the obstacle of denial and repression. We wanted to say, in the most reliable language possible: *There is torture here in Israel, all the time, and it can be stopped.* We were afraid of not being believed; we expected denial. But we could not have predicted the state's response to the 1991 report, to the seven subsequent B'Tselem reports on torture, and to the conferences we organized, the letters we wrote, and the demonstrations and petitions to the High Court: "We have no choice."

The 1991 report received extremely wide coverage in all the media. Two commissions of inquiry were appointed to examine its claims: an IDF commission headed by Reserve General Rafael Vardi and a joint Ministry of Justice–GSS commission. Vardi called me to testify. The commissions heard from witnesses who had been our interviewees in the report. Although neither commission admitted that torture had taken place, they both allowed that lessons should be learned and procedures changed.

Before the publication of the report in 1991 seven members of the board of B'Tselem telephoned me, without prior coordination between them, and asked that we refrain from using the word *torture* in the title of the report. They were afraid it was too strong a word, but Stan and I insisted: we had to call a spade a spade. Among those who approached us were those who asked us not to publish the report in English, because the intention was not to slander Israel in the world but to work for rectification in Israel, to arouse Israeli public opinion. We thought, however, that the language of human rights was a language without borders, and that the truth should be told everywhere. A year later we heard that Attorney Felicia Langer had translated the report into German and published it in Germany. A discussion was held at B'Tselem regarding whether to sue her for infringement of copyright. Only many months afterward did I understand, or admit to myself, that my anger with Langer had nothing to do with copyright but rather with my discomfort at the thought of a report being published in the German language that detailed Israeli Jewish use of torture.

After the report on torture was published in Hebrew, English, Arabic, and German, after the commissions of inquiry and newspaper pieces and wide public interest that it generated, after hundreds of people called to say how awful it was, how they had not known there was torture—after all that, very little changed. A year after the first report, we wrote a second. We documented all the responses and examined what had been accomplished after all. Palestinians were still being tortured every day in Israeli prisons. The army had changed its procedures a little, but things were the same in the GSS. And GSS people did not work alone: soldiers arrested the Palestinians and brought them to the interrogation rooms, cleaning staff mopped up the blood, doctors signed forms saying the detainees were fit for interrogation, judges refrained from intervening, lawyers defended the need for these methods—and thousands of Israelis drank beer in the popular pubs across the street from the Russian Compound in Jerusalem, where Palestinian detainees were being tortured every day and every night. They told us it was essential, that Israel wasn't Switzerland or Holland, that the country was under a security threat and that there was no choice but to use torture.

After we published the second report on torture, in 1992, I got sick. The doctors told me I needed surgery, but I asked for a second, third, and fourth opinion. Finally a doctor who practiced alternative medicine asked me what sort of work I did. When I told him, he said that perhaps my body couldn't bear any more. "How much pain do you think your body can take?" he asked me. I thought that I had never suffered real pain; I had only written about the pain suffered by others. What I experienced wasn't physical pain. It was frustration at the inefficacy of the words, frustration that our reports, which engendered such public reverberations, were not changing the reality.

Stanley Cohen, who was my partner in writing about torture, began to study denial, while I started teaching human rights and asking the questions that would lead to this book. Stan inquired into how people could live between knowing and not knowing, and what human rights organizations in the world were doing in order not only to let people know about the suffering and injustice around them but also to do something to effect change. In his book *States of Denial* he describes the state of simultaneous knowing and not knowing: how and why people, organizations, governments, and whole communities deny information that is too upsetting or threatening.[2]

I find Stan's definition of the three main stages of denial especially useful. First is not knowing. *It's not true that smoking is bad for your health. It's not true that she's being unfaithful to me. It's not true that Israel violated the Oslo agreements during Barak's term.* The role of the human rights activist is to provide information on the destruction of homes, torture, and administrative detention—distressing and threatening information that we would prefer not to know.

At the second stage of denial we say that the situation is not quite as it seems, and even if it is, there must be no other choice. In Israel people say: *It's true that there are thousands of unemployed, but that's because they don't want to work. It's true that there are very few women in the Knesset, but that's because women don't want to be leaders. And it's true that torture is prohibited all over the world, but the situation in Israel is special, it's different.* In order to overcome this stage of denial, the human rights organizations not only distribute the information they collect but also try to get us to acknowledge that these actions are immoral and not essential.

Then, at the third stage, we say, *But what can we do about it? What can I do about it? The situation is so bad, the occupation continues and everything around us is so bleak — there doesn't seem to be anything we can do to change it.* I used to believe that if we could provide the proper information, we could help Israelis pass through the first stage of denial. Then we could appeal to their sense of morality, using international human rights law to demonstrate that torture and other violations are prohibited internationally, and convince Israelis not only that these violations of human rights take place but that they are immoral and unjust. Then, finally, we could work through the third stage: how to convince Israelis to work to stop these human rights abuses. But I am beginning to worry that I am myself still at this third stage; knowing, seeing, and documenting the horror, knowing that these actions taken by our government and army are immoral and unnecessary and that they bring pain and more violence. I am trying in many ways to stop them, but without much success. How can I convince others that they can make a difference if I am not always so sure myself?

The first questions I asked when I began to write this book had to do with language. These were questions Stanley Cohen and I talked about during our years of collaboration on the torture reports. We thought that our lack of success in effecting change was perhaps related to the language in which the reports on violations of human rights were written—language that did not reflect the urgency, the cry for help, and the anger.

The small community of Israeli activists is like many human rights communities all over the world, which despite various problems and distinct cultures, speak the same international language of conventions and laws and values. But this language is devoid of the pain, anger, and urgency that I feel. I wanted to find out if we're moving so slowly, so very slowly, toward ending the Israeli occupation of the West Bank and Gaza because we're speaking a language so different from the Israeli language.

The language of human rights has been developing since the 1948 Universal Declaration of Human Rights as a common standard for all peoples and all nations. This is a language that was developed as humanity's response to the trauma of the Second World War, out of a need to reach an international understanding that such atrocities—the murder of children, women, and men, of nations and hopes—would not recur. In a series of paragraphs, the leaders of the world formulated the declaration, one that belongs to all of us. This declaration created a new language: a translation of liberal thought into standards accepted by the international community.

All the countries of the United Nations accept that the declaration reflects our worldview regarding good and evil. All world leaders recognize that people cannot be sold into slavery, that torture is prohibited, and that every human being is entitled to a fair trial, food, and education. Of course, since the Second World War, despite the declaration and the conventions that were signed in its wake, millions have been murdered in Rwanda, Burundi, Kosovo, Bosnia, Chechnya, and elsewhere. This means that the tools we have to enforce these international standards—economic sanctions, or UN and other forces sent to stop the atrocities—are certainly neither adequate nor effective.

What is the source of authority for human rights? The religious perception of rights, morality, good and evil, draws on an authority that is beyond us, beyond human beings. But the modern perception of human rights proposes that we are the authority: the convention between us, the consensus regarding the basic common values of human dignity, is itself the source.[3] But from what is this consensus constructed? What is our common humanity? How do we know that the international law of human rights is moral? And how do we convince Israelis that international law, the same international conventions that the State of Israel signed and ratified, is valid even when Israeli law says otherwise?

I thought that if I could understand what motivated my fellow human rights activists to see the reality of Palestinian suffering, to acknowledge that Israel's actions in the Occupied Territories are unnecessary, and to try to stop them, I might learn how to make more people feel the same. I interviewed almost thirty Israeli human rights activists and asked them why they employed the language of human rights, what they believed to be the source of authority for human rights themselves, and what motivated them to act.

I asked attorney Andre Rosenthal, who has submitted dozens of petitions to the High Court to stop the torture of Palestinian clients, what motivates him to get up every morning and go to court when he knows that he will lose again. "What makes you angry?" I asked him.

Andre said that *angry* wasn't quite the right word, but that he is outraged by the racism: the knowledge that the torture exists because the people being tortured are Palestinians. "You think they'd let them do what they do to Palestinians to Jews? Systematically like this? When every Palestinian detained on suspicion of hostile terror activity—placing bombs in Mahaneh Yehudah or even theoretical membership in a student organization in Romania—is a suspect whose innocence has to be proven? Where does it come from? Does it come from understanding the country's special security situation?"

I asked attorney Yael Stein, who is responsible for a significant part of the writing and research at B'Tselem, why she writes and researches and struggles for change, even against house demolitions and the revocation of identity documents, which are entirely legal according to the laws of the State of Israel. Yael told me that this fact, that everything is legal according to the State laws, is precisely what horrifies her. "The answers that we constantly receive," she said, "are 'This was approved by the High Court, this meets legal standards,' as if the moment it's written down in law it becomes acceptable. Awareness of how law can be unacceptable is nonexistent."

DAPHNA: Aren't you playing the same game? You say it's against international law—but why should that take precedence over the laws of the State of Israel?

YAEL: It's clear to me that international law takes precedence, but try persuading the average Israeli that a law determined by foreigners takes precedence over the laws determined by the Knesset that he elected. Why should he be convinced by such a claim? That's why I don't like those claims, and I really try hard to keep them to a minimum in my reports. Usually I use other arguments and only mention that it's against international law.

DAPHNA: So how do you mean to persuade them? It's not good because it's not moral? How do you explain it? Why are administrative detentions not acceptable? Who gave you the authority? What is the source of your justification?

YAEL: My justification is a moral one. It's a moral justification.

DAPHNA: Don't you feel that the reports of the human rights organizations focus largely on legal language?

YAEL: Of course they do. Stanley Cohen says in his book that in human rights organizations today we don't say, "Killing is prohibited," but "The right to life according to item 6A in convention M-66 shall not be violated." It's true. There's a kind of pull in that direction, and that is, in my opinion, very, very dangerous. There's a problem here: who would that convince? Killing is wrong! Period! You can't kill a thirteen-year-old boy, and that's that!

Dr. Naama Carmi was one of the women involved in the Open Doors organization, which was established to work for the release of administrative detainees. I interviewed her in October 1998 after eleven administrative detainees adopted by the organization had all been released, with the exception of Ossama Braham, who had been in jail for five and a half years. By means of a brief but intense media campaign, including an art exhibition and a lot of public pressure, the organization had succeeded in creating serious media interest in a subject—administrative detention—that had never made headlines before, penetrating Israeli public consciousness.

NAAMA: What happened was that Ayelet Ofir got up one day and said this couldn't go on, that something had to be done. She read a newspaper article by Gideon Levy and she happened to be on sabbatical at the time. So a very small group of people was organized, most of them lecturers in Tel Aviv.

DAPHNA: Why was this group organized at that point in time? Do you know how long these detainees were in prison?

NAAMA: I think it was organized because someone got up and said we had to do something.

DAPHNA: And that someone was Ayelet?

NAAMA: Yes. I think it always works like that. And now it's . . . not falling apart but it's fading, because Ayelet went back to work. It rises and falls on a center, on that drive. Little by little it expanded, and we started being more active, then it expanded more. When I came in I undertook to handle increasing media exposure, which was not really successful until then, and also to make a little more contact with Knesset members. There are two directions at play: one is actually moving things [writing letters to army and prison officials, appealing sentences in court, trying to intervene through Knesset members]; the second is public opinion. Public opinion is important because administrative detentions, for example, are legal and approved by the High Court.

DAPHNA: So you said: "Look, B'Tselem speaks on a certain legal level, and we're trying something different"?

NAAMA: B'Tselem, the Association for Civil Rights [in Israel], HaMoked: Center for the Defence of the Individual, and Physicians for Human Rights gave us the institutional reinforcement. We wanted to arouse public opinion, appeal to people's sense of justice. The latent underlying assumption is that this is how you recruit public opinion, and public opinion in democracy is a tool of the first order for changing policy that remains legal. There were people here who were personally committed to this issue. It became something incredibly personal, and it was really clear to us that this stubbornness would pay off. It was a slightly different approach, really, than the established one. There was personal contact with the facilities, and letters, these letters with detainees who corresponded, provided material for the media, a different kind of material. The appeal was, to put it more accurately, not so much to the sense of justice as to the human issue.

DAPHNA: The human issue?

NAAMA: Yes, the basic human issue. We published a small notice in *Ha'aretz* three times a week: "Ahmed Katamsh has been in administrative detention for X number of years and X days without trial." By the way, in our stupidity, only in the last notice before his release did we include a telephone number, and that's how we found out. Aharon Barnea called me and said: "Do you know they're releasing him tomorrow?" Before that we hadn't included a telephone number, only an address for donations.

DAPHNA: Did people make donations?

NAAMA: Yes. As long as there are notices people donate. It's a very interesting thing. That's how some people contribute to the struggle. They're not active but they donate. In this case the line that proved truly successful was: you have to give the administrative detainees—this thing that everyone knows has been happening for years—a human face. You have to give it a name and a surname, belonging to a person who has a wife and a daughter and comes from someplace and did something beforehand and had plans and aspirations and dreams. In my opinion this really worked and generated a lot of interest. I think it's a really good tactic now as well. It also becomes clear that the more you say that this phenomenon exists, you see that educated people, enlightened people—for example, every journalist I have spoken with—really didn't know that there was such as thing as holding people without trial. They respond with "Why?" and "How?" and "What a thing!" and "It shouldn't be!" People didn't know. There was an act of education here, dissemination of information.

DAPHNA: Did you really believe they'd release them?

NAAMA: Yes.

DAPHNA: Yes?

NAAMA: Although we didn't think it would be just because of our activities—there shouldn't be that kind of hubris.

DAPHNA: So why did they release them?

NAAMA: Look, a journalist who specializes in the GSS that I talked to in the middle of the campaign said, "That's not it. I talked to the GSS and the GSS . . . had made a decision, there's a trend toward releasing them." He did say though, among other things, that they do see the pressure. The pressure of the families makes it hard for them.

DAPHNA: So why didn't they release Ahmed Katamsh a year ago?

NAAMA: I know that they told him—the GSS told Ahmed—
that it really irritated them, disturbed them, disturbed
their work. Suddenly there's interest, suddenly this thing,
suddenly Knesset members are involved, suddenly we're
on their backs. Yossi Sarid was suddenly calling the GSS
when Ahmed's brother had a heart attack, and Knesset
members were coming to visit more often and bringing
letters, and we keep coming and asking questions. All of
a sudden it's something that is brought out into the day-
light. Not entirely, but there's some public exposure, and
then there are journalists, and then a photographer
shows up, and there was a giant color article in the [Is-
raeli daily] *Yediot Aharonot* supplement *Seven Days*. It
started in the beginning with Amira Hass putting in one
line, two lines, that was what she could get in. It didn't interest anyone at first—and then when Ahmed was released it was a main headline in *Ha'aretz*.

The language of human rights is neutral, dry, legalistic,
and devoid of the tempestuous feelings of the victims, the fer-
vor of religious orders, and the color of different cultures.
Many women have complained that it does not make suffi-
cient reference to the rights of women, to domestic violence
and rape during wartime. The African Charter on Human and
Peoples' Rights was written in the seventies in order to add
the cultural rights that people in the Third World felt were
missing from international conventions. The view that positions the individual at the center ignores collective rights,
which are no less important.

In the language of human rights every person has rights
by virtue of being a human being, and it is the basic duty of

all of us to protect the rights of each. But most Israelis feel that this language is extremely remote to them. What causes a small handful of Israelis to focus their lives on protecting the rights of Palestinians?

I began to write this book in English, calling it *Defending the Rights of the Enemy*—which doesn't sound as good in Hebrew. This title is what drew most of the interviewees. Amos Gil, who for many years managed the Association for Civil Rights in Israel—the largest, oldest, and most well established human rights organization in the country—told me the title was wonderful: "It represents my feeling about our work exactly." Amos has no problem with his Israeliness, nor with the fact that the Palestinians whose rights his organization defends are the enemy. Orna Cohen, an attorney who was one of the association's legal advisors, initially refused to be interviewed because of the title. She wouldn't give an explanation either. When I eventually met her at the premises of her new organization, Adalah: The Legal Center for Arab Minority Rights in Israel, in Shefaram, I took the opportunity afforded by the prohibition against smoking in the building and spoke with her outside, each of us with cigarette in hand.

"Why enemy?" she asked. "How can you call the Palestinians the enemy? I don't defend Palestinians. I defend people."

Tamar Peleg, an attorney who left the Association for Civil Rights in Israel (ACRI) after many years of activism and now works for HaMoked, told me the title had bothered her for the same reasons. "I'm only willing to meet with you because I know you," she said. Tamar defends administrative detainees and lives between the worlds of Gaza and Tel Aviv. Some of her Palestinian clients became her good friends, and sometimes friends who were detained without trial became her clients. During the last ten years I have joined her on tours of Gaza and the Ansar III jail. Tamar helped me to write the B'Tselem report about administrative detainees. I understood perfectly why she didn't like my title.

Neta Ziv, an attorney who left ACRI after ten years to write her doctorate and establish a legal aid clinic at Tel Aviv University, stressed to me that some of the attorneys at the association feel they are defending human rights as a concept rather than individual Palestinians before the High Court.

The many reactions to the phrase "defending the rights of the enemy" vary along with the different perceptions Israeli human rights activists have of their own work: there are those who feel they are part of the Israeli collective and see their work, the defense of Palestinian rights, as a reinforcement of Israeli democracy. Some feel responsible or guilty because their government is violating the rights of Palestinians, while others think that human rights have no boundaries and that there is no point in differentiating between Israelis and Palestinians.[4]

I asked Neta if there were moments when she debated between her affiliation with Israel, her identification with the state, and her work defending the rights of Palestinians. Neta told me about one morning after a bombing, when she was asked to give a radio interview presenting the position of the ACRI in Israel on the demolition of the houses of the terrorists who were responsible for the attack.

NETA: I think I'm also part of the public that was shaped by
the various kinds of ethos and mythos that make it easier
for us to see things in black and white, see things as a conflict between those who are wrong and those who are
right, the resurrection of the Jewish people against terrorists, Palestinians against Jews. The emotional dimension is also very strong. So when the emotional dimension
is very strong, you want to be connected, you want to
pass on a message in the emotional dimension, you don't
want to connect with the intellectual dimension. You
don't want to explain to people who are feeling something
really strong that it's not right [to demolish houses] because there's power and the use of that power has the potential to be abused. So the trick is to try and get the
message across in a dimension where it's really possible to
explain why human rights are sacred, something that
can't be compromised. And because I know the public
I'm addressing — I'm actually part of that public myself —
I know how hard it is. And I really am part of that public
because I myself have traveled this whole path.

DAPHNA: Let's take, for a moment, the radio interview where
you said, "We as a human rights organization are opposed to the demolition of houses." Were you really saying, "I, Neta Ziv, it's hard for me right now, today, to tell
you that I am defending the murderers, but we have a job
as an organization all the same"?

NETA: We have to have a role, and there has to be someone
who does that job and that's me. I don't exactly want to, I
have a hard time with it, but I stick to it. I stick to it not
because this is my station, but because I think it's critical

that someone takes this station. I want to make that clearer because I think my claims that human rights are in everyone's interests are justified. It includes your children—perhaps not today, perhaps tomorrow—and it also includes your cousin, who might get arrested tomorrow. Human rights are everyone's, and because human rights are for everyone, the Association for Civil Rights always says, *We're just like you, that is, we care about the same values.*

Tamar Peleg told me that particularly as an Israeli she feels guilty for what the government is doing in the Occupied Territories. "They tell me to say *responsible* and not *guilty*. So I'll compromise and say *responsible*," she corrected herself.

Roni Talmor was one of the founders of B'Tselem and wrote the organization's first report on house demolitions. We used to laugh uncontrollably when Roni and Bassem cracked strings of terrible jokes. Roni had a special talent for relating the horrors of reality in a manner suffused with humor. In 1998, when Roni came back to work at B'Tselem after a long break, I asked her what had brought her to the organization.

RONI: Why did I start working at B'Tselem? I think it's because I really cared about what's happening in the territories, what's happening to the Palestinians, what we're doing to them. I think, at the beginning, years ago, that it was both: both what's happening to us and what's happening to them. Today it's much more about what's happening

to the Palestinians. We don't interest me so much anymore. I've given up. I think the problem is what's happening to them. In other words, I'm not here to save the
Israelis from anything. The Israelis can save themselves
if they want to. The occupation isn't corrupting—it's corrupt. To say "the occupation corrupts" is to refer to what
it's doing to us. That doesn't interest me. What the occupation is doing to them interests me.

DAPHNA: What it's doing to us seems to you like a lost cause?

RONI: Yes. There was a time when I used to say "the occupation corrupts." Today I say the occupation is corrupt. That
is, you have to be corrupt in order to be an occupier. Of
course, I'm not talking about the situation after the Six-
Day War, which—at least at the time—was considered
an unavoidable war. But maintaining the occupation for
thirty-one years is corrupt. I've given up because I worked
out that every person between the ages of twenty and
sixty in the country has been an occupier in one way or
another, with the majority of the men having actually
gone to the territories and been active participants, beyond the fact that we're all participants because we live
here and pay taxes.

DAPHNA: Can you recall a particular point at which you
started to think that the occupation is not corrupting but
corrupt? The point at which you said to yourself: this society is already entirely corrupt?

RONI: You know what it's like? It's like a rapist who has ex-
tenuating circumstances. You don't care only about the
victim; you take care of the rapist as well. What led him
to rape? Why is he violent? Well, it doesn't interest me in

the case of rape, and it doesn't interest me in this case. I care about the victim.

Leah Tsemel, a private attorney who defends hundreds of Palestinians, told me the proposed title of my book was insignificant. "I fight for my life," she said.

Rabbi Jeremy Milgrom, of Rabbis for Human Rights, and Eitan Felner, then the director of B'Tselem, told me that their commitment to human rights came from Judaism. Eitan told me that in Argentina the Jewish community was the framework within which he learned the values of commitment and mutual assistance, and only when he grew up and left Argentina did he understand how little he knew about that country's politics. Jeremy told me how the group in which he is active, Shomrei Mishpat—Rabbis for Human Rights—was formed.

JEREMY: One day the Palestinian landscape engineer who worked in the office of Hebrew Union College was a few hours late to work. He said that there was a roadblock between the Dehaishe refugee camp, where he lives, and Jerusalem, and that a soldier stopped him at the roadblock and asked him to prove that he paid his taxes. None of us walks around with all of our tax receipts, so like any one of us, he was not able to prove that he paid his taxes, and they took his car. He made it to work on foot quite a bit later, and the director of the program, a Reform rabbi from America named David Forman, was outraged by this story. He said, "Of course, you paid your taxes. We pay your taxes for you. We withhold your taxes. That's how it works when you're a salaried person."

And so he went down to the roadblock and he argued with the soldiers. I don't even know whether he got the car back that day. But David had an unforgettable encounter with the reality that Palestinians live. Even though he had lived in Israel for twenty years, David had never seen anything so ridiculous, or at least not up close. So he decided to act. He called a few of his colleagues, Reform rabbis—I'm a Conservative rabbi, he called me—and a few Orthodox rabbis that he knew. And he said: "Look, it is an embarrassment to me, as a rabbi, that these things take place, so maybe we should protest, as rabbis."

The questions I asked the friends that I interviewed were the questions I asked myself: Why do I fight for the rights of others? Who gave me the authority? What is this international language of human rights? Where is my voice within this language? What does my Israeliness have to do with this issue? How does this Israeli component of my identity affect my actions in defense of Palestinian rights? How can I explain to students that Israeli law permits the military governor to prohibit Palestinians from reading certain books—and that I still think it's wrong to forbid people to read books? When did I learn this language? Why is it relevant for me?

My years of activism in human rights organizations and peace groups have mostly coincided with the raising of my children. And the questions my husband, Amotz, and I asked ourselves were questions about how to raise good and happy children: How do we teach them to ask questions and believe in their power to effect change? How do we explain to them that not everything the teacher says on Jerusalem Day corresponds with our view of reality? What do I tell my son when he asks why Palestinians haven't got their own money? And what do I say to my daughter when she asks why I take my politics with me wherever I go?

FOUR

A VICTORY AT THE HIGH COURT

February 3, 2004

In my human rights classes at the Hebrew University, I told my students about the struggle Israeli and Palestinian human rights activists waged against torture—one of our most successful campaigns—in order to demonstrate that they could make a difference. They knew that the High Court ruled in 1999 that torture is illegal in Israel. But they asked if this meant that fewer Palestinians were tortured in Israeli prisons after the decision.

I wanted to tell them a success story. I wanted to tell them that they could make a difference. We read the theory of human rights, we learned the international conventions. But the reality these students lived was one of fear and despair. We went to see the security wall that they had heard so much about, which is not even a ten-minute drive from our campus; they had never seen it, and they asked me, "How can it be?" And what difference could they make when such a wall was being built right next to them, a wall that cuts through people's homes and splits the campus of nearby Abu Dis University in East Jerusalem in two?

My students were Jewish and Palestinian Israelis, many of whom, in all their years on campus, had hardly talked to each other. In class they shared their experiences and tried to find ways to cope with the difficulties they encountered during the course of their work with local human rights groups. In their work, my students were exposed to the harsh reality of growing poverty, violence, and fear in Israel. They asked me how I kept going, and they asked me to tell them some stories that were not so depressing. So I told them about the victory at the High Court of Justice, about how, after many years of relentless work by activists and human rights organizations, the High Court did indeed rule that torture in Israel is illegal.

But I couldn't tell them that there is no more torture in interrogation rooms in Israel. Thousands of Palestinians are still not allowed to see their lawyers, are deprived of food and sleep, and are kept for hours with their hands and legs tied to small chairs, exposed to extreme heat and cold.

On September 6, 1999, a few minutes after ten in the morning, a GSS investigator entered an interrogation room at the Russian Compound and removed a stinking sack from the head of a detainee. Moments earlier, on the other side of Jerusalem, the president of the High Court, Justice Aharon Barak, had just finished reading an opinion signed by all nine High Court justices stating that the interrogation methods of the GSS were illegal.[1]

This lawsuit was originally filed in 1994, and it took five years for the High Court justices to reach their decision — five years in which torture continued to take place while the justices slowly deliberated. The High Court ruling did not stop torture, but it ended some of the horrible practices that had routinely been employed. And it sent a clear message to interrogators that the use of torture is illegal. Even though the court allowed that the GSS could still invoke the "necessity" defense, it made clear that the GSS does not have the authority to torture every Palestinian that it arrests and interrogates.

In 1991, when we published the first B'Tselem report on torture, Israel was in denial.[2] Israelis did not want to know that their "best men" were torturing thousands of Palestinians in interrogations. We hoped that if Israelis found out what was happening in their backyard, they would do something to change it. After all the publicity generated by our report, people no longer said that torture did not happen. Instead they said, "We have no choice. We have to use torture to ensure our security."

Tens of thousands of Palestinians have been held and interrogated by the GSS. Most of them are barred from meeting their lawyers; they may not receive visitors in the first month of detention, or until their interrogation has been completed. HaMoked is the only organization that is given information from Israeli authorities as to where prisoners are held. One of the most common problems faced by the families of arrested Palestinians is determining their whereabouts; HaMoked provides this information to families, and represents detainees in court. During the time that detainees are held incommunicado, the only legal recourse available is to petition the High Court to allow the prisoner to meet with a lawyer; Palestinian lawyers cannot appear before the High Court, so these appeals must be filed by Israelis.

Since 1991 Israeli lawyers have submitted hundreds of these appeals, asking the High Court to permit them to meet

their Palestinian clients and to order the GSS to stop torturing them. Some of these appeals were funded by and submitted in the name of the Public Committee Against Torture, an
Israeli organization founded in 1990. Petitioning the High
Court had two main goals. The first was to provide legal
representation and try to help individual detainees. The second was to pressure the Israeli High Court of Justice into
outlawing the use of torture and other cruel and inhuman
treatment by flooding the court with appeals aimed to remind
the justices that torture was a routine practice in Israel and to
suggest that by permitting the GSS to torture prisoners, the
court was in fact legitimizing these actions.

For years these appeals were rejected uniformly, and
then one day Allegra Pacheco filed a petition—the forty-
ninth or fiftieth case that the Public Committee Against Torture in Israel had brought before the court—that was not
rejected on the spot.[3] She was representing a man charged
with a bombing in Tel Aviv that had killed three women her
own age, and like many lawyers before her, she had re-
quested that the court issue an order forbidding the use of
torture in detention cells. The justices, who had heard dozens
of petitions of this sort, suddenly decided to group several together and hear them before an extended nine-judge panel.

The international community prohibits torture, period. "The
prohibition against torture is absolute," said Nigel Rodley,
head of the UN Commission Against Torture:

> The drafters chose not just to use the word torture,
> because they did not want the assault on human dig-
> nity, the offense to human dignity implied in that

word, to be construed too highly. They wanted a prohibition of all attempts to break the bodies and minds
of people whom it was in the interest of those captur-
ing them to break. They had in mind the sort of practices that the SS and the Gestapo had inflicted, for
example on the French partisans whom they called
terrorists during the occupation of France.

But they also knew, as they knew later when they
came to draft the Geneva Convention, that torture was
not something that could be done by good guys to bad
guys even though it should not be done by bad guys to
good guys. They knew that torture was something that
had to be prohibited whoever the captor, whatever
good cause its government may represent and whatever evil cause the detainee may be suspected of representing.[4]

Why, in view of this absolute prohibition, did it take the justices of the High Court of Justice nearly five years to reach a
verdict?

No such discussion has taken place in the courts anywhere else in the world. This is not because torture does not
occur in other countries, but rather because no country has
ever presented a claim akin to the one the State of Israel submitted to the courts.

The argument, simply put, was this: Israel's interrogation
methods did not really involve torture, and they were essential
for the security of the State of Israel. Shai Nitsan, counsel for
the state, stood before the High Court on January 13, 1999,
and did not deny that prisoners were tied up for hours, held
with sacks over their heads, shaken or beaten. Instead he

argued that these methods were legitimate. He admitted that the GSS shook the heads of the prisoners, a practice that had resulted in the death of Abed Suliman Harizat in April 1995, but he said, "The danger involved in shakings is low and the benefit is very great indeed. Three heads of the security services submitted statements to this effect, as did four different ministerial committees. There is a consensus—shaking is far from torture. Low risk. High benefit."[5]

As such, argued Nitsan, the GSS's interrogation methods were not actually torture. It was true that there were shakings, and true that Abed Suliman Harizat had unfortunately died as a result of shaking, and true that the prisoners were shackled to small stools for long hours, and true they were deprived of sleep for long periods, and true deafening music was played while their heads were covered with sacks, but when the state gave the interrogators the authority to interrogate, it also gave them the auxiliary authority to do these things. Nitsan promised to change some of the procedures: the bags would be more aerated, the handcuffs looser.

Instead of telling Nitsan that there is no such thing as "acceptable" torture and that torture is prohibited under any circumstances at any time—that every interrogator should have to wear an identification tag, that the GSS's interrogation chambers should from then on be subject to public scrutiny and frequent visits by people sent to ascertain that no torture was taking place—the nine learned judges sat, deliberated, and deferred ruling until September 1999, almost five years after the trial had commenced, after we had written and published several reports on torture, after years of public knowledge that Palestinians were being tortured.

Throughout all the years of the trial it was clear that the

justices of the High Court of Justice were unhappy with the task imposed on them. They repeatedly proposed that the state pass a law to make these practices legal. "You say it's essential and legal—please, enact a law that reflects that; if it's so clear then pass a law. When you want to, you can get a law through in three days, a week," Justice Cheshin said. But as Shai Nitsan had responded, "Enacting such a law—which has never been done anywhere—is complicated. It takes time." What Nitsan did not say was that it would run counter to international law, against the international perception of justice—and would bring worldwide condemnation on Israel.

While there was no law making torture legal, it had been explicitly permitted in 1987 by a state commission headed by a former High Court justice. The story began in 1982, when Izzat Nafsu, a Circassian Israeli army officer, was sentenced to an eighteen-year prison term for treason and espionage. In his trial he maintained that he was innocent and that his confession had been extracted by force during the GSS interrogation. The GSS officers denied this under oath. Nafsu persisted in his claim, and in May 1987 the Supreme Court ruled in his favor, finding that the investigators had lied to two earlier Military Courts, and ordered his release. An official government commission headed by former Supreme Court president Moshe Landau was set up in June 1987 and issued its report four months later. The commission was asked to investigate the interrogation practices of the GSS as well as the validity of GSS agents' testimony at the trials of accused terrorists. The commission established that GSS agents had systematically lied to the courts for sixteen years about using force to extract confessions, and it condemned the perjury. "The GSS," the commission reported, "failed utterly, in permitting itself to violate the law systematically and for such a long period by assenting to, approving, and even encouraging the giving of false testimony in Court."

The commission discussed three ways to deal with the conflict "between the vital need to preserve the very existence of the State and its citizens, and [the need] to maintain its character as a law abiding state which believes in moral principles":

> The first way is to recognize that because of crucial interests of State security, the activity of the Security Services in their war against terrorism occurs in a "twilight zone" which is outside the realm of the law, and therefore these services should be freed from the bonds of the law and must be permitted deviations from the law. The second way is that of the hypocrites: they declare that they abide by the rule of law, but turn a blind eye to what goes on beneath the surface. . . . Or, in the figurative language of one of the GSS witnesses: "It is convenient for the citizen to sit on the clean green grass in front of his house, while beneath him the refuse is washed away in sewage pipes."

The commission opted for the "third way—the truthful road of the rule of law." They wrote: "The effective interrogation of terrorist suspects is impossible without the use of means of pressure. . . . GSS interrogators should be guided by setting clear boundaries in this matter, in order to prevent the use of inordinate physical pressure arbitrarily administered by the interrogator." To this end the commission issued secret guidelines for approved forms of "moderate physical pressure."[6]

The commission made clear that the right to use "moderate physical pressure" was granted in cases involving "hostile terrorists," that is, Palestinians. Israel became the only state in the world in which torture was legal, and probably the only state that licensed different treatment of Arabs and Jews. Although the commission did not specify that all Arabs should be treated as potential terrorists, it opened the door for that interpretation, which we know has been practiced in Israeli jails.

On January 13, 1999, the human rights lawyers presented their closing arguments to the court; each one presented a different facet of the case against torture. Avigdor Feldman, the first of the petitioners to speak, gave a brilliant presentation describing how the GSS had created a separate system independent of the legal one. The state, according to Avigdor, essentially acknowledged that the methods the GSS used violate human dignity and freedom, but it wished to let the GSS act on the grounds of the "necessity" defense.

> The necessity defense befits our feelings, living in this society. The necessity defense belongs to the ancient dimension of the justice system, the laws of nature. The necessity defense is society's right to protect itself, and the basis of every law regarding clandestine surveillance, arrests and searches.

However, Avigdor went on to detail the restrictions that the justice system must apply to the use of the necessity defense:

> The law of arrests . . . does not say to a policeman — there is a criminal before you, do whatever you want to. If you need to, arrest him for as long as you want. Instead, the law places restrictions on the policeman — how long you can arrest him for, and in what manner. The necessity defense is limited by laws that determine the means that can be employed, how long they can be employed for, and when they can be used. All this is under legal supervision.

"This is the system we are familiar with," Avigdor said. "The right one." Outside this system there is another one being constructed by the GSS, which sets its own directives, over which there is no judicial supervision because it is outside the law. As Feldman said at a conference in Jerusalem a year earlier:

> The state was established together with the GSS. Just as we have water, earth, and air, we have the GSS. The GSS dealt with areas that are extremely intrusive with respect to human rights. The GSS investigated, arrested, held people in detention facilities, submitted classified material to the courts, made recommendations for appointments in certain positions, and had unlimited control over the Arab sector — but there is no legal framework for the GSS's activity. The GSS succeeded without difficulty in creating the

normative vacuum in which it operated and continues
to operate to this very day. All the other institutions
that were meant to serve as counterbalances did not
work against it.

Who authorized the GSS to investigate? Who
authorized them to take people to the GSS investigation facilities in the middle of the night, and to hold
them there? The GSS operates in the justice system
like a parasite feeding off a host. The GSS has drawn
on the powers of other bodies. If it was necessary to
arrest someone, the GSS would go with policemen,
and the policemen were the living host carrying the
leech of the GSS. The GSS is not authorized to receive a search warrant or warrant for arrest. To the
best of my knowledge no policeman ever asked:
"Why should I be a subcontractor of the GSS?" The
GSS interrogation and detention facilities were created in regular prisons. The GSS has autonomy in
the regular prisons. The prison warder only went in
to deliver meals, bringing prisoners in and out.

I asked the director of the Ashkelon prison about
the GSS interrogation wing, and he answered: "I've
never been in the GSS interrogation cells, it's a given
that I don't go in there." The GSS is not nurtured by
the powers of the law. Here is a state, making its way
democratically, measured by civil society's ability to
resist the GSS's wish to operate through that society's
authorities—and no one opens their mouths to object.
The GSS is in effect responsible for the realization of
all the laws dealing with state security. All the laws
aimed at democratic defense of the society against

the threat to its security—the realization and implementation of them are in the GSS's hands. The GSS runs the trials in crimes against state security. A lawyer is present, but behind him sits a civil GSS representative, who manages the trial by remote control. And the justices accept this as a given. This is also the case in the justice's chambers. The defense counsel stands by the door, not allowed to enter, and the GSS representative goes inside. It never occurs to the justices to ask the question, "Who are you? What is your authority?" Why? It's like water and air, like nature in this state.[7]

Avigdor Feldman made his argument with clarity and courage, and his words pose the question of what kind of society we are living in. Is this a society where a small group of people can decide how many blows to deliver, a society that has a clandestine world of its own that even justices are not allowed to enter, a society where the justice system says, "Give them their territory, they know what they're doing"? How much power do we give this group of people whose actions are not rooted in law and not subject to judicial oversight?

Six GSS men were sitting right behind me during the closing arguments in January 1999. They were not wearing any uniforms, of course, but I had been sitting beside them at the court cafeteria in the morning and saw them talking with the representative of the state. I tried in vain to see how they reacted during the trial. Like most Israelis, I know people who serve at the GSS—a neighbor, the father of one of my son's friends, a cousin. Once they retire from the service many of them are nominated to key positions, running education systems, or companies, or security services in developing countries. And many of them, such as the former GSS heads Ami Ayalon and Yaacov Peri, retire and become involved in politics, and then suddenly claim that Israel cannot continue the military occupation and must negotiate with the Palestinians.

Leah Tsemel from the Public Committee Against Torture in Israel followed Avigdor. She has defended thousands of Palestinians who have been arrested, tortured, or deported, or who have had their houses demolished. Despite having appeared before the High Court many times, she was very nervous. In Israel, she said, a loss of shame has taken place. "The denial of torture was good because it implied condemnation— we're not doing this. The old standard was derived from the hypocrisy: no torture is allowed. The loss of hypocrisy creates new standards." She spoke about a new technique that had developed with the loss of hypocrisy, where professional records of torture are kept. There are charts on which the investigators record how long detainees have been tied up "waiting," and there are forms on which doctors write what can be done to the detainees. People are actually tortured in many countries, but the standard is universal: torture is prohibited. Leah finished with a request: "Don't let us be the first to determine that torture is permissible."

While Leah was speaking, I recalled what I had been told by South African human rights lawyers such as Geoff Budlender, the director of the Legal Resources Centre, about what they called "the losing case." Each year tens of thousands of black South Africans were arrested under the pass laws, which barred blacks from living in areas designated for whites only. The Legal Resources Centre filed thousands of appeals in these cases in the hope that one day the judges would no longer be able to look themselves in the mirror and approve actions that, while legal, were so clearly unjust. Leah Tsemel, Avigdor Feldman, and the other lawyers who spoke before the High Court that day hoped that in Israel too one day, the judges would no longer be able to endorse tactics we all knew to be immoral.

But how could we reach the conscience of each judge? What could make these High Court judges—who had declined to rule on so many previous torture cases—realize they had to make a clear ruling against torture? How could we convince the justices, who had constantly been unwilling to take a stand against the army or the security services?

In the days of apartheid, a South African judge told me, "At international conferences, no one wants to sit next to us apartheid judges. We are isolated at lunches, and at breaks no one wants to be seen talking to us—but the Israeli judges are always welcome. Why is that?" I had no clear answer. But I think that the case on torture was one of the very rare cases in which the Israeli High Court judges knew that a ruling in favor of the state, their approval of the continued use of torture, might jeopardize the warm reception they receive overseas. Following the advice of Arthur Chaskalson, who headed the Legal Resources Centre under apartheid and is now the president of South Africa's Constitutional Court, we invited international judges to observe each of the court hearings. Their presence—with translators by their side—could not have been ignored.

I do believe this international presence had an effect. Perhaps the justices on the High Court were indeed concerned about their international reputation—worried about a future conference at which no one would sit next to them. At the

end of the long decision that the nine judges signed, they
added the following:

> Deciding these applications weighed heavy on this
> Court. True, from the legal perspective, the road be-
> fore us is smooth. We are, however, part of Israeli so-
> ciety. Its problems are known to us and we live its
> history. We are not isolated in an ivory tower. We live
> the life of this country. We are aware of the harsh re-
> ality of terrorism in which we are, at times, immersed.
> Our apprehension that this decision will hamper the
> ability to properly deal with terrorists and terrorism,
> disturbs us. We are, however, justices. Our brethren
> require us to act according to the law. This is equally
> the standard that we set for ourselves. When we sit to
> justice, we are being judged. Therefore, we must act
> according to our purest conscience when we decide
> the law.[8]

And they went on to outlaw the methods of interrogation that
had been used daily by the GSS.

I do not know what eventually touched the judges. But I
was moved by the last human rights lawyer to speak, Andre
Rosenthal. Andre has represented the largest number of tortured Palestinian detainees—in 1998 alone he petitioned the
High Court eighty-eight times. Each time he asked the court
not only to stop the torture of his client in the interrogation
room but also to issue a verdict that torture was prohibited in
principle. He had already said the same things so many times
before the justices who were present that, this time, after five
attorneys had repeatedly explained why the High Court should

rule unequivocally, Andre just kept asking loudly, *"Ma ze?* What is this?"

As Andre repeated, "What is this?" it seemed to me he was asking about the racism in our society, a society where a representative of the state justified the arrest, interrogation, and torture of tens of thousands of people—just because they are Palestinians.

FIVE

AN ARAB HOUSE

September 4, 1999

It was a beautiful Saturday morning. I could hear the quiet of a Shabbat in Beit Hakerem through my turquoise curtains. The thought of going out to the West Bank to build a house on such a beautiful day wasn't exactly appealing. Amotz wished me a muffled good day and rolled over to resume his Saturday morning shut-eye. I knew that although the weather was pleasant then, by noon it would be searing. I imagined myself hauling rocks in the midday sun and could barely bring myself to take the icy water bottles out of the freezer. On the table were the bowls of sweets I prepared for my children every Saturday morning so that they could watch TV while we grabbed another hour of sleep. This was their weekly sweet-eating time, and that day three of Gali's friends were sleeping over as well.

It was only an e-mail announcement, I told myself. *That's not compelling. How can they expect people to come if they only send e-mail invitations? Had they called I would have felt guilty and gone for sure, but it's going to be so hot. . . .*

I forced myself to leave the house and then realized I'd

forgotten to bring a hat—clearly a sign that I didn't want to go. These demonstrations, where a few dozen Israelis rebuilt Palestinian houses that had been demolished by the municipality or the Israeli Ministry of the Interior, were all that was happening at the moment. It was important not to sit home while the government spoke about peace and sowed the seeds of hatred at the same time, I told myself.

I ran into Uri on the stairs, coming back from a sleepover at a friend's house. At nine, he rarely slept away from home, and he'd come back early to see me. "You're leaving already?" he asked, crestfallen. "It's not fair!" I went back in the house with him. Everyone would be late anyway, I figured, and by the time they got organized I'd be there. But when Uri saw the sweets on the table he remembered a television show he wanted to watch, so I went out again, on my way to rebuild this demolished Palestinian house.

The Israeli authorities have destroyed over eleven thousand Palestinian houses since 1967, and the pile of rubble that marks the place where a house used to stand is a harsh sight to behold.[1] This particular house I was setting out to help rebuild had been destroyed not long before—on August 11, 1999—while Barak was leading the government and peace negotiations were under way, and I knew it was important. But in the car I kept thinking that it was too hot, that I'd already been to a million demonstrations and that no one would really notice if I didn't go. *Perhaps I should go to the museum instead*, I thought.

The world-renowned Israel Museum is close to my home and I often plan to go, but somehow, because it's so near, I always end up postponing it. Besides, the museum always irritates me a bit. The last time I'd treated myself to a day at the

museum had been almost a year before, on my birthday. I'd
gone to see a wonderful exhibit entitled *To the East: Orientalism in the Arts in Israel.* Never before in Israel had I witnessed
such a serious discussion about Orientalism and the dilemmas faced by Israelis living among Arabs in Israel and surrounded by Arab countries. The exhibit examined the
different attitudes of Israeli artists toward Arabs, the "other,"
and the relations between Jews and Arabs in Israel. Some of
the artists, such as David Riv and Larry Abramson, seemed
remarkable and courageous to me. A photograph by Pinhas
Cohen Gan taken in the Jericho refugee camp on February
10, 1974—of a green tent planted by Israeli artists in the
midst of the mud houses of the refugees in the desert—was
stronger than anything I could have written about house demolitions and the humiliation of being homeless.

In the catalogue, the curators of the exhibition, Yigal
Zalmona and Tamar Manor-Friedman, explained that they
had chosen to show not only how the Arab is depicted in Israeli art but also the manner in which the Arab is absent, the
blurring of the Arab presence, his state of "present absence."
Yigal Zalmona wrote about Ein Hod, the Israeli artists' village not far from Haifa, which was built in houses deserted
by Arabs in 1948. Many of the residents of Arab Ein
Hod live in a nearby village that is still not recognized by the
government—as if it didn't exist. Zalmona wrote,

> Old Jaffa is another example of a ruined place—an
> Arab settlement that was turned into an artists' quar-
> ter and a tourist highlight, a bourgeois convention of
> good taste. The combination of the exoticism and the
> sense of local authenticity, together with the fact that

the area is emptied of its original inhabitants, enables
its possession and conversion into part of a system of
aesthetic values for Israelis, a system that communi-
cates an Oriental, Mediterranean beauty and a feeling
of home, community, "Israeliness." Yet all the while,
these homes preserve a different memory, of another,
absent collective.[2]

The wonderful exhibition, however, contained not a single
word of explanation in Arabic. The catalogue was printed in
English and Hebrew, and the works were accompanied by
descriptions only in Hebrew and English. I thought about
calling Tamar, a childhood friend from Beer Sheva, and asking her why there was no Arabic. In a country where Arabic
is the official second language, in a city where a third of
the inhabitants are Palestinians, at an exhibition on the subject
of Orientalism, why was there no translation into Arabic?
She'd probably tell me there were budget constraints. Nothing
good would come of the conversation, I was pretty sure of that.
No doubt she'd tell me that Arabs don't come to the museum
anyway, and that the few who do know either Hebrew or English. So why call? (When I did call, more than a year later,
Tamar told me there really had been a budget problem, and
not only had they tried to translate, but they had invited the
participation of several Arab artists, who had declined.)

Still, that early Saturday morning was lovely, and I
imagined myself strolling up the long pathway to the museum's sculpture garden, watching the well-dressed visitors
and listening to the birds chirping in the cypress trees. *Where
are they building this house?* I wondered, jogging myself back to
the other reality. *Maybe I'll drive there, help out a little, and then*

come home in the early afternoon. It's probably nearby, but I haven't got a clue where. I know the big cities and the refugee camps on the map of the territories, but I have no idea where this village is. I don't even remember what it's called. No, I'm not going to go. I'm going to the museum instead. After that I'll do something to make up for it during the week.

The museum wasn't open yet, but the line at the ticket booth was already long. They were showing a Kandinsky exhibition—not a good enough reason to stand in line. I did a U-turn and headed home, deciding that after a nice breakfast I would write about why I didn't go to the house building.

I didn't go because I was afraid it would be terribly hot and I remembered the march I had organized in Hebron in October 1996, when I got dehydrated, and the dozens of Women in Black vigils I had participated in over the years on Fridays between one and two in the afternoon (and the dozens of vigils I had *not* participated in, which made me feel bad about the women who had stood there week after week for years). Then I thought about the demonstrations at Har Homa, the Palestinian-owned hill southeast of the city that had been torn apart and sliced up into neat apartments for young Jewish couples to take out mortgages on. I remembered all the letters, the reports, the speeches and debates, and I just wanted a Saturday free of the complicated outside world. Even the museum had become a complicated place for me. Although I felt it would be self-indulgent on my part to go home to my wonderful apartment in a green neighborhood, where the birds chirp all day long, that was what I wanted, more than anything. So I went home, where I felt good.

I have been an activist in peace organizations and human

rights organizations for many years. I have always wondered
how to persuade more Israelis to attend demonstrations, write
protest letters, do something against the continuing military
occupation that makes millions of people miserable, forcing
them to live by laws that prevent them from leading normal,
reasonable, dignified lives. I have participated in hundreds of
demonstrations, organized dozens of them, and written reports
on human rights violations in the territories. I have always
wanted more Israelis to say, "Enough! Let's do something different here—let's redistribute the region's wealth, and allow
more people to fulfill their dreams." I thought once that if
more Israelis knew what was going on in the territories, we
would surely have to withdraw, to facilitate the establishment
of a Palestinian state, and finally achieve peace. I thought
that if people demonstrated and protested and pressed, something might change. Not like what Prime Minister Barak's
so-called peace government tried, but rather something more
just, something based on the idea "We are all human beings—
let's see how we can live together" rather than "We are
stronger, but because the acts of terrorism committed against
us hurt us, we are willing to reach an agreement with you."

The controversial negotiations over deployment in 9 percent or 3 percent or 50 percent of the territories, in this settlement or that—this is not the kind of peace I dream of. This
map composed of different-colored patches—Areas A, B, C—
reminds me too much of the Bantustans and not enough of
opportunities for peace. Here too, just like in South Africa
during the eighties, there are white belts around orange areas
on the map. Any child could tell you that these cartographic
gymnastics—maps and roads cut up into ours and theirs—are

impossible. In South Africa the Bantustan plan to build small enclaves and call them independent "homelands" did not work—why should it work here?

When we established B'Tselem at the beginning of 1989, we thought that if we only knew more, informed the Israeli public more, the oppression here would end. We asked how we could reach more people, how we could not only make them aware that Palestinians are tortured in prisons every day but also allow them to comprehend the awfulness and realize that they could do something to stop it.

When I think about house demolitions, I am always reminded of Roni Talmor. Within the small community of human rights activists, each person has a particular issue that drives him or her especially nuts. Tamar Peleg and Ilana Hammerman were always outraged by the administrative detentions—how could people be detained without trial? For Roni it was house demolitions—the barbarity of it, the unnecessary evil and stupidity. Roni wrote the first B'Tselem report on house destructions during the First Intifada, when the bombing or bulldozing of houses as a punishment or deterrent was de rigueur.[3] I interviewed her a decade later, and she still voiced the same rage over this barbaric practice. I asked Roni why house demolitions in particular made her so hopping mad.

RONI: I'll tell you why. Look, this is something that no other country in the world does—not even the regimes we think of as the darkest, the most crazy. Saddam Hussein dropped mustard gas on the Iranians, he blows people's heads off, but he doesn't destroy their families' houses. It seems to me the most primitive thing, something that goes beyond the violation of conventions. I'm ashamed that the courts in the state I live in permit such a thing.

DAPHNA: But why? Why house demolitions especially?

RONI: Because how can such a thing be? Who ever thought up this barbaric idea? They always demolish the house of someone who's either in prison, dead, or run away where they can't find him. He's not in the house by definition. If he was, they'd take him to prison or kill him. Yet even though he's not there, they come along with explosives, take the family outside, with all their possessions, and blow it up. It seems to me higher up on the cultural ladder to kill someone you know is a terrorist, a fugitive, or whatever . . . that's much more cultured than razing a house. How can they even do it, physically? How can the soldiers execute the orders? How can they take out the mattresses, the children's schoolbags, the oilcans, and blow it sky high? That's not taking action against the criminal—say it was a terrorist who killed Jews, put a bomb in the market—it's an act against his family. There are small children wandering around there. How can they do it?

DAPHNA: How do you think they can do it?

RONI: Because I think that everyone, the entire society here, is fundamentally corrupt. Brainwashed, corrupted, that the occupation is corrupt.

DAPHNA: But what you're saying is astonishing. Somehow house demolitions bother you more than mustard gas, even though they're less violent—no one gets injured, no one gets killed.

RONI: The whole picture, of all the family's belongings outside, and the house being blown into the air, as punishment, as what . . . ? They say it's a deterrent. I don't believe that. I think that it sprouts another ten new terrorists. But even if it were a deterrent, so what? Is that the criterion for anything? To me it seems like stooping to the lowest level of cultural abasement.

By 1999, when Roni and I had this conversation, very few houses were demolished to punish the owners—though this practice, tragically, would resume with great frequency during the Second Intifada.[4] Instead they were leveled on the grounds that they had been built without permits. Of course, for the vast majority of Palestinians, it is impossible to get such a permit.

Bilhah Berg, director of legal services at the Association for Civil Rights in Israel, handles the cases of people whose houses were demolished for lacking permits. Ostensibly, each municipality or government is authorized to destroy houses that were built without permits. The only thing is, Palestinians in Jerusalem and in extensive parts of the territories have no chance of getting permits to build their homes. A significant part of the Palestinian land in Jerusalem—the land that was not expropriated to build Jewish neighborhoods—is colored green on the map. In other words, building there is prohibited. The shortage of houses for Palestinians in East Jerusalem is so severe that an estimated twenty thousand families are homeless. Young people starting families cannot get building permits, even on their family land.

Bilhah led an initiative to reach an agreement between the Palestinian residents of two neighborhoods and City Hall. She hoped to achieve an agreement whereby the residents would agree not to build without permits and the municipality would undertake not to demolish existing structures.

BILHAH: I see house demolitions as one of the more severe phenomena. Not just the demolitions themselves, but everything: the absence of a planning system; the absence of investment in infrastructure in East Jerusalem; the collection of municipal taxes in East Jerusalem despite the failure to provide services; the education system, which has failed, throughout the years of the occupation, to handle East Jerusalem. In one area, however, the municipality is very active—house demolitions. They don't plan, or if they do, it's in a manner that restricts building on the one hand, yet on the other they're really good at enforcement, really diligent and active and engage all their resources. This is the demolition of a house, a very severe blow to a person's human rights—the basic right to live. And the people have no alternatives. I tried to think of, or recall, examine verdicts and the press, for cases where the state demolished Jewish homes, or the courts had refused to prevent a demolition, or the authorities had ordered a demolition when the person didn't have alternative accommodation. I don't know of any such case. Even the tents and shacks they put up opposite the Knesset weren't dismantled. The state also destroys tents when they belong to the Bedouin in the territories and the Negev, tents built according to the planning and construction law. The fact that the state doesn't ensure the right to minimal accommodation is a severe blow to people's rights. The state would never conceive of destroying the tents of the Jewish homeless and throwing them onto the streets. But it doesn't think twice when it's Palestinians in question. I can't weigh up human rights and say this is the single most severe violation, but in my view it is one of the worst.

DAPHNA: There's a racist element to this, isn't there? Why do they enforce it in East Jerusalem and not with respect to Jews?

BILHAH: The entire approach to the issue of land is fundamentally discriminatory. It didn't begin with house demolitions. Land was expropriated from Arabs for Jews, a very large amount of agricultural land was given to kibbutzim and moshavim, and Arab land is very limited. There's already discrimination from the word go. In the neighborhoods of East Jerusalem, a large part of the planning, when any is done, is aimed at restricting construction rather than facilitating it. We [at ACRI] also went over the existing building plans for East Jerusalem with town planners. All our studies show that a great many of the plans are based on purely political considerations rather than design requirements. The opportunity is provided to use land, as much as possible Arab land, for the benefit of Jews, either by expropriation on the one hand or limiting their construction on the other in order to prevent them from expanding. The very essence of the planning is discriminatory.[5] If from the start the idea is to allow Jews to build as much as possible and restrict Arab building as much as possible, so as not to enable them to live here, then it follows that the way to implement this policy is to demolish the homes of the Arabs, not of the Jews.

Simultaneous with the rebuilding of demolished houses by activists from the International Coalition Against House Demolitions and Israeli and Palestinian peace activists, the Association of Civil Rights in Israel tried to find a different solution, through agreements, for Palestinians who wanted to build.

BILHAH: In Jabel Mukaber—a neighborhood in East Jerusalem, close to Talpiot—two-thirds of the landowners cannot build because their lands are marked as green areas, although there is no planning logic to this. The land is marked green to restrict building, motivated by a long-standing political agenda on the part of the authorities. Our idea was to organize a new plan, which would allow restricted building in green areas, according to the needs of the community.

When we [the architects Tali Shapira and Ayala Roneal and the Association for Civil Rights in Israel] started this work, the Municipality of Jerusalem gave us a gentleman's agreement that they would immediately start implementing the idea. This meant that even before we signed the convention we would work toward mutual agreement: representatives of the neighborhood would act to stop new illegal building, and the Municipality of Jerusalem would examine all the existing buildings and work to approve building permits for houses that had already been built. No promise was made to approve all the houses, but the municipality agreed to examine each case and make an effort to approve, adapting the plans in process. If there was a case where a house was located in the path of a huge road that was being planned, a road that could not be rerouted—and here we're talking mainly about the eastern ring road around the city—according to the municipality there would be no choice but to destroy it. However, they meant to approve most of the houses. The Ministry of the Interior, at the first stages, was not a partner in this agreement. We approached them separately, along with the planners, the architects, and representatives of the neighborhood, and we asked them to participate in this project, with a view to accomplishing things through coordination, and we received a general declaration from the Jerusalem district supervisor that they welcomed the plan a great deal and would be glad to participate as it progressed. They also agreed to notify us in advance should a demolition be planned, so that we could approach the courts and ask for postponement so as not to damage implementation of our program. But they didn't meet their commitments. After the date of the gentleman's agreement between the sides, the Ministry of the Interior demolished two houses without giving us any advance notice and the Municipality of Jerusalem demolished another two. Of course, these four demolitions really shook the inhabitants' trust in our project. This also happened in Beit Hanina. At the height of the attempt to formulate an agreement between the residents and the municipality, they went and demolished a house.

At some point, the Ministry of the Interior cut ties with the Municipality of Jerusalem completely and, while these agreements were being signed, brought in its bulldozers and demolished another house. I can't see any justification for that, even when I try to look at it from the authorities' point of view—I can't see any justification for destroying a house from any point of view, let alone when there's an agreement between the residents and the municipality with the involvement of the Ministry of the Interior. In the agreement the municipality undertakes not to remove people living in their own homes, and not to destroy the homes, and then the Ministry of the Interior comes in and does it instead. Now, one of the Municipality of Jerusalem's claims is "There's nothing we can do, it's the Ministry of the Interior, it has different authority." This is one of the absurd claims. One of the difficult things is that there are multiple authorities here; there's a double authority to destroy: both the Municipality of Jerusalem and the Ministry of the Interior, and each one does whatever it sees fit. I can reach an agreement with the Ministry of the Interior today that is not binding on the Municipality of Jerusalem and vice versa.

I feel that I am fighting all the time, that my job is a war. In the day I think war and at night I think war—all the time. I don't finish working when I go home. It goes with me, this terrible situation. I open a newspaper, and that is what I see before my eyes. All I think about is how to be more effective, make more progress, what more can be done to change this situation. Often I don't even read the weekend newspaper; I haven't got the strength anymore, I can't take it; I need that time to do something for myself.

September 5, 1999

An article by Gideon Levy stared at me from the morning newspaper.[6] It told the story of a woman whose house was demolished. Levy writes a weekly feature in *Ha'aretz* called

"Twilight Zone," in which he depicts the bleak daily reality in the Occupied Territories, where people's dignity is trampled upon every day by laws and regulations and court orders, all of which purport to represent the "rule of law." Moving photographs accompany each article, providing a look at the other side, for those who want to see it—the face of a bewildered child in the hospital whose parents are not allowed to visit him, or a young woman who didn't get a permit in time to give birth in a hospital.

During the first few years of the Intifada the impact of B'Tselem was tremendous. It played a central role in supplying reliable information to Israeli journalists, Knesset members, the diplomatic community, and activists. It filled an important niche for the Israeli public too, as an entity that could be trusted because it consisted of "our guys"—Israelis who covered what went on in the Occupied Territories. The Palestinian human rights organizations were perceived by most of the public as instruments of propaganda for the PLO, the enemy. When they reported the death tolls, most Israelis believed they were inflated. But when B'Tselem published a report, people listened. We examined all our information—cross-checked our testimonies, as we liked to say. Our most important goal in the beginning was to attain credibility. If someone died from a heart attack as a result of the stress caused by soldiers' presence, we debated whether we should include that person among the numbers of those killed or not. As research director, I felt that it was my responsibility not to fail. We sent each report to the IDF spokesperson for a response prior to distribution. They would generally squirm before claiming that this or the other detail was inaccurate—in other words, *What you are saying is correct, but we are still right.*

After the organization's credibility was established, people knew that if B'Tselem announced that three houses were
demolished without prior warning, that people were being
expelled from their homes and country without trial, that
thousands of children in Jerusalem were not entitled to
health insurance because they were not registered as residents of the city in which they lived, it was true. The information was always reliable. But *Ha'aretz* provided its readers
with the information in a more approachable and accessible
fashion. It's not that Gideon Levy's articles are easy to read.
Often I have to force myself to read them; I can't bear the
horror. But Gideon writes every week, and if people want to
know what's going on there in the Occupied Territories—
that place that most of us, most Israelis, don't want to know
exists—then they can read Gideon Levy. Amira Hass, the
only Israeli journalist who lives in the Occupied Territories,
also wrote almost every day, sparing her readers nothing.
It's not that people don't know. We all know, even if the editors of the Hebrew newspapers provide us with less and less
news about what is happening there. Still, we know—but
what do we do with that information? What can one possibly
do with that information?

Hol Ha'moed Sukkot, September 27, 1999

I was glad I went to the rebuilding of a demolished house in
Walageh. No one would have noticed if I hadn't, and there
were slightly too many people for one building site. Still, it
was interesting, and it made me happy. *Happy,* of course, is
not the appropriate word here, because the whole thing was

so bizarre and unclear. In order to reach this village, which is officially part of Jerusalem, you have to go through two checkpoints. We went through the tunnel to Bethlehem and then cut back toward Jerusalem, reaching Walageh by a small winding road. City Hall claims that the area below the road falls under its jurisdiction, while the upper part of Walageh belongs to the Occupied Territories.

The five hundred people that live in the part of the village that is now part of the united Jerusalem are not considered residents of Jerusalem. In fact, they carry the orange identity cards of Palestinian residents living in the Occupied Territories. In other words, the municipality of Jerusalem can send bulldozers to demolish their houses, but because of their orange identity cards, the Ministry of the Interior won't let them have access to Jerusalem. It doesn't make sense, it doesn't seem reasonable, but that's how it is—the land belongs to Jerusalem, and the residents don't.

Before we started the rebuilding we were briefed by Khalil El-Atrash, one of the residents of the village, who pointed out the houses that had been demolished or were slated for demolition. Of the seventy houses in the village beneath the road, fifty-one were earmarked for demolition. Twelve had already been destroyed. The courts had so far ruled on eighteen cases—in each case issuing demolition orders for one year later and fines ranging from NIS 7,000 to 49,000 ($1,800 to $11,000). The narrow asphalt road that the residents had tarred at their own expense was about to be destroyed because it had been built without a permit, as was their mosque.

The Israeli and Palestinian volunteers organized themselves into two rows, passing the bricks from hand to hand.

Two young Palestinian men laid them one after the other, straightened them, and cemented them, as if to say, *We're used to this line of work, leave it to us.* Most builders in Israel are Palestinians, but the contractors are Jews. In Walageh, the two young Palestinians, men in jeans and T-shirts, made sure to keep their distance from us. We handed them the bricks. They built the walls. The new house we were building was already slated to be demolished in October.

After about an hour of work, Rivka, Zohara, and I went to prepare lunch in the nearby tent that served as the Halifa family's kitchen and dining area. Rabbi Arik Ascherman, who organized the rebuilding, had made sure to bring tomatoes, cucumbers, and kosher salads—hummus, tahina, and coleslaw—in large plastic containers. Someone pointed out with a smile that one of the salads was a brand made in the Occupied Territories by settlers, and Arik apologized for not having noticed. Miriam Halifa and her daughters, whose demolished house we were rebuilding, washed and chopped vegetables with us. "You need to learn more Arabic," Miriam told us in rapid Arabic, "and we need to learn Hebrew." When we brought out the lunch, the wall of the Halifa family's house was almost finished.

Three rabbis were building with us that day in Walageh. Rabbi Arik Ascherman, Rabbi David Rosen, and Rabbi Jeremy Milgrom are members of Rabbis for Human Rights, and they are also involved in leading the Israeli Coalition Against House Demolitions (ICAHD). Because we were building the Halifa family's house on Hol Ha'moed Sukkot, the Jewish harvest holiday, they associated the building of the house with building the sukkah—a small hut that Jews build every year to celebrate the exodus of our ancestors from Egypt, to remember how they lived in the desert on their way to the promised land. They spoke of the significance of the sukkah of peace.

Jeff Halper, the man behind the Israeli Coalition Against House Demolitions, is also the person behind the e-mail messages I receive. He drove me to the house-building demonstration in his old car. I have seen Jeff in action in many protest movements over the years, but I have never seen him as motivated as he has been since he started "producing" (as he likes to say) these events. I asked him where the passion was coming from. What gave him the strength to organize the rebuilding of a demolished Palestinian house every few weeks?

JEFF: For us, house demolition was not the sole issue of the occupation. We started with that, but as soon as we got into it we understood that everything was connected with the occupation. Every house demolition is a microcosm. There's the land issue, the roads issue, the settlements issue, the economic welfare issue—they are all contained in the house demolitions. I think that's one of the reasons we were so effective in recruiting an international lobby, because we always put the demolitions into the wider context of the occupation. Why are they demolishing this house? What is the policy behind the action?

House demolition is the essence of the occupation: the humiliation, the trauma, the cruelty. The analogy we make is to rape. I mean, you're violating the very essence of the person. It's more than just another political issue. They destroy 150–200 houses a year. The impact of that on the families and the surrounding villages is so huge. It's like a ripple effect. And for the Palestinians, what is the meaning of the occupier who comes in and does this? He has the power that enables him to do this to you. It's not just rape—it's serial rape. The guy comes again and again and feels he has the right to rape you. And it's not even a criminal act—it's like he has a license to rape and humiliate people. So I think that from the Palestinians' point of view, the meaning and implications are much wider than the house demolitions themselves.

Jeff spoke with passion about the cooperation between Israelis and Palestinians to oppose the house demolitions and rebuild Palestinian houses that had been destroyed. He told me how he learned to know the villages in the territories. "If you had asked me two years ago where the Arab village of Anate is, I wouldn't have had a clue, although I have been active in the peace movements for years." He added, "I have the same fears that Israelis have. I have a car. Is it safe? But now I know the territories." Jeff told me that through dealing with house demolitions he learned about the gray bureaucratic mechanisms of the occupation—the mechanisms that we can't understand, that seem so boring to study. "Do you know, for example, what E1 is?" he asked me. "Do you know that the area of the settlement of Ma'ale Adumim, E1 on the map, is larger than the area of Tel Aviv? That piece of land marked on the map cuts the West Bank into small pieces; that's why there's no chance of an agreement with the Palestinians."

I told Jeff I hadn't believed that e-mail messages could get people out of their homes, and I told him why I hadn't come to the previous demonstration. Jeff told me that the international influence of their e-mail messages was huge because they told the stories of the people whose houses were demolished and also expressed the political significance of the demolitions in the context of the Israeli-Palestinian peace accords. In practice, he said, activists have lost all hope that Israelis can do anything, and they're turning to the international community. Jeff said that in one month the U.S. State Department had received more e-mails about house demolitions in Katana village than it had about the entire war in Kosovo.

In Hebrew, the phrase "Arab building" connotes shoddy, substandard work. By contrast, the phrase "an Arab house" brings to mind an old, well-built, expensive house. So what happened? When did we start appreciating the Arab houses and belittling the people who built them?

Sometimes when I'm not careful where my thoughts wander, I think there are so many Israelis from many different cultures who have lost their homes, in the deepest sense of the word—family, culture, language. All they have in common is this imaginary phrase, "building a home for the Jewish people," to the point that they don't really care what happened to the houses that were destroyed at Tantura or Jerash, or those being demolished in Walageh today.

On February 25, 1996, a bomb exploded on a bus on the number 18 line in Jerusalem, killing twenty-five people. Dozens were injured. The day before that, Natan the contractor had come to our house with three Palestinian laborers to take up the tile floor in preparation for renovation. Most of those killed on the bus were from the Katamonim neighborhood, a working-class area where Natan lived. When Natan returned to our house after the bombing, he was furious: "I'll never vote for the Labor Party again in my life," he told us.

We all agreed that these suicide bombings were a response to the order that Prime Minister Peres, the leader of the Labor Party, had given a month earlier to kill Yahya Ayyash—a Hamas leader known as "the Engineer." But we did not agree on what could be done to stop the horrible attacks on Israeli civilians. Every morning Natan would arrive with his transistor radio, drink his coffee, and moan about how his laborers couldn't get in because of the tight closure. On March 3 another bomb exploded on the number 18 bus line. Nine people were killed, seven injured. The next day thirteen people were killed and over a hundred injured in a bombing in Tel Aviv. Those were days of utter despair. There were constant rounds of telephone calls to see if everyone was all right: *Bus 18 comes to our neighborhood. Is my mother all right in Tel Aviv? Who was injured?* We sat for hours in our floorless apartment, in the midst of the never-ending renovation that no one had patience for, in deep depression. The talk was about politics, funerals, and the upcoming elections. Avi, the carpenter, was a diehard Likudnik, and he bet me that the right-wing Likud Party and Binyamin "Bibi" Netanyahu would win the next elections. Yehudit, the architect, was a Meretz voter and she didn't want to give up on the dream of peace that was starting to come true. Natan, the contractor, said he'd always voted for Labor and he was glad to see them in power—but would no longer give them his vote.

The renovations continued sporadically for months, months during which the Likud's Netanyahu did win the elections, as Avi had prophesied, months during which Yehudit and Natan never stopped arguing about politics or the optimal height of the balcony's ceiling. Eventually, after Natan called her "sweetheart" one day, Yehudit told me she couldn't take it anymore and that she refused to work for him. She said we had to get rid of Natan. Natan was glad to go, and Yehudit brought in another Jewish contractor with another set of Palestinian laborers to finish the job. When the renovations were finally completed, it turned out that there was no electricity or phone line in the apartment. The first electrician had built the fuse box and phone connection in one place, and the second had put them somewhere else. Only a meter separated the boxes—but who would connect them? I invited both electricians for coffee. Herzl, the first contractor's Israeli electrician, blamed Hassan, the Palestinian brought in with the second group. He claimed that Hassan wasn't even a certified electrician and announced he wouldn't touch wiring installed by someone who didn't have a clue. He finished his coffee and cigarette and left. Hassan kept quiet until Herzl departed. He told me that he was an electrical engineer trained in Bulgaria and promised that he would fix the problem the next day.

But Hassan didn't come the next day, nor the day after. When he eventually returned, he apologized and explained that his daughter had been in the hospital and that he had to be with her. He didn't make a big deal out of it, and he didn't want to talk about it. After some prodding he told me that he was married to his cousin from Jordan. They had been married three years when his daughter, Amal, was born with a rare genetic defect that required frequent hospital visits. He took a wrinkled piece of paper out of his pocket and was persuaded to part with it only after I swore to photocopy it and return it immediately. It was a certificate from Hadassah Hospital, stating that Amal needed frequent and special care. "This document doesn't help me," he

said, "but I keep it anyway. At Hadassah they give Amal excellent care."[7]

Since their marriage, Hassan, who is a resident of
Jerusalem, had tried without success to arrange a residence
permit for his wife, Eva. But from the Israeli authorities'
point of view, she is a foreigner. She has to leave the city
every three months, cross the border to Jordan, and submit a
renewed request for a visa to return home again. But the last
time she went to Jordan they told her she couldn't come
back. "Wait three months," she was told, while ten-month-old
Amal was hospitalized at Hadassah in West Jerusalem.

I found an amiable clerk in the Foreign Ministry who
promised to help. He arranged a visa the next day. When you
know whom to call and you speak unaccented Hebrew, there
are nice Israeli officials to be found in every ministry.

A soldier at the border crossing looked at Eva's new visa
and said it wasn't possible that she had received a visa for
three months. He marked a big X on the visa and wrote,
"Valid for 10 days only."

"We'll manage," Hassan told me when he saw the look of
horror on my face. "It'll be okay. At least Amal is getting
good medical care here."

Palestinian children whose mothers are from Jerusalem
but whose fathers are not aren't even entitled to be registered
as residents. They don't exist as far as the Israeli authorities
are concerned. They are not eligible for education or health
care. There are approximately ten thousand such children in
Jerusalem today. Luckily, Amal was born to a father from
Jerusalem and a Palestinian mother from Jordan. She is
therefore registered as a Jerusalem resident and gets excellent
care at a hospital in Israel. When Eva came back to Jerusalem

to be at her daughter's bedside, Hassan came to connect our electricity, and the renovations were finally completed.

I try to remember when I started to ask questions. I can't put my finger on the turning points in the progression from an entry in my journal of the 1967 war—written when I was ten—that says, "We'll show them," to my present position. I asked everyone I interviewed for this book about the moments when those changes took place for them. When did it first seem that what officials were saying on the radio wasn't completely true? I asked about the moments that followed, when they understood that something had to be done. Were they the same moments? When we hear or see something wrong, such as these houses in Walageh being demolished even though they could never have been built with a permit in the first place, do we want to do something good?

I remember one moment in 1981 when I understood that something was wrong. I was listening to the 1 a.m. news in the shower: "All our planes returned safely." How many times had I heard that phrase on the radio? It was winter, and heavy rain beat down on the low roof of the bathroom. I asked myself, *What about the people in the houses that have just been bombed?* I pictured them standing in the rain with their children, scurrying to find shelter, frightened. *But all our planes returned safely.*

When I was sixteen I had a boyfriend, Uzi, who was a pilot. It was the dream of every teenage girl in Beer Sheva—a boyfriend from the air force base at Hazerim. "All our planes returned safely" was kind of a trick to tell me that Uzi—and Ron, who sat in front of me in class, and all the other handsome boys who had become pilots—had not been hurt while dropping bombs in Lebanon. Sometimes we saw bombed houses on television—houses that were referred to as "military targets"—but who were these people that our fighter planes were bombing before returning home safely? What did they do after their homes were destroyed? How did they survive? Where did they find shelter from the rain? Where will they live? I stood there in my cute little rented Jewish Agency house in Ir Ganim—which seemed like a palace to me—and looked in the bathroom mirror. The rain beat loudly on the low roof, and I thought, *Where will they live?*

SIX

ON FOOD, FRIENDSHIP, AND NORMALIZATION

In September 1993, after a Tel Aviv rally in support of the Oslo peace accords, we organized a dance party. Some fifty thousand people were at that party, in the square where two years later Yitzhak Rabin was murdered because he led the way to peace. I never thought that the Oslo accords were perfect. In fact, I knew the Oslo accords were arrogantly formulated, avoided any mention of human rights or dignity, and were devoid of compassion. But Yitzhak Rabin and Yasser Arafat recognized that two nations claim possession of this land. After decades of struggle, the leaders of these warring nations came to understand that compromise was necessary. Although the Israeli right and radical left disagree with the likes of me, I maintain that the Oslo accords were important because they constituted recognition that previously had not existed, recognition that there are two nations, each with a significant claim to the land.

This is why we danced—because the accords symbolized hope and change. Anyway, I said at the time, we had better dance, for who knows what tomorrow will bring?

Even then, many Israelis were opposed to the peace accords. The same right-wingers who are now running the country called Rabin a traitor. Many cars bore "Indict the Oslo Criminals" bumper stickers. But I was in South Africa in 1984 when the white government tried to survive by offering limited enfranchisement to Indians and "coloureds" (people of mixed race) because they thought they could crush the black struggle for human rights in a united, democratic South Africa. Here too, offers of this kind are made by leaders who know that the oppression cannot continue in the same vein for long. They're trying to reduce the pressure, to adapt a little, because force alone is not adequate to rule over millions of Palestinians. In both cases, despite the inadequacy of the government's offers, the psychological influence was significant. For years the whites in South Africa believed they had special privileges by virtue of their race. But suddenly the people whom they taught their children to regard as subhuman were receiving the right to vote. The destruction of the lie had been initiated, and it opened the door for a larger transformation. It's that way here as well. When I grew up, there were no Palestinians in this country. Prime Minister Golda Meir said so, our teachers and parents told us so, and we all believed it. We were told that Palestinians had no special connection to this place and that they could go and live in one of the Arab countries around us. Years later, when Israeli peace activists stood in public squares calling for talks with the Palestinians, they called us traitors and prohibited us, by law, from talking with Palestinians identified with the PLO on the grounds that it was a terrorist organization. Then all of a sudden Prime Minister Rabin was talking with Yasser Arafat and with the same Palestinians with whom only months earlier it had been illegal to talk. All of a sudden I could meet Suad for a glass of cold lemonade at her home instead of in Belgium.

Despite their patronizing tone, the Oslo accords were a breakthrough in Israeli consciousness. They allowed us Israelis to see, for a few years, how peace would feel—what a thriving and rich country we could live in. The country experienced wonderful economic prosperity. Millions of tourists came to Israel. Investments flourished. For the first time in my life I was able to travel to Arab countries. We, who had been born with a passport almost as despised as the South African one, could now travel to almost anywhere in the world. Can you imagine what a great experience it was to cross the border to Jordan by bus—the border that had been out of bounds to us for so many years?

But while we were celebrating, the Palestinians still lived under occupation, and their situation only got worse. Israel continued to build settlements (doubling the number of settlers during the period of the peace talks) and added more roadblocks, which prevented Palestinians from traveling between different parts of their own territory.

When I heard, a few weeks after the signing of the Oslo accords, that an Israeli-Palestinian women's peace organization was going to be established, I thought we would finally be able to institutionalize the friendship and joint work we had pursued for so many years. After years in which we had been forced to go abroad in order to work together, the accords—and American and European recognition of the importance of encounters between the two nations—made it possible for us to have a joint organization and joint meetings here in Jerusalem.

After years of writing about violations of human rights in the Occupied Territories, I wanted to do something to bring about change—not just to write and document. I wanted to cooperate with Palestinians on an equal basis, not from the problematic position of a defender of victims' rights.

Three months after the signing of the Oslo accords I was elected to take part in establishing this Israeli-Palestinian women's peace organization. We did not yet know what exactly the organization would do, or how it would work. The application for funding to establish the organization was submitted to the European Union months before the signing at Oslo, before I came into the picture. All I knew was that Israeli and Palestinian women had agreed to set up an organization called Jerusalem Link, comprising two parts—Bat Shalom, an Israeli women's group in West Jerusalem, and the Palestinian Women's Center in East Jerusalem. We looked for an office, discussed how to furnish it, and asked ourselves how we could translate the idea of cooperation into real mutual practice. During the four years that I directed Bat Shalom, we organized meetings between dozens of Israeli and Palestinian women with the aim of learning to know and understand one another better. Young girls who went to joint summer camps in Europe and the United States came to know and respect one another. Women from refugee camps visited kibbutzim and hosted women from the kibbutzim in their homes. Israeli and Palestinian authors and artists met and worked together. We organized demonstrations, seminars, conferences, and in-service training programs. Despite all this, we continued to argue persistently about the order of our priorities as an Israeli and Palestinian women's organization.

We held a contest for female writers and artists, along with workshops for young girls, young mothers, and mothers with teenage children. We founded a fair for Palestinian artists to present and sell their work; we supported and organized art exhibitions—and we never stopped arguing. At one of the first meetings in which I participated, eight Palestinian and Israeli women were discussing the inaugural event for the Jerusalem Link when the question arose as to whether food would be served, and if so, what kind of food. We were sitting in the grayish lobby of the National Palace Hotel in East Jerusalem, in old armchairs, and the waiter brought us small cups of Arab coffee and tea. I was the newest and youngest member of the group, and I learned quickly that the question of what food (or if any food at all) would be served at the event was more significant than I had presumed. The group of Israeli and Palestinian women that established the Link had already met, in Brussels and in Jerusalem, and they called for two states, side by side, at a time when nobody—not even groups such as Peace Now— was talking about a two-state solution.

I never took an interest in the details of written points of agreement between the Israeli and Palestinian women. I wanted to find other ways, women's ways, of translating the agreement between the nations into cooperation. I believed we could build a model of cooperation between the two women's centers on the two sides of the city and prove that it was possible to build neighborly relations out of mutual understanding and recognition. I thought I would meet new women, new friends. But neither my Israeli friends nor my Palestinian friends joined the organization we established.

My Israeli friends found it very hard to understand why instead of celebrating the peace, we insisted on the release of Palestinian political prisoners, demonstrated against the closure of the Occupied Territories, and kept going out on the streets every week wearing black when our leaders were talking peace. My Palestinian friends thought that it was time to build their own society, to write a women's charter, to make sure that their leaders marched toward democracy. As long as the occupation continued, more settlements were being built, and more checkpoints restricted their movements, they felt there was no point in talking about peace.

Although we called ourselves the Jerusalem Link: A Women's Joint Venture for Peace, peace was not in the offing.

The inaugural event was carefully planned to coincide with International Women's Day on March 8, 1994. Simone Susskind from Belgium, who had organized the first conferences for Israeli and Palestinian women in Brussels, made sure to put us in touch with female European ministers, who took a great interest in the new organization and promised to attend the opening. And then on February 25, Baruch Goldstein, a Brooklyn-born settler, murdered twenty-nine Palestinian worshipers at the Tomb of the Patriarchs in Hebron; another twenty-six Palestinians were killed in the riots that ensued. Our event was canceled, as were dozens of others in the following years, many of them smashed by the violent reality that we did not manage to change.

While I hoped that our organization would build a culture of peace, we never stopped protesting against the ongoing occupation. In fact, my close working relationship with the Palestinian Women's Center only made me more aware how far away peace truly was. It took the Palestinian center months to get a phone installed at their office in East Jerusalem because the Israeli telephone company, which has a monopoly on telephone lines, would not send a person to install it. Their office was situated right at the northern border of Jerusalem near a checkpoint, so that the women who lived outside the city and lacked entry permits could have access. But the only store nearby was on the other side of the checkpoint, so buying water or food for our meetings meant asking the soldiers at the checkpoint for special permission to cross. While most Israelis were celebrating peace, we knew that it was still far off. We had not forgotten that the occupation was still in effect. We reminded our government again and again that it had promised, but failed to deliver, the release of women political prisoners. We demonstrated against every new settlement that was built. During those years, surrounded by celebration, when most Israelis believed we were on the road to peace, I stood in Jerusalem's Paris Square every Friday with Women in Black, holding a sign that said, "End the Occupation."

People who passed our weekly vigil called us evil black widows. They cursed us and spat at us. They asked why we were spoiling their happiness after the peace agreements. I organized dozens of women's demonstrations during those years of Oslo-inspired joy. I wrote dozens of signs protesting Rabin's continued curfew in the Occupied Territories and his construction of settlements. We tried to work together — Israeli and Palestinian women — to create fellowship and understanding between ourselves, to end the occupation, and to protect the status of women in both societies. We were not terribly successful. In November 1995, when Rabin was murdered, I wept my heart out. We turned over the signs we had used in many demonstrations outside his home—calling on him to speed up the peace process, evacuate the settlements, and release political prisoners—and used the other side to write slogans against Shimon Peres, who replaced him. We protested against his efforts, like those of Rabin and other Israeli leaders before him, to try to solve the conflict through killing, occupation, and detention. "Talk peace," we called, "and stop making war. You can't make peace through war."

Cooperation between Israeli and Palestinian women is difficult, fascinating, annoying, and full of ups and downs, corresponding to shifts in the political situation, the number of attacks, the tightness of the closure, and the rest of the troubles that make the promotion of peace in our region almost impossible.[1]

Palestinian members of the Jerusalem Link thought that their national struggle took precedence over our joint struggle as women. I remember a conference on women's rights that was held at the Beit Berl Teacher Training College in the midst of this strange reality. When I finished my lecture on solidarity among women and how together we could bring about change, I was approached by a young Palestinian lawyer who said, "For three years now I have not been able to receive a permit to live with my husband in Jerusalem. We were married three years ago, and I am still in Ramallah and he is in Jerusalem. Can you help me get a permit before we talk about feminism?"

Throughout the years of joint activities between Israeli and Palestinian women, we spoke about the order of precedence. I don't really remember all the arguments or all their nuances, only the general tone of members of the board of the Palestinian organization. They said that our concern with feminism was a luxury that they could not permit themselves as long as their national struggle for liberation continued. And anyway, they used to say, when the time came they would manage their feminist struggle alone, without us.

It was an irresolvable argument—and we often avoided talking about it. The relations between us were so asymmetrical and so loaded that we spent most of the time trying to define our joint agenda, without much success. I think we could have done differently, done better, although I haven't yet worked out how.

The number of Palestinians was usually smaller than the number of Israelis. We Israelis would always arrive first. Almost all our meetings took place in East Jerusalem, in the last building on the outskirts of the city, close to the West Bank. They were always late, always with good reasons: the checkpoints, the roads, they were members of a lot of committees and worked very hard. Hanan Ashrawi, the Palestinian spokesperson during the peace talks, always arrived last of all, and everyone knew she was the most important. Zahira Kamal, the head of the Palestinian FIDA Party, tried not to be very late; Knesset member Naomi Chazan was always there and always on time, and Knesset member Yael Dayan only came when it was really important, and then only to speak up and leave early for more important places. The meetings usually began with a description of the events of the previous week and included criticism of us, the Israelis.

Today, more than ten years have passed since the establishment of Bat Shalom. I have been interviewed by dozens of newspapers and by students writing research papers on cooperation between Israeli and Palestinian women. I have written about the feminist peace movement and endlessly repeated the things that one is supposed to say about women being able to discuss things that men do not dare to; I have received awards and international recognition on behalf of the organization. We did put forward the first important model of long-term cooperation between Israeli and Palestinian women. We did lead the way to the recognition that Jerusalem must be shared between the two peoples and that each independent state should have its capital here. I believe that women can lead differently, but we have yet to find out how. I have often felt that women are no less tough on one another than men.

I love being a part of the process of founding organizations. In a country where the establishment is perceived to be corrupt and power-hungry, Israeli civil society is rich, diverse, and highly significant. But the process of establishing a feminist organization composed of two separate centers on opposite sides of the divided city was especially difficult.

Each organization has a board of directors consisting of more than a dozen women, each with her own strong opinions, and each representing a particular political or ideological stream. The Bat Shalom directorship included members of the Labor Party, Meretz, and the Communist Party; some were elected to the Knesset on the grounds of their feminist peace activism, while others held leadership positions in the trade unions or other centers of power. All decisions were to be made by consensus and not by majority vote, which meant that each meeting took hours, and the most important issues were decided in the last minutes. After the Bat Shalom board and the Jerusalem Women's Center board had separately made their decisions, each issue had to be discussed and agreed upon at a joint meeting of the two boards.

Should we make a joint logo? Should we print one set of stationery or two? Ghada Zugheir, the first director of the Palestinian center, wanted as little sharing as possible: separate stationery, separate reports, lots of separate activities. And although I heard a great deal about her and her colleagues' concern that the Palestinian public would view them as collaborators with the Israeli oppressor if they worked with us, although I heard about threats to Ghada's life for cooperating with us, there was still something about her reluctance that hurt me a little anew each time. I invested so much thought and love and hope in building these relations that it is difficult for me to summarize those years.

My memories are pictures that range from hope to desperation. I remember our family trip to Ein Gedi, to accompany a group of Palestinian and Israeli girls going to the kibbutz youth hostel for the weekend to get to know one another and learn to acknowledge, understand, and listen to one another. It was January 1996, and the Dead Sea was smiling in the desert. We had almost reached the green Ein Gedi nature reserve when we heard on the radio that the Engineer had been killed in Gaza. I knew that everything was going to go crazy again. Every time there seemed to be a little spark of light, when Palestinian girls who'd never been out of the Occupied Territories came to a kibbutz for the first time in their lives, or when Israeli girls first met their Palestinian peers for a quiet weekend—something would happen. We'd had a few days of quiet, and then Shimon Peres, recipient of the Nobel peace prize, sent murderers to kill Yahya Ayyash "the Engineer," who had planned attacks in which Israelis had been killed. They used a smart bomb, planted in a cellular telephone that exploded as he spoke with his father. And the girls, so young, did not know how to go on and talk about peace. They did not know what was said about this attack back home. They spoke from the heart, about their fears. They sat together in a circle for long hours under the trees on the green grass of this desert oasis, searching for the path to each other and to themselves. And I knew that the retaliation would be swift, the attacks and the assassinations—and that this would probably be the last weekend they spent together.

The Link's most important and significant event was a weeklong cultural and political festival, Sharing Jerusalem. Our statement was that Jerusalem belongs to two nations. When we first said this, we were the only ones doing so; today this understanding—that two people see Jerusalem as their capital—is becoming widely acknowledged, even by most Israelis.

In June 1997, to mark thirty years since the Israeli conquest of East Jerusalem, Israeli and Palestinian members of the Jerusalem Link organized a cultural-political week in Jerusalem called Sharing Jerusalem: Two Capitals for Two States. The event was sponsored and largely funded by the European Union. During that week thousands of Israelis and Palestinians participated in seminars on the shared future of Jerusalem, visited three art exhibitions assembled especially for the occasion, and listened to music on both the east and west sides of the city.

"We wanted to show the diversity of Jerusalem and attract as many people as possible by organizing events that appealed to different tastes," explained the producer of the cultural events, Jack Persekian.

There was something for everyone. If you liked jazz and wanted a moonlit night in a beautiful garden, you'd go to the Ambassador Hotel. In the mood for contemporary Palestinian music? You'd go to the Palestinian National Theater. Al-Kasaba Theater offered classical Arabic music and a live talk show from Jerusalem on Palestinian radio. In a different setting, Souq al-Kattanin (the cotton market) in the Old City of Jerusalem hosted a show of traditional Palestinian folk music and old-style refreshments. Placing the events in different parts of Jerusalem meant involving many others in the production process. This was useful, as members of the community took on the micromanagement of the different events and many more people became personally involved in realizing the project.

The production of the week's events was replete with difficulties, misunderstandings, and tensions. We were the only Israelis who called for sharing Jerusalem. Even Peace Now did not agree to participate in the events, saying that the time had not yet come to speak of divided sovereignty in the city, although many members of the movement took part as individuals.

As a result of the Israeli fear of shared life in Jerusalem, we could not find a single gallery that would host the art exhibitions, and all the cultural institutions refused to host our music performances. Even gallery owners and directors of cultural centers who personally agreed with the idea of a shared Jerusalem were afraid of identifying with it publicly. They feared that hosting our shows, which presented Jerusalem as the future capital of both states, would have cost them the crucial financial support of the municipality or the Jerusalem Foundation, both of which work to reinforce sole Israeli control over the city. In the end Philip Catherine, the Belgian jazz musician, played at Zig Zag, a gay-friendly café in the western part of the city. He had come especially for the occasion with his band, and the venue was not big enough to hold the hundreds of Israelis and Palestinians who came to listen. Sinead O'Connor, who was supposed to give the final concert at Sultan's Pool, the huge open amphitheater on the border between East and West Jerusalem, was frightened by the threats on her life and canceled the performance.

But for me, the most difficult thing—more difficult than the threats on my life, more difficult than the constant negative answers I received (from the directors of art institutions, producers, ticket offices that refused to sell tickets to our events, and the police, who made every effort to prevent the festival from taking place), more difficult than the disapproval of the municipality, more than all the negative reactions from Israelis who saw us as traitors—was the tension between us, the Israelis and Palestinians. There seemed to be no subject over which we did not argue, from the title of the event to the location of the jazz performances to whether Israelis and Palestinians should appear together on the same stage. The Israelis always wanted more things done together, and the Palestinians wanted fewer. A week before the events were scheduled to begin, when the invitations came back (late) from the printer, it looked like everything was going to fall apart. After we had decided together on every word in the invitation and translated the entire program into three languages, the Palestinian coordinator of the event, Amneh Badran, had added a few lines to the program while they were at the printing house: *The living city of Jerusalem, a symbol for peace, has suffered a lot from injustice. Let's work together to bring the second best choice of both people into reality. Sharing Jerusalem: Two Capitals for Two States is the answer.*

"There was a bit of open space on the program," she said to me, "so I decided to fill it—I didn't mean any harm." To this day, almost four years later, she is still angry with me for taking ten thousand programs out of envelopes and covering the paragraph she had added with a sticker depicting two doves of peace. How much tension, how much violence, how much anger and misunderstanding can be contained in sticking peace dove stickers on an invitation to a week of events proposing shared life in this city? It was as if generations upon generations of hostility had found expression in our inability to formulate one joint invitation, in three languages, to a different life in this crazy place.

Some of the tensions between us derived from more than suspicion grounded in the national conflict. Even though the status of women is subordinate to that of men in both societies, the role of Palestinian women in their society is even more problematic than our own. While we Israelis had grown accustomed to hearing "There are more urgent issues than the status of women," the Palestinians faced harsh criticism both for their feminist positions and for their cooperation with us. This is why, when we planned the Sharing

Jerusalem event, they invited men. Both Israelis and Palestinians invited men to participate in the events, but they involved key figures such as the late Palestinian statesman Faisal Husseini in the planning and deliberation. We hired a woman producer; they hired a man.

On the evening of the grand opening of the Sharing Jerusalem festival, we held a press conference with over four hundred people (one hundred journalists and three hundred international participants—mostly Italians—who had come to support us). After the press conference and a cocktail party in the garden of the Ambassador Hotel in East Jerusalem, the guests traveled in prearranged buses to the unveiling of the exhibitions. Tired and drunk with joy that we might succeed after all, at least for a week, in showing that we could live here together, I did not go to the openings. In the evening, when everyone returned and the opening concert was about to begin, Jack Persekian, the Palestinian producer, asked me why I had not participated in the tour. I was embarrassed, as he had labored for months to set up the exhibitions. I told him I wanted a personal guided tour without the hundreds of other guests, and we planned to go the next day, just the two of us.

At four in the afternoon, when Jack came to pick me up for our tour of the galleries, there were already two film crews waiting with me—one Israeli and one Palestinian—who were documenting the festival (and who refused to cooperate with each other). For the past six months I had seen Jack every day—we had gone together to raise funds from European ambassadors in Tel Aviv, discussed the artistic program, looked for performance venues—but I realized when I entered his gallery in the Old City of Jerusalem, I had never really seen him before. Jack told me that what he loved about the exhibition, *Home,* which he curated with an Israeli, Ganit Ankori, was that it was not clear which artists were Israeli and which Palestinian. I was confused—both because I hadn't thought there could be this kind of gallery of contemporary art in the Old City, and because until that moment I had not thought about art, only about the political encounter between Israelis and Palestinians. In my encounter with Jack, the gallery, his family, and his memories and dreams, I learned about a Jerusalem I had not known, and about my own limitations.

Several months after the events ended, we collected photos and articles about it in a book called *Sharing Jerusalem: Two Capitals for Two States,* which we edited together with Amneh Badran.[2] Jack suggested that instead of him writing something, I interview him about the process of producing the festival from his perspective, and we transcribe the conversation. But the transcript was not published in full because Amneh Badran, our co-editor, would not agree to Jack's title: "A Conversation with Daphna." Amneh's argument was political and complicated, touching on relations between Israelis and Palestinians. We didn't completely understand it, but she insisted. She would not have the interview published under that title. I was already on sabbatical in California and had come back for just a brief visit, and Jack was already busy establishing the Al-Ma'mal Foundation for Contemporary Art. After three hours of arguing about the title in the small office of the graphic artist in Ramallah, the staff there asked the three of us to leave and come back when we had made a decision. Only on the way home, in

Amneh's small red car, did I understand that the argument had not really been political, but personal. The feminist movement taught us that the personal is political, but not how to deal with the political when it becomes so personal. In the end, Jack shortened the interview and called it "Excerpts from a Conversation."

My own contribution was met with even harsher criticism, and Amneh vehemently opposed including it in the book. In it I asked why we—the Israeli and Palestinians women of the Jerusalem Link—never ate together. I wrote about the evaluation meeting of the Sharing Jerusalem festival. We had sat together, some twenty Israeli and Palestinian women, on the fourth floor of the last building in Jerusalem. The room overlooked the checkpoint where the soldiers were standing, deciding who to let into the city and who to turn away. We had intended to summarize this week of events during which we had walked a common path, thousands of Israelis and Palestinians, in order to say that we wanted a shared life in this city, with dignity and recognition of everyone's right to see Jerusalem as their capital. We had gotten together to ask ourselves what we had achieved with this week of music, exhibitions, and seminars. And there had been nothing but water on the long table between us. In my article I asked why, in these two cultures in which hospitality is so central, our table was devoid of food and loaded with politics.

Analyzing this meeting, I wondered why, sitting around that blue table with its bottles of water, we had once again turned to discussing the title of the festival. Suddenly, when everything was already all over, the divisive question of the translation of the title into Hebrew and Arabic had come up again. The English name, Sharing Jerusalem, had originally been proposed by Knesset member Naomi Chazan. It sounded great in English but in Hebrew we wanted to express sharing without the implication of dividing, at least not physically; in Hebrew the words come from the same root. We didn't want a wall through the city again. So at the time we translated the title as Living Together in Jerusalem: Two Capitals for Two States. But at that meeting after the events—when we had managed to convey such an important message about the city's future, when thousands of Israelis and Palestinians had met—why was the main question that arose how to translate the title into the different languages?

Dr. Sumaya Farhat Naser, the director of the Palestinian Women's Center, joined Amneh in objecting to my article. She focused on other questions that seemed to me less important. "Why did you write about the attack in the Mahaneh Yehudah market?" she asked me. I didn't know how I could not have written about the bombing, which killed thirteen people only hours after our last meeting on the shared future of Jerusalem.

Sumaya asked me to shorten the article so that it could be included in a book we edited together, and I asked her when we would finally be able to talk about the things that we never talk about. When would we talk about the difficulties, the tensions, and the problems between us? When would we talk about what happened beyond our pretty albums, beyond the pictures published in the world press, the films, articles, and dissertations written all over the world about this instance of cooperation between Israeli and Palestinian women? When would we find out why we never ate together?

Sumaya agreed to write an article with me about all the

issues we had repressed, and for almost a year we met period-
ically to discuss them. We made no progress, or at least I felt
we were making no progress. I wrote about my mistakes, my
pain, about how despite years of working together we had not
become friends. Sumaya also wrote about my mistakes, and
about the difficulties in Palestinian society, which opposed cooperation with Israelis. We wrote in English because that was
the language we used to communicate. Sumaya wrote:

> Recalling how we, Palestinian and Israeli women,
> rarely could get beyond stereotypical fears of "the
> other"—despite having worked together as the
> Jerusalem Link for more than three years—remains a
> bitter memory for me. Whether one belongs to the
> party of the oppressed or the oppressors, to the occu-
> pied or occupiers, surely both people suffer as victims.
>
> Such a polarized situation limits the space possi-
> ble for rational, objective dialogue. However, even
> under such circumstances it is critical for us to admit
> that two sets of facts exist, that there are two stories
> rather than one. By agreeing not to judge in terms of
> what is right or wrong in the other's story, and in-
> stead respecting that another story exists, a possibil-
> ity for dialogue emerges. Mutual respect can lay the
> foundation for later political understanding, even
> reconciliation.
>
> No doubt, this was—and continues to be—a
> painful process. Yet, through voicing our concerns,
> expressing feelings of joy and gratitude, sadness
> and fear, steps are taken towards inner liberation. A
> genuine exchange in conflict resolution, consensus

making, occurs. I must admit that at times it was re-assuring (even gratifying!) to hear the other side express worries and sorrows. At least for the moment, we Palestinians were not the only ones with problems. "Let's share depression!" I would say, and everyone would laugh. . . .

There was a special feeling of "doing the right thing" when the project idea first surfaced in autumn of 1996. Support from the European Commission and a number of other funding organizations confirmed the importance of our work. We were proud, having dared ourselves to attempt what others (namely men!) are not allowed to try. Since the issue of Jerusalem's future was so controversial, we worked hard to create venues for discussion, exploring possibilities for new, joint visions. Being women, we had less to lose than men when we veered from the general consensus. This, we believed, obligates women to seize the initiative, using the "gates of women" as entry points from which to include men in the planning and implementation.

However, before proceeding, Palestinian women had to receive a "green light" from the Palestinian Authority. The P.A. needed to approve the project slogan "Two Capitals for Two States," and the right of a women's NGO to take on such an explosive topic. Full support was fast in coming from the P.A. since the PLO and its negotiating committees are forbidden by the Oslo accords to address the issue of Jerusalem.

Of course, a "green light" from the Palestinian Authority did not quiet all criticism. Many Palestinians oppose the peace process because of its inability to secure even minimal national and political rights for Palestinians. In the *realpolitik* of the Middle East, the validity of international laws and resolutions seems to not apply to Palestinians. Such an environment promotes widespread expressions of despair, coupled with hopelessness amongst Palestinians.

The peace process postponed negotiation on Jerusalem to the final stages, also other controversial issues such as settlements, the right of return for refugees, borders and water: Jerusalem was deemed "too sensitive" to be dealt with right away. Trust had to be built up.

This waiting time was seized by the Israeli government as a golden opportunity to enlarge Jerusalem through expansion of vast settlements in East Jerusalem. Such unilateral actions destroyed any possibility for trust between the two sides, placing the Palestinian aspiration to East Jerusalem as their capital at a distinct disadvantage.

Unfortunately, current "facts on the ground" continue to deny the national, political and human rights of Palestinians. Palestinian presence within Jerusalem has been sharply marginalized. Walking after sunset through East Jerusalem, one notices an eerie quiet: shops, restaurants, even small street kiosks are shuttered and closed. A Palestinian human presence is almost invisible. Yet less than a kilometer away in West Jerusalem, the streets are bustling with Israelis off to meet family and friends at busy shops and cafes.

Into the midst of this complicated and highly sensitive area, we came up with "Sharing Jerusalem: Two Capitals for Two States." As project organizers, we were over and over again confronted with the following accusations: "How dare you divide Jerusalem! How dare you propose two capitals in Jerusalem! You are giving West Jerusalem away to the Israelis! West Jerusalem is Palestinian land, taken away by force. You want to give it away before negotiations have even started? Who appointed you to speak on behalf of Jerusalem, suggesting such a solution?"

Deciding on a title for the project seems an easy task, no? Not at all! Endless hours of discussion were required in order to find a title acceptable to both sides. We agreed (perhaps too quickly!) on the title "Sharing Jerusalem," realizing only later we had neglected to define what "sharing" means. Does it mean West Jerusalem for the Israelis, and East Jerusalem for the Palestinians? What about the settlements? What about confiscated land and Palestinian dispossession? Does "sharing" mean dividing Jerusalem, or uniting it? If we are sharing, does that mean Palestinians can return to their homes and properties in West Jerusalem? And which Jerusalem do we mean: the city boundaries of 1967? The first, second, or third extension of those boundaries? Do we refer to the current city boundaries, or to the borders of the planned greater Jerusalem?

A steering committee, composed of women from both sides, was formed to oversee planning, supervision and approval for each phase of the project.

Committee members (many overwhelmed with work at their own organizations) were unable to be as involved as originally planned. This often left staff of the women's centers—themselves weighed down with work and worries—to make decisions. The staff of each center promised to be frank and forthcoming with the other side, yet often this promise was hard to keep. Time was running out fast and some decisions simply couldn't wait.

After long days of deliberation over the design, content and production of the "Sharing Jerusalem" promotional brochure, the Palestinian side accepted responsibility for its printing. Upon dropping off the program at the printer, the Palestinian coordinator noticed an empty space near the top of the program. Finding it a pity not to fill the space with a nice thought—and forgetting to consult with the Israeli side—she added these words: "The living city of Jerusalem, a symbol for peace, has suffered a lot from injustice. Let's work together to bring the second best choice of both people into reality. 'Sharing Jerusalem: Two Capitals for Two States' is the answer."

"Let's try to open up the story of the program and the passage that Amneh added when it was already at the printers," I suggested. "Don't tell me now, so long after the incident, that Amneh Badran added a whole passage to the invitation just because she wanted to fill up a two-inch space."

Although we worked together for long months and were in daily contact, Amneh and I never managed to become close. In retrospect, I understood the cry that this addition embodied, her sense of wanting to do something without an Israeli stamp of approval. I had always understood the asymmetry in our relations, that we Israelis could write about the Palestinians' difficulties, understand them, but our lives remained more comfortable than theirs. All the same, I still couldn't get used to the fact that essential differences of opinion were not discussed, that disparities between worldviews became technical questions regarding the size of the font on the invitation. I couldn't really understand how annoying it was to work with us. I understood the violence in covering over the only passage she had written alone, and I wanted, at a distance of years from this silly incident, to try to understand what it represented. Why did Amneh feel she had to talk about the "second best" solution for Jerusalem, and why couldn't I bear that sentence? I thought perhaps that I would be able to talk to Sumaya about it. But Sumaya insisted that it was all because there were two unused inches on the invitation — and I felt that we were getting nowhere.

My meetings with Sumaya always took place at her office near the A'Ram checkpoint because she did not have a permit to enter Jerusalem. It was also, I think, because she wanted me to make a greater effort: her life was already filled with inconvenience that my government was responsible for. We did part of the joint writing via e-mail. In one of my letters to her I wrote about my pain at our inability to speak, our inability to create real friendship, and our inability to eat together. "In retrospect," I wrote, "I shouldn't have covered the sentence with the dove stickers. It was arrogant and violent on my part. I should have understood then what I understand now, that it was Amneh's attempt to make her voice heard, to voice her fears. What I found difficult at the time, and what I still find difficult to agree on, is our lack of ability to discuss the mistakes and difficulties. What's the point of cooperation between women if we don't develop a different pattern, one that's more open to dialogue? And why, after so many years of joint work, am I still the 'Israeli'? When, when will you agree to come to my house for dinner?"

Sumaya answered in a letter:

Dear Daphna,

I think this is the first time I have written "Dear Daphna"! I feel like it, after having read your comments on our article in process. I could feel the sensitivity and your strong longing to be accepted as a dear, close, normal friend, by me, by us — Palestinian women who want to work with you for peace. You see, I can do it easily as long as it is private, and I recognize that you like it. The problem is, we never speak about it, although deep in our hearts we know exactly why it is so. We would rather suffer than confront!

As long as our relations and sphere of work are not only official but also highly political, and as long as huge asymmetry continues to exist between our peoples, the one being the occupier and the other is occupied, it will remain politically unacceptable to address you as a friend. You remain in the first hand occupying a position in the machinery of the political system that suppresses my life and my people. I am very sorry for this brutal confession, which just mirrors the reality. I want to be honest and clear, knowing it hurts. I wish our struggle for liberation, homeland, political independence, integrity, and sovereignty would be over and that we could begin the process of building the joint peace for both peoples equally, so it would not be a problem at all to be friends, to feel close, to work beyond the barriers of nationalism and politics. Remember, our joint work was a pioneering step at a time where meeting and speaking to each other about politics was forbidden by both sides. Yet it was tolerated only because we claimed the work was political. Only as such is joint work possible in order to secure political and social protection for those who need it in their society. You cannot enjoy living in your society and make demands of us, who are deprived of most of what you have, as if we belonged to your society, especially when your people and state are responsible for the misery imposed on us. You dream of an open Jerusalem, one city for all, with no flags or symbols. You already have all these things and when their political role is completed, they can easily be relinquished. While we, we are deprived of all these factors deemed necessary for statehood, and you want us to withdraw before we have even tasted them. You demand things that comply with a post-statehood and post-nationalist stage, but we are still in the pre-stage, and our demands are different than yours.

A Jerusalem without walls is the desire of all. But when we insist on having our Jerusalem, Palestinian Jerusalem, it is the land and soil, the space, and thus the sovereignty we mean. You cannot just enjoy having all of Jerusalem belong to your side,

which controls everything and then allocates morsels
to us, claiming this to be compromise, generosity, and
charity.

We want the validity of our right to live in the city,
the freedom to move and visit, the right to live and
love in the city, to develop and share the planning of
its future. It is a big sacrifice for our side if somebody
says: we want only East Jerusalem. What about West
Jerusalem, which was taken by force from the Palestinian civil population? What about the hundreds of
walls put up by the issue of laws to legalize administrative and bureaucratic regulations that manifest discrimination and apartheid between our peoples and
on the basis of ethnic and religious considerations,
aiming at creating a demographic change favoring the
Israelis and depriving the Palestinians? I am sure of
your knowledge and awareness of the injustices done
by force. I understand your confusion and your asking why, why, why? It is an attempt to escape from
facing the reality, which is brutal and cruel, as you
start to feel that you share responsibility and want a
change for the sake of your own people.

I am writing to you because I feel your desire to
be understood. I feel the same way, that both of us
should give mutual understanding a chance, that you
too need to understand me. Perhaps our article will
succeed in presenting the message you wish to deliver.

You express your pain, and I respect and understand that. Do you know that in our culture and tradition it is inappropriate to express pain or to speak
about it? Does this mean that we suffer less than those

who express the pain? More likely it is an act of strength and a relief when you do it. I envy you. I have the privilege not to have had as terrible and painful a history as your people. My misery started when yours began to find its end, at my people's expense. The fears of persecution, deprivation and extinction have become part of your existence, and it seems you can hardly get rid of them, maybe you do not want to. Parallel fears thrive in my society and our dilemma is getting more and more complicated, since we are continuously dealing with two victimized peoples. Remember, when someone is strong, relaxed, and experiences stable life conditions, daily life goes on almost normally, so it is easy and a luxury to address feelings and pain. You can afford that. It is a kind of self-defense for those who are weak and oppressed not to give room or space for pain to come on the surface. Do you remember anyone who in the darkest moments of your history dared to express pain openly?

You wonder why we, the occupied, oppose and reject normalization. You expect us to act normal in a normal situation. If we do so, then we accept the imposed abnormal situation and perceive it as normal. This itself is an imposition of your interests. This is wishful thinking needed to ease the conscience of those Israelis who have feelings of responsibility, yet are far, far away from guilt. I wish the feeling of guilt would find its way into the Israeli people, which would mean the first step towards reconciliation with the Palestinians was on the horizon. Don't pretend you don't know that thousands of Palestinians were forced by the Israeli military authorities to become collaborators and endanger the lives and future of their own people, under the pretense of normalization. The Israeli secret authorities have deeply hurt every single Palestinian, injured our souls, and suffocated almost every drop of trust that has been built — even in our own society. How many years have to pass until the generations learn to heal the wounds? Even after that, many other generations will suffer because of the remaining scars. Every Israeli bears the responsibility for the consequences of this and other war crimes. And you expect us, while still under occupation, to forget? No Palestinian should ever be allowed to forget. It is our responsibility to the existence of our people. But we shall learn to forgive if we gain our rights and a life of dignity. Consider please, that you live in a state of law, which gives security, protection of the individual, and ensures freedom of expression. When you oppose or criticize, this is your right and your opinions are met with recognition. Many people are indifferent, do not think of opposing or involving themselves. They are indifferent, it is an easy life for them. In your society you, and they, can afford [to] be this or that. In my society the chances for choice are very limited. It is pressing, it is vital for us to act, the things that are happening touch on the very essence of our lives and future. Imagine, you belong to the state and society that endanger my existence and that of my people, and then you just ask so innocently, and have difficulty understanding our refusal of normalization. Our problem is not that we do not know how to eat with each other, or drink coffee with each other. Our problems are political and there is room for learning how to discuss and resolve issues. There are many experiences where coming together has been misused for personal or political reasons and led to harsh consequences for individuals.

Again, dear Daphna, you see what I have written, my thoughts which came up on impulse. I just reacted. I cannot visit you at home nor eat with you in a restaurant. This is not acceptable in my society yet, because our peoples are still enemies. Were I to do so, I would feel that I had sinned intentionally. I could never forgive myself. From a human point of view, please understand me, and do not feel hurt personally. If you feel hurt all the same, it could be an incentive for you to do something about it. My anger and bitterness come through again and again. My frustration and dissatisfaction also. My explosive desire to defend and explain is alert and ready as if I were in a state of alarm. This is my reality, which does not provide equal opportunity, even for discussing issues.

I read over what I have written to you the next day and I recognized the difficulties in addressing you just as a private person. I had tried, but very shortly reverted to talking to you as a representative and a bearer of responsibility for your society, people and state. This may not be fair, since personally we do get along. So the problems that divide us are the political, they shadow our lives, we have to address them!

Nevertheless, this painful reality should never stop us from trying. We already have come a considerable distance, filled with pain and disappointment, but we have learned a lot from each other and about each other. I am very happy to have had this experience. These are the first steps.

Dear Sumaya,

Thank you for your beautiful letter, and your courage and sincerity. My response, like your letter, is both personal and political. You write about normalization and about guilt, and my letter is a response to both issues.

It took me months to answer you. I thought about this letter many times, changed it and rewrote it and never really finished it. Christmas came and I wanted so many times to call you and wish you a Merry Christmas, but did not. Then came the New Year, the new millennium, and I did not call or write, not because I didn't think about you but because I thought about you so much.

You wrote me that you could call me "Dear Daphna" in private but not in public. You are very dear to me, both in public and in private, and it is hard for me to accept that you can address me as "Dear Daphna" in private only. I know all the arguments against normalization, and I respect them, yet personally I find it impossible to make such a separation between the public and the private. If the time is not ripe for you as a Palestinian to acknowledge that I, an Israeli, can be "dear" in public as well—then I will wait until the time comes.

You wrote me openly that in the present political situation I remain "in the first hand occupying a position in the machinery of the political system that suppresses [your] life and [your] people."

I read these sentences over and over again, asking myself whether you are really writing about me. Occupying a position in the machinery of the political system that suppresses your life? Me?

I have accepted this position of "the enemy" for ten years and I cannot take it anymore. I regret not being able to feel guilty all the time, but I just do not want to be "the other," the Israeli, the oppressor, the occupier.

I am Daphna. I am a mother. I am a woman. I am a feminist. I love to dance. I don't want to be identified as THE ISRAELI all the time. This identity is the most problematic of all for me, and yet in my relationship with you I am always THE ISRAELI. I understand your position and I respect it. You are of course right.

Identifying me as the Other, as THE ISRAELI, is your active objection to normalization. By telling me over and over again that you can call me Dear Daphna in private but not in public you are reminding me that I am first and foremost an Israeli—you are refusing to take part in the normalization process.

January 2002

Sumaya called and told me she had finished writing her second book and that it was great. It is the sequel to the autobiography she published six years ago. Her first book won a prize, and tens of thousands of copies were sold in Germany. She told me that in Beit Rima, the village neighboring her home, two wounded Palestinians who were bleeding could not get an entry permit to the city and receive treatment at a Jerusalem hospital. I called the International Committee of the Red Cross, which told me that indeed the Israeli soldiers weren't letting the ambulances in. I phoned Sumaya back and told her I could do nothing and that when I had some news I would call again. I carried on chopping tofu for the vegan dish I had prepared for my sister-in-law, and I thought about how Sumaya had been the first one to tell me she wanted me to feel guilty all the time.

"You Golan women," my brother-in-law likes to say, "you're champions at guilt." Nevertheless, I have not written about guilt at all in this book. The truth? I don't feel guilty because of this lousy political situation. Me, the one whose middle name is guilt, who imbibed this emotion as an integral part of femininity, I really don't feel part of this Israeli engine that is oppressing the Palestinian nation. I have no desire for anybody to see me as such.

In my letter to Sumaya two winters ago, before the Second Intifada broke out and we stopped meeting—before Sumaya got stuck in Birzeit and even a trip to neighboring Ramallah became an illegal journey for her—I told her about this book.

I have just finished writing a book on how this situation makes me feel, how I feel as "the Israeli." As you correctly point out, these concerns about what it's like to feel guilty all the time, to do but not to do enough, questioning my position in Israeli society—are all petty concerns compared with your life as a Palestinian living under military occupation. Again you are right, but I was hoping that beyond national borders, beyond the inequality of our situation, we could be friends. We could eat together; we could be frightened about our children's future; we could struggle together for peace. But you tell me—not yet. And that is fine with me. It was painful for years, it still is, but I will wait.

When I was in California there were days when I had terrible cravings for hummus. I lived in Silicon Valley for a year with tens of thousands of Israelis who shared the same craving. A friend used to come over from time to time with homemade hummus that tasted almost as good as that which I was imagining. All of us, the Israeli Diaspora of the Silicon Valley, shopped at Iranian stores that imported Israeli hummus and other Israeli products. I know that hummus is yours and not ours, but there, in beautiful California, there were times when I missed the smell and taste of certain foods here, and I couldn't care about the politics of colonization of food. It was then I realized for the first time that in all those years of working together we had only eaten together once.

When I was writing to Sumaya about the hummus, I already knew I would have to tell her more in order to make her understand the atmosphere that prevailed. That city, Sunnyvale, California, where thousands of Israeli high-tech people and their spouses live, overflows with abundance, big cars and lots of money and people who dream in Hebrew of hummus and barbecue on Yom Ha'atzmaut. I didn't describe the aroma of the hummus that my friend Shulamit brought me one morning when I called her in desperation: "I'm dying for some hummus like you get in Israel."

I only wrote Sumaya a little. I didn't tell her about the weekly family trips to the Iranian shops that import Israeli products, and about how much we were all missing the food at home. What would I tell her? About the excitement of seeing *krembo* in California? Or how I would sometimes go to three different Iranian stores throughout the northern Bay Area in California in order to find cucumbers like we get in Israel, not the pale American variety?

But I told her about the food because in California I understood how much I loved the food back home. I also understood, as I said previously, that we had never eaten together, and that this food question was loaded and complicated and painful.

"Don't come and eat hummus with us. We don't want to be Mahmud who mixes hummus for you," my friend Samie Sharkawi used to say to me. Samie is a Palestinian Israeli and she used to laugh at the patronizing Israeli Jews who seek "authentic" inexpensive, Arab hummus restaurants, while pretending that the warm hospitality of the owners is a sign of real friendship. Samie speaks Hebrew to me, although she gets angry with me for not knowing Arabic and insists on speaking at least some Arabic to me despite the fact that I understand very little.

I have no language problem with Sumaya. She is a lecturer at Birzeit University, and we speak English to each other. She has never said anything to me about hummus.

Sumaya has always been warm, smiling, and determined to maintain formal but cordial relations, as if we were negotiating the future of Jerusalem and the Israeli-Palestinian conflict—as if, were we to relax for a moment, it would be as if everything were already righted and there were peace and we could laugh together. Not that we didn't laugh together, but the absence of food, and the fact that we sat in long meetings together for hours and only drank coffee or water—that was something that I suddenly understood in California.

Okay, so I'm exaggerating. Sometimes at bigger events to which consuls were invited or where we hosted Turkish and Greek women from Cyprus, there would be food . . . but usually not. I know there's something supercilious about this concern with whether or not there was food at the meetings—but it bothers me when so many people here hardly have any food in their daily lives.

On December 29, 2001, eight Israeli women went to meet Palestinian women in Ramallah. By that time Sumaya was no longer running the Jerusalem Women's Center, and she did not attend the meeting. At the American Colony Hotel, we squeezed into a large seven-seater taxi and drove to the Qalandia checkpoint. There are two roads. One is new, wider, bigger, and used by Israelis. The other is worn out and used by Palestinians. The Palestinian taxi dropped us at the checkpoint, one of hundreds of yellow taxis that couldn't go out—or, more correctly, didn't want to go out because they would be unable to return to Jerusalem. We met Dr. Islah Jad, who was waiting for us by the side of the road near the checkpoint.

Islah looked as if she were in Paris, with small earrings and a red blouse. "Here's our duty-free," she said, pointing to the dozens of peddlers offering cheap merchandise on cardboard cartons beside the road where thousands of people were walking.

Believe me, everyone who cares should see it. Just go there and stand there for two minutes and see the tall fences, the confused soldiers with their weapons who are unable to check everyone, and the hundreds of cars crawling through the checkpoint. I can't describe the bedlam. It's frightening. We walked to the other side of the checkpoint, a few hundred meters, and took three yellow taxis to the Women's Center in Ramallah. On the way we stopped at the northern Ramallah checkpoint because we'd had a call from a friend who had not managed to make the rendezvous because the checkpoint was closed and the soldiers had thrown smoke grenades at a group of demonstrators.

At the Women's Center we met with twelve Palestinian women—leaders from Fatah (Arafat's party), the Communist Party, aid centers for women—and spoke about what we could or should or wanted to do and whether there was something we could do together.

That long meeting was fraught with a lot of anger and tension. At the end we decided to meet again to speak about the many questions and how we could do something. I left home at 10:30 that morning and returned at 4:30 in the afternoon, starving. After I had seen the checkpoints, the tanks in my friends' garden, the destroyed houses, the roads full of potholes, and the gas grenades at the northern Ramallah checkpoint, how could I make a big deal out of the lack of food at the meeting?

But let me return to the letter I wrote to Sumaya two years ago:

I'm telling you these details because I am aware of the luxury of my situation. I know that I can decide I've had enough of feeling guilty, but that you cannot simply leave your struggle and go. I know. But I want at least to tell you my story. I want you to know how I feel about your inability to eat with me. I had to leave the country and write a book to begin to understand it myself. The book was almost finished when I received your letter about guilt and normalization, and I realized that I was writing an entire book about those very issues without actually using the words.

Something is very wrong here. You do not need theories of colonization and the legalistic language of human rights to know that nothing is normal here. Living in Jerusalem, you know that something is very wrong. It is too tense, too full of people who know they are absolutely right, too many people living together back to back. I wish I could write in the clearest of voices, of the kind that I sometimes hear from my children, asking why. Why do the streets in East Jerusalem have signs in Hebrew? Why can't your son come into Jerusalem? Why? Reading Jamaica Kincaid's writing about growing up in Antigua made me think it's okay to ask questions that we usually ask ourselves quietly, some of which are not considered interesting, aloud.[3] Simple questions like why nine-year-old Palestinians are turned away from public schools on the grounds that there is no room for them. But I don't have the childlike, beautiful voice that Kincaid has, and of course, as you keep reminding me, I am the colonizer, not the colonized. So I can only ask different questions, although I'm not sure you would find them interesting.

I was hoping that we'd be able to reach each other as women, as mothers, but we did not. You are right, the obstacles in your path are much more difficult than mine. I can choose to say goodbye to the struggle for peace and for human rights, you cannot. We often talked about the tension between the feminist message of our relationship and the national one.[4] We wanted to have feminist discussions, you wanted to struggle to release the Palestinian political prisoners; we talked about leadership courses for women, you talked about the closure of the territories. This tension was always there, and when we worked together on the Sharing Jerusalem event we realized how each word, each decision has different meanings for each of us. We have been having this dialogue on friendship and interests and the abnormality of the situation for quite a few years now. We have managed to accomplish things together: the meeting of young Palestinian and Israeli women, the Sharing Jerusalem week—a demonstration that this torn and divided city can be shared, at least for a few days, by Palestinians and Israelis alike and that we could live in peace in this city while respecting the right of both peoples to build their capital in Jerusalem.

But this tension between us, this dialogue about distance and closeness, about alone and together, came up again and again in different versions, in different

tones, sometimes in angry letters, sometimes in small
gestures. Your words always implied, do not come too
near, you are still the enemy, and my response was always that you were, of course, right. Albert Memmi,
in his beautiful 1957 essay on Tunis, *The Colonizer and
the Colonized*, called people like me "the colonizer who
refuses."[5] This long letter to you, which I will make
part of my book with your permission, is indeed about
my refusal, and the refusal of my Israeli friends, to accept colonialism. But it is also about my refusal to always be identified as the "colonizer who refuses."

On July 12, 1987, my daughter, Gali, was born
and I became a mother. A few months later marked
the beginning of the intifada. The intifada reminded
all of us Israelis, even those who didn't want to
know, that millions of Palestinians living under military occupation could no longer bear the burden,
and that you are struggling for your independent
Palestinian state, your human rights. A few months
later I finished writing my Ph.D. dissertation about
South Africa. In the next few years I continued to
teach at the Hebrew University while at the same time
helping to form B'Tselem. As the research director of
that organization, I wanted everybody in Israel to see
and know what our government and army were doing
in the territories. We believed that people should
know so that no one could later claim that they had
not. We hoped that justice would follow knowledge
and acknowledgment.

Now I am writing about those years: the questions,
the dilemmas that we faced as women, as Israelis, as

human rights activists, and for some of us, as mothers. When we founded B'Tselem in 1989, hundreds of Palestinians had been arrested and were held in prisons for months without trial, all the schools and universities in the territories were closed, and people were killed in the clashes every day. We thought that if only people knew, things would be different, they would do something to bring about change. We thought that if we could provide the information, thousands of Israelis would take action. Sometimes it worked. When we published a report about the banning of books in the territories and told the public how soldiers had burned the banned books in a library, people were outraged. The Israeli association of writers organized an event condemning the policies. People were angry and ashamed because they could not understand how Jews could burn books.

Ultimately, however, we witnessed a strange situation. B'Tselem was so successful in conveying the information, in showing journalists around, producing reliable reports, and organizing press conferences, that we could now be certain that Israelis knew what was happening. Ignorance of violations was no longer the problem. But we were less successful in actually changing the policies. After the signing of the Oslo accords in 1993, it seemed as though the time was ripe to institutionalize the cooperation between us, Palestinians and Israelis. As you correctly write, the women of the Jerusalem Link were pioneers, setting up a long-term relationship to work together for peace and justice. But peace has not come yet, nor justice, and despite all of our sincere attempts to work together, "the situation," "the oppression," "the occupation" have always stood between us.

I'm still not sure whether I really understand the difficulties or can reconcile myself to them. I haven't written about our joint enterprise because for me, your reservations about calling me dear in public are a sign that we did not choose the right way. Not that I know what the right way is, but as I already wrote, if we—Israeli and Palestinian women—cannot eat together, then this is not the way I want to work for peace. . . .

I believe in the power of women to communicate beyond the boundaries of nation and state. But I also believe that we have not yet found the way, perhaps because the time is not yet ripe. I'm glad that we can finally raise the questions that we didn't touch on before. The exchange is difficult for both of us, but I hope it will lead to new understandings.

I look forward to meeting you and working together on our article. Even if we cannot answer all of our questions together—even if we know that in this harsh reality we cannot be friends—I hope that we can at least talk about our difficulties and raise the issues of future cooperation in the hope that a just peace will come someday.

The next time I came to the office at the edge of the city, beside the checkpoint, I sat with Sumaya to discuss our article and the new difficulties in cooperation between Israeli and Palestinian women. When we met, we decided to keep writing together, documenting, recording, questioning. "We can't give up," Sumaya told me. "We've invested so much in the dialogue between us, learned so much about each other, that we can't just say that misunderstandings blind us to the possibilities for peace and reconciliation. We have to find other means of communicating, thinking about the problems between us. When we started writing together, we decided to write about the misunderstandings between us. We need to admit that they exist; we need to discuss them, acknowledge them. Acknowledgment is the starting point for reaching each other. Let's have something to eat," she said. In the small kitchen, a big Palestinian meal awaited us. We sat down together, Sumaya Farhat Naser, Amneh Badran, three other Palestinian women who work at the center, and I—and we ate. It was delicious.

SEVEN

SEPARATE BUT NOT EQUAL

October 12, 2000

I am famous in the Agnon family for my tehina. Amotz's mother says my tehina is the best. But that day I stood mixing the lemon into the tehina and wondering when Samie Sharkawi would get here and what she would have to say about my tehina. It had been a long time since she'd called and said she'd be right here. On the radio, there were reports of the lynching in Ramallah — two Israeli soldiers murdered. I didn't think soldiers could be murdered, only killed, but that was before I saw the awful pictures over and over again on television, a Palestinian youth standing at the window of a police station showing off his hands soaked in the blood of the killed soldiers.

This was in cosmopolitan Ramallah, of the restaurants, the jazz on Thursday nights, where, before the intifada, we used to go. *And where is Samie, why hasn't she arrived yet?* I thought. Samie is a Palestinian Israeli. That means she is an Israeli citizen, she understands Hebrew, and no one will stone her as she makes her way to my house. *Anyway, why should anything happen to her?* All the same, when she didn't call again, I started to worry.

When she arrived she said the tehina was excellent and she just got lost on the way, which was really annoying because we had so much to talk about and so little time. This was the first time I'd seen her since the Second Intifada had begun some weeks ago, and although we'd spoken on the phone I wanted to see for myself that everything was all right, make sure that she still believed, as I do, that someday everything will still work out here. In the past few weeks, Palestinian citizens of Israel have demonstrated in sympathy with the inhabitants of the Occupied Territories, the first time that the unrest in the West Bank and Gaza has spread into Israel. On October 1 and 2, demonstrators in the heavily Arab north of Israel were met by live fire from the police, and thirteen Palestinian Israelis were killed.

My friendship with Samie is one of the best things to come from the four years I ran Bat Shalom. This wasn't even Bat Shalom's main aim, or Samie's. She taught me about what she scornfully calls "hummus and labaneh friendship," which made me think of Memmi's analysis of colonized Tunis and how the colonizers, even those who "refuse to be colonizers," love most of all the food of the colonized.

The cooperation between Israelis and Palestinian women from the Occupied Territories involved workshops, dialogue groups, meetings, demonstrations, and joint events. The place of Palestinian Israelis in these meetings was always somewhat vexed. Palestinian Israeli women who belong to the Arab minority—which constitutes some 20 percent of the

Israeli population—always felt neither here nor there. In formal terms they were always part of the Israeli group, but closer in language and culture and identity to the Palestinians from the territories.

Samie would ask me, "What are you looking for in the territories? Have you taken care of everything there is to do at home?" She was reflecting on many dialogue groups of Jews and Arabs in Israel that did not do much to change the inequality between Israeli Jews and Israeli Palestinians. The small minority of Palestinians who were neither deported nor ejected from their land in 1948 became citizens in a state that they did not want—nor does it want them. Most of their land was confiscated—today they own only 2.5 percent of the land in Israel, and are not allowed to buy houses in the kibbutzim, moshavim, or any other of the new Jewish-only settlements in the Galilee. Since 1948, more than seven hundred new towns and villages have been built for Jews—and not a single one for Palestinian Israelis.[1] At Bat Shalom, most of our work was focused on the relationship between women in Israel and women in the Occupied Territories, but we also held ongoing dialogue groups inside Israel. Samie moderated Bat Shalom dialogue groups in the Galilee, where Palestinian Israeli and Jewish Israeli women met. While the meetings in Jerusalem between Palestinian women from the Occupied Territories and Jewish women from Israel were always tense, the meetings inside Israel itself were usually relaxed. Too relaxed, Samie taught me. "We've internalized our subordinate place, our role as hummus mixers, to such an extent that few of us ask questions about our place in these dialogue groups. Look at who makes the decisions, who runs the groups in all these Jewish-Arab coexistence organizations.

Why do the Palestinian Israeli women speak Hebrew, a foreign, second language to them, while the Jewish women can't
speak Arabic?" (Discussions with Palestinian women from
the Occupied Territories are held in English, a second language for all of us.) She would continue, "Why, why do Jews
always want to be invited to our festivals, our weddings?
How many Israelis invite Arabs to theirs?"

That was in 1995, years before Prime Minister Barak
publicized his short trip to eat hummus in Tira, a small Arab
town close to the Green Line, in order to curry favor with the
Arabs in his arrogant and gauche manner after alienating
them throughout his term in office. It was years before events
would prove that if we don't rethink the partnership here inside Israel between Jewish and Palestinian citizens, we will
never be able to live in peace.

Samie and I worked together at the Ministry of Education. She had told me about her meetings with Palestinian
teachers who are afraid to let the children talk about their
pain and anger, and about her own similar feelings. Two of
those killed by the police in October 2000 were high school
children, but not a single official of the Ministry of Education
came to the families to console them, and not a single psychologist was sent to their schools. She has told me about visiting
her uncle in Nablus and sitting in the car at the checkpoint on
the way back. "We sat there waiting and waiting," she said,
"and my son ate a banana and tried to throw the peel out of
the window into a big garbage can nearby. He missed, and a
soldier came up and yelled at him through the window to pick
it up and put it in the bin." He was a big soldier with a rifle,
she said to me, getting angry again as she repeated what she
said furiously to the soldier at that checkpoint: "Don't speak

to my child like that." I love her so much. She has also related an encounter she had with a settler who stopped at a roadside shop in the West Bank, took a bunch of bananas that were hanging outside, and without paying for them gave them to his children, who were waiting in the car. Samie demonstrated exactly where his handgun was tucked into his belt, and his gait as he entered the place as if he owned it. She described how surprised he was that she dared to ask him why he thought he could take bananas without paying.

Samie joined me in working at the Ministry of Education after much hesitation and long deliberations about whether to work for the establishment. For hours I tried to convince her that there was no choice, that if we wanted to effect change we had to work in the education system. "It's easy," I told her, "to say that this is a discriminatory system, but come try and change something in order to give more children a chance." She never felt at home at the ministry. Neither of us had worked for the government before, but while I found the freedom to ask questions, to make many new friends among those who did not question the system there, Samie could not stand the long drive to Jerusalem, the ugly office, and the loneliness that came with being virtually the only Palestinian in a building of thousands of people. For me it was coming home, in a strange way: my mother worked at the Ministry of Education for thirty-five years, and when I arrived I met many of her old colleagues, mostly women, who adopted me as their daughter and told me many things they never would have said on the record.

When in 1999 Yossi Sarid, the head of the liberal Meretz Party, was appointed minister of education under Barak, he promised, in an eloquent torrent of words, to focus all his

efforts on equality in education—or, as he called it, bridging
the gaps. I was hired to develop a plan for the Ministry of
Education to address inequality.

I devoted about two years to studying the ways that the
education system aggravates the inequality between the center and the periphery, between the poor and the rich, between Arabs and Jews, and between boys and girls. The
more I learned, the more alarmed I became at the growing
disparities. I tried to translate them into simple questions:
how can we give third-grade students in a poorer community,
in a wealthy settlement, in an Arab village, and in the big city
equal chances of a decent education? There are no private
schools in Israel, and the state is supposedly providing a good
education for all, but only 8 percent of students accepted to
universities are Palestinian citizens of Israel, and the percent-
age of Jewish students from development towns is not much
higher.

Early on in my work I was told that my job was not
meant to address Arab education: "By equality in education,
we mean the gaps between underprivileged and rich neighborhoods, the periphery and the center in Jewish education.
In Arab education there are so many gaps that they have a
five-year plan."

The five-year plan, which proposes an addition of 50 million NIS (some $10 million) per year for five years, amounts
to a small tranquilizer administered too late and doesn't even
pretend to solve any of the problems that have emerged from
years of neglect of Arab education. As one of the Arab superintendents told me, "It is like giving a child a dollar out of
your salary and asking him to believe that you have just
opened up a world of opportunity for him." Unlike Sarid's

statements about the need for an approach that promoted social justice rather than charity, the five-year plan was based neither on a sense of justice nor on long-term change. It contained no addition to the basic budget for Arab education, it did not empower the Arab teaching personnel for the long term, and it was not even managed by Palestinian Israelis. A retired Army captain was hired to direct the implementation of the five-year plan — not a single word of which was ever translated into Arabic. It was astonishing that even a minister who presumes to be on the left, who heads the Citizens' Rights Movement, did not see fit to appoint an Arab educationalist to head the designated plan for Arab affirmative action. In the spirit of Margaret Thatcher's education reforms, the five-year plan was contracted to large private companies. But the bid was publicized only in the Hebrew newspapers, and the requirements were such that no Arab company could have competed. One of the companies to win a contract to improve the reading capacity of Palestinian Israeli students was a college in the West Bank settlement of Ariel.

I therefore insisted that, in addition to the five-year plan — parallel to it — my recommendations would be to address the entire education system in Israel, both Jewish and Arab, in the plans for equality in education. The intention was not only to speak about social justice but also to build plans for more just distribution of resources and empowerment of teachers so that they could lead the required change. For that purpose we formed the Committee for Equality in Education, which I coordinated, with key bureaucrats of the ministry, academics, teachers, and principals. Through long sessions we proposed fundamental changes in budget allocations: poor schools would receive more than rich schools;

teachers' status and pay would be raised, mainly in development towns and underprivileged neighborhoods. We proposed and developed programs for training teachers, and suggested changes in the curriculum to reflect the presence of many cultures and two national identities in Israel.

The discussions of the Committee for Equality in Education were part of the Ministry of Education's dialogue on renewal and change, a process called Michlolim. The title cannot be easily translated into English, as even in Hebrew the word is not clear. But what it meant was that the ministry should go through a holistic change.

One of the meetings of the Michlolim team took place in the hall of a hotel in Zichron Yaakov. Sixty-two senior members of the Ministry of Education were in attendance. The conference was devoted to change and the fear of change and was facilitated by three organizational consultants, all of them formerly organizational consultants in the military. We sat at six round tables, about ten people per table. One of the facilitators asked those sitting at my table to change places with those at the next table. "Why should we?" I asked. The facilitators used our refusal to change places to demonstrate the different stages of the fear of change. Using diagrams they had prepared in advance, with accompanying transparencies, they explained the fear of change that exists in every organization.

"Meaningful change," I suggested, "would be if everyone at our table were to get up and leave the room and other people, Arabs, were to come in and replace us. There are sixty-two of us, senior staff of the Ministry of Education, and only two of us are Arabs. Today the Arabs make up about a fifth of the population of the State of Israel, and there should therefore be at least twelve Arabs in the workshop run for the top echelon of the Ministry of Education." My words were met with utter silence.

These questions about Palestinian Israeli representation in the leadership of the Ministry of Education have never asked. The two Palestinian Israeli representatives were never given any budget or power to make a difference. And it was agreed that the education of Palestinians in Israel should be run only by Jews.

I soon found out that although the tenure of Yossi Sarid provided opportunities to talk about injustice, lack of equality in the country, and how the education system nurtures, facilitates, and preserves that lack of equality, he did very little for change. He was so occupied by his battle against the educational system of Shas (a religious Mizrahi party) that he missed the opportunity to produce real change in the state education system, and he resigned after a short time in office.

I knew there was very little I could do myself, but after months of conversations with the administrators who preserve this inequality by allocating less money to Arab schools and fewer Arab superintendents (each of them supervises more than twice as many teachers and students as their Jewish colleagues), I could see that most of the people at the ministry had never been challenged to rethink these policies. So I asked Samie to join me at the ministry to try to work for change. I wanted her to help expose the inequality and to plan programs that would allow Arab schools and Palestinian Israeli teachers to get more funding, more programs, more hope.

Looking for the sources of inequality in education and

trying to understand why so few Palestinians graduate from high schools with grades that allow them to enter university, I employed diverse questions and methods used by feminists to explain and combat the inequality between men and women.

Women from the first generation of feminism focused on questions of representation, access, and quantity. How many women hold key positions in government, the parliament, and other public offices? How many women writers are taught in schools? How much do women earn in relation to men? These questions touch on the formal aspects of equality and are based on the assumption that the greater the representation of women in key positions, the more their status will improve. The task of the struggle for equality is to create numerical equality between women and men in pay, positions, opportunities, representation, and access to key positions.

The question I asked was, how much does the Ministry of Education invest in one student in Yeruham or Dimona or Raanana or Jedida? And although they kept telling me this was not a good question, and that there was no answer to it anyway, I kept asking how much the Ministry of Education invests in Arab education. It took me months to arrive at the numbers.[2] But the figures clearly show at least some of the discrimination: Arab education receives inferior allocations for training, supervision, nature, and art lessons. In general, the physical infrastructure of the schools is more dilapidated, and the money invested in educating an Arab student is on average only one-fifth of the amount invested for Jewish children. The educational situation of the children in the "unofficial" Bedouin villages is extremely dire. Many students are forced to walk kilometers to the nearest bus stop and then travel large distances (up to seventy kilometers) in order to reach their schools. The physical conditions in the schools are bad, and the children lack basic study aids. The Arab schools have significantly fewer of the unique programs in which the Ministry of Education invests. In a study we planned with the Israel Central Bureau of Statistics, all school principals in Israel had to reveal the budgets they have, not including teachers' salaries. We found that for each Jewish student, schools have an average of 4,935 NIS a year ($1,097); for each Palestinian–Israeli student schools have an average of 862 NIS ($191). In the south, for each Palestinian–Israeli child there are some 270 NIS ($60), compared to children of Jewish settlers in the West Bank, where there are some 6,906 NIS per year ($1,535).[3]

How much money is invested in Palestinian children in Israel as opposed to Jewish children? The data are hard to find, and the discrimination they reveal is tough to explain. Why are classes more crowded in Arab education? Why does the State of Israel fund fewer school hours for Palestinian Israeli students? Do they need to learn less?

When we talk about our children, I kept asking at Ministry of Education board meetings, do we not include the Arab children? Bedouin children? Are they not also our children? Then why are some of our children studying in such poor conditions? Why do we invest less in them?

But the discrimination in budgets cannot lead us to understand the whole picture of inequality. Just as women learned that the liberal notion of equality is not good enough — that it is not enough to make the same salary — to create a society in which women are equal, I added some questions, in the spirit of the second wave of feminism, that asked why the female voice is marginalized.[4] Considering this feminist discussion of the diverse qualities and different perceptions held by men and women which could enrich our society, I asked, "How could the education system benefit from equal representation of the voice of Arab leadership?"

Palestinian Israelis are not partners in the Ministry of Education's decision-making system, in the outlining of policy, or in planning. There is no Arab district manager, no Arab administration head, and no Arab representation in the ministry's management. Of the thousands of people who work in the ministry's administrative headquarters, not even ten are Palestinian Israeli—and most of them work in the cafeteria. The education system that purports to teach our children democracy, human rights, and active citizenship does not apply these values itself.

One of the Ministry of Education board meetings was held during the Muslim holy month of Ramadan. I asked if they could open the cafeteria for the early dinner of breaking the fast and, in an unusually generous gesture, they did. It was the first time that such a request was ever made. I invited to that meeting a number of Palestinian Israeli intellectuals, and one of the senior participants from the ministry told me,

> I have been working here for twenty-five years, and I have never met such Arabs—people who are intellectuals, and not appointed as yes-men or collaborators with the security services. Not only does the head of the Arab education system have no authority or budget, he never says anything in the meetings. Between us we call him "the plant." His deputy, a man

appointed by the security service, actually runs the department.

The fear of the Arab voice is so great that even today every appointment of a Palestinian Israeli teacher requires the approval of the General Security Service via the deputy supervisor of Arab education. My attempts, as well as those of human rights organizations who appealed to the High Court, to stop this situation in which each teacher needs the approval of the GSS have not been successful.[5] This situation creates fear and lack of trust in the Palestinian Israeli teachers and principals and increases the sense among the Palestinian public that the education system discriminates against them and neglects them.

The fact that Palestinian Israelis have no representation in the Ministry of Education reflects their absent presence in the lives of most Jews in Israel and especially in the lives of most of the decision makers. The inequity in budgets, curriculum development, and subject materials that respect the culture and identity of Palestinians are the problem not only of the Palestinians in Israel but of Israeli society as a whole. There can be no education without empowerment, and this situation in which Jews make decisions and develop curricula is one that oppresses not only the Palestinian minority but also the Jewish majority.

Many Palestinian Israelis claim that equal representation of Arabs in planning and management positions will be possible only if an autonomous Arab administration is established. Why not acknowledge our different voice? the Arab educators ask. To preserve the unique interests and characteristics of the Palestinian Israeli population, and to determine the

order of priorities and the content of study materials, perhaps autonomous administration is necessary.[6]

When I asked Samie to join me at the ministry and invited
other Palestinian Israeli intellectuals to advise and participate
in developing the plan for change, I was hoping that some of
them would become the much-needed leaders of the new education system for Palestinians in Israel. But it did not happen.
Samie was mostly interested in trying to change the curricula
at Arab schools—until now no significant effort has been
made to facilitate curricula that reflect Arab culture, history,
and literature in Arab schools. "Why do we have to learn Bia-
lik and all the Jewish poets and literature, learn history from
a Zionist point of view, when there is not a single textbook at
school that is devoted to our own Palestinian history?" she
asked. Samie led a group of Palestinian Israeli educators in
writing and planning their own curricula in history and civic
education—they tried to develop programs in Arabic (not just
translations from Hebrew) based on Arab culture.

This emphasis on Jewish-Zionist values, without respect
for Palestinian national identity, has increased the sense of
alienation between the two nationalities and the Arab minority's sense of being disregarded in Israel. The Arab education
system in Israel institutionalizes fear: fear of connection with
the past, fear of sharpening the sense of cultural and national
identity, and the teachers' fear of engaging current affairs.
Not only the Arab schools are damaged by this discriminatory education policy; the denial of Palestinian history is also
a characteristic of the Jewish textbooks.

Samie is particularly pained by the lack of respect with
which school curricula address the identity of Palestinian
students in Israel. When I asked Samie to write an article for

a book I edited on inequality in education, she wrote about her experience, as a child, of negotiating the disparity between the story she was told at home and the story she was told at school. She wrote about the poems that her father, a poet, created about their family lands, which today are the lands of Kibbutz Metzer, and about her teacher, who was afraid to read those poems in class. Throughout the months we worked together at the Ministry of Education, Samie told me that very little has changed since her own days in school; her children go to schools that are still driven by fear. She concluded her article thus:

> At home I was pulled towards my roots; at school, consistently and powerfully, I was uprooted. Looking back I can smile at how home won in the end. Education—that was the magic word, the key word. That's where we have to bring both the light and heavy tools and continue to work. An old saying is lodged in my consciousness, thanks to my mother, who was my yesterday, today and tomorrow: "You can't hide the sun with a net." For more than fifty years the establishment has been trying, mainly by means of the Ministry of Education, to do so. It hasn't yet understood that this is impossible.[7]

EIGHT

LETTER TO SUSAN SONTAG

February 7, 2001

The night Prime Minister Barak lost the election to Ariel Sharon, Amotz and I sat with our friends Micha Odenheimer and Naama Zifroni, drinking wine, comforting each other, not listening to the radio. We didn't want to know. After a lot of eating and smoking and drinking, I said: "Tell me, isn't it strange that American Jews come here because of these old stones?" Micha, who is an Orthodox rabbi, almost had a heart attack. "What are you questioning? All of Judaism? The whole basis of it?"

One Friday evening in December 2000, during the month of Ramadan, I happened to be in the Old City at the time when tens of thousands of worshipers were returning home from prayers. I found myself a lone woman among hundreds of men hurrying home, and I asked myself, *What do I have to be afraid of?* And also: *What do Israelis think will become of these tens of thousands of Muslim worshipers—that they'll disappear? Can't everyone live here in tranquility? Can't everyone just pray wherever they want to and let us dance in peace in this city?*

Perhaps this city is a little too loaded, too tense, I thought.

Amotz always reminds us that we are located on the active Syrian-African Rift and that in the twentieth century more people died from earthquakes in this region than in California. Amotz is an expert on earthquakes, and he says that although they can't be predicted, a big one is anticipated in this area in the next hundred years.

"Why are Israelis blind?" Jack Persekian asked me one Friday as we walked in the Old City, and I did not answer. Several Saturdays later he asked me the same question again, as if the conversation had never been interrupted: "Can't they see that this road isn't leading anywhere good?" I told him I didn't really know where Israelis thought this was leading, where we'll get to, and that everyone feels that something bad is happening here, that things are bad. I told him I'm scared, that all my friends are worried and depressed. I also told him that the Palestinians that most Israelis encounter are either the few low-skilled manual laborers who manage to get in, terrorists who plant bombs, or Arafat and his people on television. These three representations are not very appealing.

"They are not very appealing to me either," he said, and laughed. At that point Henia, Jack's wife, called and asked him to pick up her father from the Augusta Victoria Hospital. Since our meeting had just started, I joined him on the ride to the hospital in East Jerusalem and then to the Palestinian neighborhood of Beit Hanina.

Jack and I live in the same city but in two entirely different worlds, with two different languages and two different cultures. Two or three times a week, on my way to the university on Mount Scopus via Road Number One, I pass the New Gate in the Old City walls, near the Anadiel Gallery. It takes me five minutes in traffic. Jack took roads through

Mount of Olives that I hadn't known existed. After picking up Henia's father we drove past the gate to the university parking lot, the one that I use. I asked myself what Henia's father—with whom I could not converse because I don't know Arabic—thought of me. Sitting behind him in the little car, I felt like a dumb tourist. Jack offers me a glimpse into his parts of the city, which since the intifada have become so threatening, so full of secrecy and anger and tension. He introduces me to his friends who create, show, and promote contemporary art in the city and dream of opening galleries that show artists from all over the world, who will come and hold workshops and teach the youth.

The next time Micha and Naama came over was in May 2001, on Independence Day. The children wanted to draw, so I gave them a pile of scrap paper. On the back of the pages were drafts of the letter I wrote to Susan Sontag, the American author, essayist, and playwright who was invited to receive the Jerusalem Prize for literature—a prize given biannually at the International Book Fair in the city. In the letter I asked her to consider attaching some conditions to her acceptance of the prize. Micha read the first page of the letter from the pile of scrap paper and got angry with me. Why shouldn't Susan Sontag come and get her prize? My letter was very long. I dared to send her eighteen pages because in 1997 she had endorsed the initiative of the Jerusalem Link and, together with a few dozen international celebrities, signed a petition supporting cooperation between Israeli and Palestinian women and recognizing a shared Jerusalem as the capital of two states, Israel and Palestine.

This is what I wrote:

Dear Ms. Sontag,

I read in the Israeli newspapers that you have been named the Jerusalem Prize laureate for 2001. In Hebrew, when a woman receives a prize she is called the "bride of the prize." I hope that you will lay down some conditions before entering into a marriage with Jerusalem these days.

I would like to suggest that you come to visit us in Jerusalem and see for yourself how cruel this city is, how deep in denial. Please, don't marry into that without seeing it for yourself. Could you delay your acceptance of the prize for maybe a year, and say you will come back for it when municipal services in East and West Jerusalem are equal? Could you listen to the voices of Israelis and Palestinians in Jerusalem who want this city to be shared?

Could I invite you for tea? I know that sometimes it is interesting to meet with typical residents of a city you are visiting. I am a typical Israeli. I am the mother of a daughter and a son, I am happily married, I grow herbs for tea on my rooftop, I served in the army as an officer, my parents are Ashkenazi and Mizrahi respectively, and I love Jerusalem. I live in Jerusalem and I love this city. I also admire you, your books, and your courage, but the Jerusalem that now seeks to honor you is a city that treats one-third of its inhabitants with cruelty. Jerusalem, the city yearned for by millions of people around the world, excludes children from its public education system every year just because they are Palestinians.

We need your help. We need the help of concerned Jews, of intellectuals, of human rights activists, of feminists, of anybody who cares about justice. We need your support in joining the voices of Israelis and Palestinians who believe that we can share this land, that we can share Jerusalem, and that we should allow both the Jewish and the Palestinian diasporas to regard this land as their homeland. The last few months have been worse than the other hard times that I remember. For a few years I had some hope for peace and justice in this region. Now I am more scared than I have ever been before. Let me tell you about my Jerusalem. . . .

Since the 1967 annexation, Israel has claimed that Jerusalem is "a united city, the eternal capital of the Jewish people." As a result, it crushes any symbolic Palestinian attempt to make the city their capital too. And so for the last thirty-four years Israelis have celebrated the reunification of Jerusalem while ignoring the one-third of its residents who do not recognize Israeli control and who believe, like most of the three million Palestinians in the Occupied Territories, that the city is theirs too.

The difference between East and West Jerusalem would be evident to you too, if you came to visit. On one side of the city, you have a choice of dozens of different films, plays, concerts, and art exhibits at any given time. On the other side, in East Jerusalem, the city streets are deserted and there are hardly any cultural events. The venue of the International Book

Fair that invited you is at the western entrance to the city, but a short walk or drive away you will see the paradoxes of this divided city.

Every year my children are asked to wear blue and white to school on Jerusalem Day, as the schools mark the reunification of Jerusalem. Jewish children are taught about the heroic liberation of Jerusalem in 1967 and the significance of its reunification. They are never taught about Palestinians who live in East Jerusalem and what this day means for them. Israel celebrates a reunification that does not exist.

When my son was six I took him to a work meeting in East Jerusalem. On the way, he asked me: "Why don't they have street signs, and why don't they have traffic lights, and why are the children walking on the streets, why don't they have pavements?" Indeed, the difference in the infrastructure is easy to see: this year the Jerusalem Municipality's budget comes to some $500 million. Only 14 percent of that is directed at East Jerusalem, which is home to 33 percent of the city's population.[1]

The statistics show that in West Jerusalem there are 710 people for each kilometer of paved road, while in East Jerusalem there are 2,448. In West Jerusalem there is one kilometer of pavement for every 690 people, compared with 2,917 in the East. A public garden is shared by 447 people in the West and by 7,362 in Palestinian East Jerusalem, and of the 4,589 public benches in the city, only 170 are in East Jerusalem. Of the 302 water fountains in Jerusalem, just two are in East Jerusalem.

Classrooms are too crowded and the education services are inadequate in West Jerusalem, but the situation is much worse in East Jerusalem. The head of the Jerusalem education system told me that the shortage of classrooms is so severe that he has to turn children away and tell their parents that there is no room for their children in the schools. "You wouldn't dare tell me that there is no room for my daughter or my son in the public education system, would you?" I asked the city education chief, and he admitted he would surely have found room for any Jewish children. "But," he added, "even though I know I am breaking the law every day, there are just not enough buildings in East Jerusalem, not enough classrooms." Indeed, some 20 percent of Palestinian children of school-going age are not registered in either public or private schools.

In response to a High Court appeal against them by hundreds of Palestinian children who were turned away for lack of classrooms, the Ministry of Education and City Hall claimed that there was just not enough public land to build on.[2] Take a look at a map of Jerusalem. It is a map of denial. In the middle, at the heart of it, is the small area of the Old City, neatly surrounded by walls, completely distinct from the rest of the city. It houses several different quarters: the Jewish Quarter, the Muslim Quarter, the Christian Quarter, and the Armenian Quarter. And around this delicate Old City, the map shows spots in different colors. The large blue spots indicate expropriated Palestinian land. There are not enough schools built for Palestinians, but thousands of new apartments have sprung up for Jews. How is it there are enough classrooms for the people who live in the blue spots and not for those who live in the red areas of the map? Why, in thirty-four years of united Jerusalem, have hardly any libraries or community centers or clubs for the elderly been built in East Jerusalem?

Is that the Jerusalem you want to marry?

I took a short break from writing to go up to my rooftop to water my plants. It is the end of a very hot day, Shabbat, and the roof is starting to cool down. I love to spend the last hours of Shabbat listening to the birds and drinking tea made from the herbs I grow. Very few cars pass by. As I was appreciating the first new leaves of the lemongrass plant — *luisa* in Hebrew — which almost died during the winter, the phone rang. I didn't feel like answering. My daughter was at a Scout meeting in the neighborhood, so she should be safe. Amotz took our son to the movies. There are only three cinemas that operate on Saturdays in West Jerusalem — all pretty close to the *teffer*, as we call the invisible borders within the city. A bomb exploded at the *teffer* a week or so ago. Bombs usually explode in the mornings, I told myself, and it is too early for the after-dark shooting to start. Still, maybe I should answer, I thought, and rushed down from the roof inside to pick up the phone. Maybe someone was in danger. But by the time I reached the phone it had stopped ringing. So I dialed *42 [call-back] and asked the man on the other end if he had just called me. He spoke little Hebrew and in a heavy

Arabic accent said I must have a wrong number. I observed to myself that these days, when we Israelis and Palestinians are planting bombs in mobile phones, a "wrong number" sounds bizarre. There was a message from my Palestinian friend and colleague Rana Nashashibi on my answering service asking me to call as soon as possible. Rana is the director of the Palestinian psychological services in East Jerusalem, and when I dialed *42 again and asked for her she was indeed there. The last time I talked to her was a couple of weeks ago, when I called and asked her what she thought we should do—"we" meaning Israelis who are sick of this crazy war that is going nowhere but is causing so much suffering, or we Israeli and Palestinians who have been working together to end the occupation. "I don't know," she said. "We'd better think of something insane, because all the normal things haven't worked."

But when I heard her voice I knew that this call was about something else. "I am afraid there might be another kid like Muataz and Jaber," she told me, and my heart sank. "He is in Shaarei Zedek Hospital and they [the hospital authorities] won't let anyone see him." I told her I would go and look for him at the hospital. I knew if I walked fast I would get there before Shabbat ended and the receptionist would still be an Arab. Shaarei Zedek is an ultra-Orthodox Jewish hospital, and on Saturday you cannot buy coffee, use the phone, or watch TV there. Most of the workers on Saturdays are Arabs, allowing the Jewish staff to observe and enjoy the Sabbath. The Arabs serve as the *goy shel shabbat,* the Gentile who performs duties Jews are not permitted to do on Saturday.

At this point in the letter I went on to tell Sontag about our first encounter with Jaber and Muataz, the children with their arms and legs shackled to their hospital beds. I also wrote about Haled Abu Dayeh, who was beaten to death by security personnel at Shaarei Zedek Hospital in 1997.

The two receptionists in the emergency room were indeed Palestinians, or Arab Israelis, as they are called by the majority of Israeli Jews. The woman was on the phone, so I talked to the man. He could not find the patient on the computer. He was probably brought in by the police or soldiers, I told him, not knowing from where he had been brought. The receptionist said he did not remember anybody coming with the police or the army except for a drug addict. But I was insistent. I called Rana from my mobile phone and convinced the receptionist to talk to her. A few minutes later, he found the file, and he remembered the youth who was brought in by soldiers late at night and then taken back to police headquarters for interrogation.

What did I do next? Well, nothing. I called Rana with the information, told her to let me know if there was anything I could do, and walked home to make dinner. I told myself for the millionth time that I should improve my Arabic by now, that it is a shame that after so many courses my Arabic is so poor. And even more importantly that I should do something, that this situation cannot be allowed to continue. Making the lives of Palestinians so miserable, so painful, cannot be the way to peace.

I do not know what to do, so I am writing you this letter. We need your help. Don't leave us alone. Don't forget all your values, your beliefs, when it comes to Israel. If you accept the invitation to be our bride, would you at least embrace our understanding that Jerusalem should be shared and should be the capital of both Israel and the Palestinian state?

Can I invite you for tea on my rooftop? The view is not as nice as it was eight years ago when we first moved into the apartment. The new Begin Highway was built in the valley, and there is a lot of new construction going on—a high-tech park at nearby Givat Ram and new buildings for the Ministries of Foreign Affairs and Education, just near the Bank of Israel and the prime minster's office. If you come, I will show you the top of the High Court of Justice, by the Knesset building. If all these buildings are going up near my house on the western edge of Jerusalem, maybe even those who plan our city know that someday it will be divided between a Palestinian and an Israeli state. Maybe there are not enough classrooms because the Jewish mayors of Jerusalem and the heads of the education system have known all these years that one day Palestinians will run their own education system in Jerusalem—that one day Jerusalem will be theirs, too.

Former mayor Teddy Kollek, who is among the initiators of the Jerusalem Prize, was responsible for the policy of discrimination against Palestinians in terms of municipal services for too many years, while at the same time claiming Jerusalem to be a united city. He is responsible for the massive building of neighborhoods for Jews only. In one 1987 council meeting he explained his policy toward Palestinians — one-third of the residents of his city: "I don't want to give them a feeling of equality. I know that we cannot give them a feeling of equality. But I want, here and there, where it doesn't cost us too much, and where it is only an investment of money or something, to nevertheless give them a feeling that they can live here. If I do not give them this feeling, we will suffer."

City councilor Anat Hoffman, a member of the left-wing Meretz Party, calls this policy "municipal blindness." She recalls:

One day during Kollek's administration, I was sitting in a supervisory committee that had the great honor of reviewing the status of public toilets. I had the temerity to ask how many rolls of toilet paper the city dispenses. The official's answer intrigued me: "Forty eight rolls every seventy-two hours in the western part of town, but none, of course, in the eastern quarters." "Why?" "It isn't necessary, since the Arabs aren't used to modern flush toilets."

A rowdy debate ensued. It had, I am gratified to report, positive results. Directives went out to install flush toilets with plastic seats, and to ensure the regular provision of toilet paper to all the city's public toilets, regardless of the ethnic origin of their users. But this is all beside the point. The point is that among the tens of participants in the debate, not one was an Arab. Indeed, the only useful information at the meeting was provided by the Palestinian who serves the council members their tea.

Ms. Sontag, I have always admired your struggle against denial. Please help us by not accepting the policy of blindness that comes with the Jerusalem Prize.

In 1997 you were kind enough to join the international advisory board of an event entitled Sharing Jerusalem: Two Capitals for Two States. This week of cultural and political events, organized by Palestinian and Israeli women of the Jerusalem Link was an attempt to show that Jerusalem can be shared, that the interests, needs and dreams of the two peoples can be met in Jerusalem and that both can have their capital in the city.

For one week Palestinians and Israelis attended jazz concerts and art exhibitions in East and West Jerusalem. An open public discussion among Jerusalemites about the future of their city was held. We invited you then to come and speak at our symposia; that invitation still stands. I wish you could come and see the thousands of people who marched from East to West Jerusalem calling for an open and shared Jerusalem. Were we successful? I guess not. If we had been, we would now be living in a Jerusalem of peace, a city administered by Israelis and Palestinians, men and women, Christians, Jews, and Muslims. If we had been more successful, we all would have been happy to welcome you as the bride of Jerusalem.

But what we managed to do then, Israelis and Palestinians together, I am not sure we could do today. The war has torn us further and further apart. We encountered a lot of resistance to our project in 1997. No theater, no public hall, no art gallery in West Jerusalem agreed to host our public events. "Personally, we agree with your slogans," we were told by most Israelis, "but if we host an event under the title Sharing Jerusalem: Two Capitals for Two States, we would probably lose our municipality funding, or the funding from the Jerusalem Foundation," which supports most of the cultural events and venues in West Jerusalem.

This is exactly the reason that we needed your support and were grateful to the 125 intellectuals, writers, Nobel laureates, and actors from around the world who supported our call to share the city. It is for the same reason that we need your help and support now. How do you see the future of our city? What does Jerusalem mean to you? When Jews around the world say Next Year in Jerusalem—at this time every year, on Seder night—what Jerusalem do they mean?

During the week of the Sharing Jerusalem events I often thought of your comments on art being something that exists in the world, not just a text or commentary on the world. I thought about your critical work when I visited the exhibition entitled *Home* at Anadiel Gallery in the Old City. "You know what I like about this exhibition?" Jack Persekian, the owner of the gallery and one of the curators of the exhibition, asked me. "What I like is that you cannot tell which artists are Israeli and which are Palestinian."

Come and visit us first and hear the different voices. I am sure you will appreciate the photography book about to be published by Jack's group, Al-Ma'mal, a contemporary art center in the Old City. The book, entitled *Exposure*, contains very little text, but the photos, taken by Palestinian youths who participated in photography classes given at the art center, tell stories of Jerusalem you might want to see.[3]

We must not—any of us—forget their Jerusalem, as well as mine, nor the city of peace Jerusalem can be.

Thank you,
Daphna Golan

May 11, 2001

Naama called me in the morning to tell me that she had invitations to the prize-giving ceremony for Susan Sontag at Binyanei Hauma. I was still thanking her for giving up her invitation for me, and we were laughing about how her partner, Micha, and I would probably not stop arguing even when Susan Sontag was making her speech, when I heard her voice change, like night to day. "Steve just came in," she said, "and he's completely in shock. He says they murdered the son of his good friends from the Tekoa settlement. Did you hear the terrible story this morning of the murder of two children in a cave in Tekoa? That was Kobi, the son of Steve and Andrea's friends."

Susan Sontag kissed Mayor Olmert before and after receiving the prize. Olmert gave a fiery speech, at the end of which he made the following call to Palestinians: "If you would stop shooting, perhaps you would be able to listen." Sontag gave an impressive, smart, profound speech. What I remember about it is that she addressed me, and all of us who wrote to her asking her not to come, or not to accept the prize, or asking her to say that she was accepting the prize and donating it to an organization working for peace in Jerusalem, or a women's organizations, or to say any goddamn thing about the occupation in Jerusalem. For our benefit, she quoted the African American poet Dudley Randall, who gave this reply when reproached by fellow African Americans for not writing about the indignities of racism: "A poet is not a jukebox."

NINE

IN SEARCH OF AN OPTIMISTIC ENDING

February 5, 2000

For months I wanted to finish writing this book. The confusion between writing and life oppressed me. Keren Segal and Devorah Manekin, my wonderful research assistants, told me that I needed an optimistic ending. "You can't end with something depressing," they said, and they're so charming, such beautiful, aware young women who smile upon the world so. They're the beauty of Israel, to use a local turn of phrase.

So I waited for an optimistic ending, hoping that something would happen. Keren and Devorah and I had coffee at the Meirsdorff Faculty Club and spoke of possible endings. It was too cold to sit on the large patio overlooking both old and new Jerusalem, so we sat indoors. Keren told me about the millennium celebrations in Bethlehem, and it sounded so lovely to me that I wanted that to be the optimistic ending. Bethlehem 2000, music and dancing—what could be more optimistic than that?

A few days later Jack Persekian visited me to pick up a draft of the book. He too told me about the Bethlehem celebrations. Jack had produced the event and spoke excitedly about the huge New Year's Eve party in particular. Twenty thousand people had danced in the square in Bethlehem and the decorated and festive streets leading to it. This picture of people dancing in the streets is so different from the usual sight of empty streets in Bethlehem and East Jerusalem at night that it seemed to me a wonderfully optimistic ending — so far removed from the destroyed houses, torture, and administrative detentions.

"Perhaps I could interview you," I asked Jack, "for my optimistic ending?"

He laughed and told me he didn't want to be my optimistic ending. "If we're talking about endings," he told me, "this one's not going to be good. The Israelis are acting as if they have all the time in the world, as if everything will eventually work out. They talk and talk and fail to understand that the Palestinians have no more strength, that they can't take any more suffering even if they're told that it'll be all right in the end. It's going to explode soon."

A day later we went for a stroll in the Old City, and while walking down one of the alleys I asked him if we should do something together again — perhaps a sort of festival like the one we had in 1997 — in order to show that it's possible to live together in Jerusalem.

Jack laughed so hard that I was infected too, and we walked among the tourists for a good long while, roaring with laughter. "It won't work," he said. "It won't work. Let's sit down for a minute and talk about it." We sat among a horde of Danish tourists eating falafel sandwiches, and he explained to me why he thought the two groups can't live together in this city.

"I want a wall between us," he said, "a high wall that will separate us from each other. We can't have the Israelis running our lives anymore. We don't want to live in fear any longer—and until the Israelis understand that, there will be no resolution here. Let's build a beautiful wall, maybe a wall made of glass."

"And how will we meet?" I ask.

"I don't know. Perhaps there'll be a special gate for that."

One evening Dafna Galia, my best friend, called to say that she was coming right over. Dafna has been my friend since army days, so I know that "right over" means in an hour or two.

Her visits always begin with a telephone call, around 10:00 P.M. "Have you put the children to bed?" she asks me, amused because the bedtime ceremony takes hours in our house. "What a big deal you make of it! Only two kids!" Dafna has five children and is unfazed by anything.

In the hour and a half that passed before she knocked on the door, I sat down once again to finish the book. I wrote about friendship. I wrote about friendship because that's also the other side of Israel—the side I didn't present to my American students. There's something about Israeli friendship, something warm, something good, and I don't know whether students who come to Israel for a month feel it. It's the lovely side of this crazy country.

There are many words that sound good in English but contrived when translated in Hebrew—*human rights, compassion, solidarity.* But the Hebrew word for friendship encompasses something of all of these, something that works for me. It includes partnership, faith, warmth, and a moral code that says—although it is not formulated anywhere—that there are things you don't do to friends.

This friendship is problematic in many respects as well. Like anyplace, Israel has its old-boy network, or as we say, "people who ate from the same mess tin"—in other words, people who were in the army together. If there's any reason the infractions of human rights in the Occupied Territories are so severe, or for the bombing of "terrorist targets" or "infrastructures" in Lebanon, it's because the people who ate from the same mess tin are running this country. Our country is run by generals—lots of them. Not only is the prime minister a general, but his advisors are military figures and too many ministers and Knesset members and mayors are former senior officers.

And now there's a new trend—discharged officers are whisked into positions as school principals. If they know how to manage a tank unit, they must know how to run an education system; that's the logic. It's the same logic that spirited Prime Minister Barak from the head of the army to the head of the government.

These officers, the buddies, scare me, and their loyalty to each other does too. Whoever does not belong to this circle of protectors of the state is considered a little inferior. That of course includes all the women and all the Palestinians in Israel, as well as the immigrants who did not serve in the military. After that the circles of friendship get tighter—and at the center is the secret society of the Sayaret Matkal, the elite commando unit. "The unit" is so secret that no one outside it really knows what goes on in it. Amotz was a member, and although I've lived with him for sixteen years now, I still don't know what they do in that unit. Anyway, everything's so secretive that nobody's supposed to know who's in it—although it is such a big deal to be in it that all the neighbors know anyway. This hush-hush business of men who talk so importantly frightens me terribly. They always say they know better; they say it's not as simple as we mothers think. Year after year they sacrificed a few dozen more children in Lebanon, a country that didn't belong to them and which there was no reason to be in, killing people and embittering thousands of Lebanese. "But it's more complex than you imagine," they told the Four Mothers, a group of mothers of soldiers who called for the withdrawal of the army from Lebanon. They form a military system of government that runs the lives of people who don't speak their language and don't recognize their authority and don't want their occupation. They say it's essential and that it's the most enlightened rule of occupation that could possibly be constructed.

Of course not all those who ate from the same mess tin are like that, and there's also something beautiful about the friendship between them—something I will probably never understand if, after all these years and meetings, I haven't yet understood. Amotz's best friends were with him in "the unit," and despite having been discharged twenty-three years ago, they still meet often.

On Amotz's birthday I was thinking about the friendship he and I share. In the morning we went down to the market and bought berries and tangerines and kohlrabi and many different kinds of lettuce, and the smell of the fresh fruits and vegetables the week after a snowfall was marvelous. After lunch, sitting on our roof in the warm winter sun reading the paper, with Amotz so handsome in his hat, I thought I had found my ending.

But that was my personal happiness, not an optimistic ending. So I kept looking, and in the meantime, things have only gotten worse.

September 5, 2000

Hagar Rublev, one of the founders of Women in Black, died, suddenly, at forty-six. I remember her laughing, with a cigarette in her hand and a voice filled with questions. And now she is gone. So young and beautiful.

A short time before she died she asked me to speak at a conference she had organized on Israel and apartheid. I don't know what she knew about my opinions on the subject. I don't really know myself. Perhaps my opinion is that although Israel and South Africa are not the same, they are also very similar.

"In South Africa," I've said over the years, "the struggle is for a shared life. Here we're struggling to achieve an amicable divorce." The population numbers are also different. There are many other differences as well, but still, it's worth learning what happened there, what worked and what didn't.

I'm not afraid of using the word *apartheid* to describe what's happening here, but I'm not sure the term helps us to better understand discrimination in Israel or know what to do in order to change it. Do we want to say that there's discrimination in Israel and that the Palestinians in Israel, Palestinian citizens of Israel, do not have equal rights? When we talk about apartheid are we referring to the Palestinians in the Occupied Territories, who have no rights, just as the blacks in South Africa had no rights? Or do we want to say that the situation here is as terrible as it was there, in South Africa?

From my point of view, the most frightening similarity lies in the precise and consistent use of the legal system to normalize the abnormal state of discrimination. The apartheid regime was terrifying, offensive. Not only did millions of people live without minimal rights, in ongoing impoverishment, but the discrimination was anchored in a complex system of laws: laws that prohibited marriage between blacks and whites, laws that prohibited blacks from living in cities declared white, laws legislated in a pseudo-democratic process and enforced by a well-oiled system of attorneys and courts and a gigantic bureaucracy constructed to maintain the discrimination.[1] Israel is also a state governed by laws. The Occupied Territories have legal systems and hundreds of laws, directives, and regulations: regulations left over from the British and the Turks, Israeli legislation, Jordanian and Egyptian law, international humanitarian law that doesn't really apply although the High Court saw fit to adopt its humanitarian spirit, military edicts, the laws of *sharia*, and now legislation enacted by the Palestinian Authority. What a lot of laws. Like in South Africa. Here too, the state employs hundreds of attorneys and lawyers and consultants to explain how what is unjust is also legal.

The thousands of regulations and laws and edicts—both here and there—don't make the injustice any more just. They just make it more legal. They threaten our basic understanding that law is more than an agreement between the powerful. South Africa was not the only country in the world with discrimination, but it was the only country in the second half of the twentieth century where racism was entrenched in law, where discrimination was part of a regulated and orderly legal system, and apartheid was perceived globally as something that had to be ended. I'm not sure if the use of the term *apartheid* helps us to understand the discrimination against Palestinians in Israel and the oppression of Palestinians in the Occupied Territories. I'm not sure that the discussion about how we are like or unlike South Africa moves us forward toward a solution. But the comparison reminds us that hundreds of laws do not make discrimination just and that the international community, the same community we want to belong to, did not permit the perpetuation of apartheid. And it doesn't matter how we explain it and how many articles are written by Israeli scholars and lawyers—there are two groups living in this small piece of land, and one enjoys rights and liberty while the other does not.

But Hagar didn't ask me what I think about Israel and apartheid. She just complimented me on my outfit and told me she'd let me know where the conference would be held and that she would be glad to see me there.

Everyone is talking about the fragmentation of the left, the internal conflicts. From the outside we appear similar. We're all leftists, even though *we* think there's a lot of ideological disagreement and diversity among us. I always feel as if I don't quite belong. These categories that have developed for defining exactly which pigeonhole each of us on the left fits into are even more diverse than the bigger goddamn categories. Zionist, non-Zionist, anti-Zionist, post-Zionist, disappointed post-Zionist — none of these categories really describes me. If I had to choose an appropriate label from a list, I'd have to choose "none of the above." I'm really not there.

In the mid-1980s, when I was a student at Berkeley, we participated in dozens of demonstrations that seemed more or less like our demonstrations here in Israel. There were a few dozen, sometimes hundreds, and on rare occasions thousands of demonstrators. The call was to withdraw investments from South Africa. This was the third phase of the boycott against South Africa, following the cultural boycott and the economic boycott. This was after Mandela's banned African National Congress (ANC) called in 1985 for South Africa to be made ungovernable. The call resulted in a wave of demonstrations, protests, a state of emergency, arrests, and eventually the end of apartheid.

The combination of resistance in South Africa — most of which was nonviolent resistance by hundreds of organizations that included millions of people (women's organizations, youth, church, trade unions, human rights organizations) — with the guerilla activity of the ANC and Pan-African Congress (which were banned and operated mainly outside the country, in military camps in neighboring countries, or in exile in Europe or the United States) and international pressure was what led to the fall of apartheid.

So perhaps in these difficult times it's worth being encouraged by the thought that international pressure and the belief in the universality of human rights can be translated into action. If we can learn anything from the struggle against apartheid, it's that even demonstrations that appear to be small are effective — that people on one side of the world can worry, think, protect, and influence the rights of people on the other side of the world, and that maybe, maybe, international pressure will help us too.

Hagar did not live to attend the conference she had organized on Israel and apartheid, which was held on September 5, 2000, shortly before the Second Intifada began. This is what I said there:

> Dear Hagar,
>
> You remember, the night before you went to Greece, we talked about optimism? "What are you so optimistic about?" you asked me on the phone, and I imagined your hand gesturing interrogatively. Your smile.
>
> We talked about the Camp David agreement, and about sharing Jerusalem. You observed that we never say it in Hebrew. Sharing Jerusalem. It sounds right only in English.
>
> "And if they sign the agreement, then what?" you asked me, and for a moment I felt that I had to justify how happy I would be about it.
>
> I can't remember exactly what we talked about. I lay in bed, exhausted from another day of work at the Ministry of Education, with more and more numbers flickering through my head. All day long I had looked at numbers, and seen how every page, every column of numbers screwed the Arabs. I remember that we had talked about the checkpoints, and the funny patchy state that the Palestinians would have — a state made up of disconnected parts. "Is that a

state?" you asked me, and I saw the map of the Bantustans in South Africa—lots and lots of dots, large
stains and then tens of smaller dots. I remember not
wanting the conversation to end.

I was so exhausted by the numbers tallying discrimination against Arabs in Israel: the number of
hours Arab students study, the number of buildings
that house schools, the number of teachers. I was also
exhausted by the question of what to do about it.
How can I work every day for a system that oppresses Arabs every day?

I remember really wanting to talk to you. Not because we agreed, but because we didn't. I really
wanted to tell you why I am optimistic, because I also
wanted to tell myself. I wanted to say to you, "Hagar,
look what a long way we've come, all of us, Israeli society, in the direction of a society built on equality, a
society that lives in peace with the Palestinians who
live within it and next to it, a society where everyone
will feel they are not living under occupation."

I wanted to tell you because I wanted to tell myself too that it's impossible to live here—and impossible to try to make it different—without being
optimistic. I wanted to tell you, Hagar, that the black
sign shaped like a hand that the Women in Black
carry, the hand that says "End the occupation," is a
hand that I and many others associate with you and
your voice. That hand that says "End the occupation"
is what they were talking about at Camp David.
Once, when you said, "End the occupation," they
didn't know what occupation you were talking about.

Today even Barak admits there's an occupation, even in Jerusalem.

Hagar, would you want them to name a square after you in Jerusalem? I really wanted to talk to you, but I was a bit scared. How would you feel about my job at the Ministry of Education? I wanted to know whom you considered "us" and "them" because I myself don't know how I feel about working for the establishment. Apartheid was not only a discriminatory system but one that determined discrimination as the norm. In apartheid South Africa I would not work for the Ministry of Education.

Later you called and said you weren't feeling well, and couldn't come and drink wine with me on my roof. We never managed to speak about optimism, or anything else.

I am optimistic because our reading of reality—our reading that something is far from right here, that we're living in a country where Jews have more rights than Arabs, living in a country built on another nation's land, that imposes a rule of oppression on millions of Palestinians and makes their lives miserable—is today not the exclusive domain of a scattered handful, as it was when you started standing at the square dressed in black and calling for an end to the occupation.

The agreement that will be reached will be constructed on this recognition. Perhaps the solution will not be exactly right. Perhaps the agreement will not be signed this month, perhaps we will have to go through another sea of anguish and war before it is achieved. Perhaps when it is achieved it will be partial and the map will still appear crazy, something that cannot survive for the long term.

But at Camp David, even Barak recognized that the only way to live here together is to read history not only as the story of the Jewish people returning to their land after protracted suffering and their persecution and destruction in the Holocaust, not only as the story of the Jewish people building a new and egalitarian home here, but also as the story of hundreds of thousands of Palestinians who were chased from their homes so that we could establish a state, and the story of millions of refugees who dream of returning to their land. And the story of millions of Palestinians living with identity documents that are written in a language they don't understand, living under the control of soldiers and officers and courts and a government that are not theirs. Barak and his people at Camp David, like most of the Jewish public in Israel today, have understood that its impossible to continue maintaining a rule of occupation in East Jerusalem-that this city belongs to two nations and we have to learn to live together.

It could be that it will still take time before they decide how many refugees will be allowed to return, the extent of compensation, and how exactly Jerusalem will be divided, but our biggest achievement (and we should be proud of it, glad, even for a few moments, even for a few months) is that this insight into reality that many share seems simple to us all today. This is an

insight that you and many movements and friends
helped develop. Among those who contributed were
the peace movements End the Occupation, Gush
Shalom, and Peace Now; the human rights organizations B'Tselem, HaMoked, the Association of Civil
Rights, the Alternative Information Center, the Public
Committee Against Torture, and Physicians for Human Rights; tens of activists, movements, and other organizations; the new historians who told the story of
the establishment of the state in different voices; and
Palestinian intellectuals in their writing and publications. Of course the shift in world opinion contributed
to this, as did the intifada and the impossible reality
of the Israeli army continuing to govern the Occupied
Territories.

The way the South Africans read the history of
South Africa influenced their course of action. What
kind of state did they want? How did they see their
future? What needed to be done to effect change?

The historiography of the Afrikaner rulers of the
apartheid state begins with white settlement in 1652,
and describes the Boer treks to establish the white
republics as journeys to the Promised Land. The
black inhabitants of that land are described in chap-
ters devoted to "difficulties encountered along the
way," together with the natural and climatic obstacles facing the chosen people. For them, the story of
South Africa was the story of survival of the chosen
people in the midst of a hostile population.

When white liberals, most of them English-
speakers, wrote the history of South Africa, they told

a story of struggles between races and cultures, and hoped that education and burgeoning fellowship would create a more egalitarian future. Instead of a Eurocentric perspective, black historians began to focus on African cultures. They began way before the Common Era, before the settlement of Afrikaners and before British colonialism, and continued by creating common insights for the various African nations, and discussing relations with the white minority in South Africa. Since the 1970s Marxist historians have written the story of South Africa in terms of economic exploitation. Frederick Johnston describes how the largest diamond and gold mines in the world made a small group rich on the back of cheap labor.[2] The story of South Africa, he argues, is like the story of Little Red Riding Hood: dressed up as something it isn't. This history of apartheid is less a story of white racism than an attempt to preserve the relations of economic exploitation and ensure small groups of wealthy people access to unconditional cheap labor.

There are of course various other readings of South African history, and they influence the perceptions of the present and shape the answers to the questions of what the main explanations are for the development of inequality, and the ways in which it can be changed.

In the first lesson I attended about South Africa the lecturer drew two circles on the board, one within the other. "The internal circle," he said, "is where the whites live. They have democracy, they have rights,

and they elect their leaders. The larger circle, the ex-
ternal one, is where most of the black inhabitants of
South Africa live. They have no rights." I was very
young, but still it didn't seem to make sense. How
could the whites in the internal circle have democracy
if the blacks didn't? "Can there be this magic line between those who have and those who do not, in a
democracy?" I asked. Later, when I taught Introduction to South African History, I was pleased to dis-
cover that in every class, without me saying anything,
there were those who learned something about our
situation here in Israel. It's not that everything is so
wonderful in post-apartheid South Africa: we know
that there's crime and violence, that most of the capital is still in the hands of very few, the gaps are vast,
and there is still a long way to go. But South Africa
managed to recognize that it was impossible for one
group of people to have rights and another to be denied them. They created something more just, a country that millions of people feel a part of—feel part of
its future. And it will happen here too. It's already
happening a little.

Hagar lived in the very heart of the conflict. And
her heart could not bear the occupation. She could
not contain the lack of justice any longer. Her house
was on the wounded and torn seam between the two
parts of the city: the West—ultra-Orthodox and secu-
lar, the openness of pubs and the Russian Compound
with its torture rooms, and the East—the slave market behind Paratroopers Street, the Ethiopian church,

the Italian hospital, the Ministry of Education, and her house on Prophets Street. How many significances and conflicts can one place hold? Her place was so lovely, with plants and colors and her smells and those of this city that is so filled with contrasts and tensions.

Hagar, I don't know if thousands more women will stand in the squares all over the world and cry, "Enough!" And I don't know if thousands of Palestinians and Israelis will march in a parade from East to West Jerusalem like they did in the parade you organized with Rana Nashashibi in 1997. I don't know whether the slogan will be what it was then — "Sharing Jerusalem" — or whether it will be a little different.

I don't know if there will be an agreement soon, or how the city will look, but I know that we'll live in this city together after the occupation has ended. I know that this city can be open and beautiful and not so pained. And I know that your stubbornness, your insistence on standing there every week dressed in black, in the weekly mourning you took upon yourself, saying, "End the occupation! End the occupation! End the occupation!" helped bring that day closer. I promise you it will come someday — there will be no more occupation. Like in South Africa, it's impossible to continue the oppression — here too it can't go on.

I promise you, Hagar, that your place in Jerusalem will be a meeting place for good neighbors rather than the center of hatred. I promise that, just as you believed, we will live together in Jerusalem, free of the occupation.

The Night After Yom Kippur, October 2000

The television was filled with the chaos of the start of a new intifada: Israeli soldiers shooting at people, rocks being thrown, the uprising in the Occupied Territories, and the demonstrations of Palestinians in Israel.

What mother in the world could bear the pain of seeing her child slaughtered in a barrage of gunfire, hiding behind a barrel? What for? It's enough already. What mother could bear the sight of her son shooting at children? What for?

We've had enough of this craziness. Leave us alone. Let us mothers make things a little quieter. For years you told us we had to be in Lebanon. Why? Thousands of people were killed there, and for what? It's enough now. Let's sit down and divide up this country, its water, its land, and sacred buildings, and that'll be that.

What logical person could explain why Israelis simply have to grow their lettuce in the Jewish settlement of Netzarim, in the Gaza Strip which is in one of the most congested regions in the world, a region where Palestinians have no water to drink? It's just enough already.

I was frightened when I saw all these generals on television. "We'll win," said Prime Minister Barak that night. "We'll win," he repeated, pointing his finger as he explained what he told French president Chirac. Still pointing his finger, he said to Sheli Yehimowitz, the interviewer, "Maybe for *you* it's just a game."

Mr. Prime Minster, I wanted to say to him, *if Sheli Yehimowitz were prime minister, she'd be doing a better job than you are, so don't talk rubbish. Pull those poor soldiers out of Joseph's Tomb in Nablus, and tone down your puffed-up ego. Even if that idiot Yasser Arafat with his corrupt regime is not your ideal partner, he's all there is. There's no time. Hurry. Finish it already. Let us live quietly, with flags of all colors flying in Jerusalem, so that we can go and listen to jazz in the eastern city.*

Whom do you think you're fooling with these lies of yours? This city is divided. Believe me, I've lived here for many years. There aren't many Israeli taxi drivers who are willing to take me to Shuafat, just across the seam line in East Jerusalem. So come, let's not kid ourselves. We know that the garbage is removed less often from the streets of East Jerusalem. We know that we throw children from East Jerusalem out of school every year, telling them there's no place for them. So why not let them govern their own world? How many shootouts do we need before we understand that this city will be divided, and that if we don't restrain the madness around us, the Temple Mount will explode?

When the chief of staff said on television, just after the start of the uprising, that this could develop into a war, Amotz's red boots sprang into my mind. I never want to see him in uniform again. Never. It's enough. He's forty-five, he's handsome, he loves nature, and I don't want to see him in uniform. Enough. I don't want to see my children in uniform either. Never. I didn't have children in order to put them in uniform. In fact, I'm sure all mothers feel this way, don't they? We've just been brainwashed. Lebanon, infiltrators, terrorists—security, security, security. With pompous self-importance Barak again spoke of our impressive security, our unity, and the holy of holies. Let us live in quiet. Don't cheat us. Send Ariel Sharon to his farm. Send the generals out to pasture and stop shooting. Divide this land between the two nations in a dignified and amicable divorce, not by war. No one will win a war.

The Evening After Sukkot, October 2000

"What if there's a war?" Uri asked me.

"Look," I said, "there's a meeting with Arafat, Barak, and Clinton. They're meeting, and that's a good sign." At the very same moment I was thinking that I should fix up the shelter and shop for supplies at the supermarket. I thought about why I was frightening the children; I shouldn't have spoken with Uri about what was happening, about hearing "Prague"—a well-known Israeli song about the Russian invasion of Czechoslovakia, usually played at tense times—on the radio. I didn't tell him that I too am afraid. I said it would be all right; I said there would not be a war. But he heard me tell Gali not to go to the mall or downtown because it's too dangerous now.

How can we raise children in these awful days? How do we tell them not to be afraid when the ambulances rush noisily past the house every day? How can we tell them not to be afraid when we are afraid? No one will win this war. No one ever wins a war. How can you raise them when they know that Rami and Amir are exactly like them, only Palestinian? What does that mean to them? Jack says that the way home

to East Jerusalem is like a battlefield. He suggests we think
about California all the same. We have a kind of sad joke
about this—that we'll take our families and children and go to
California if there's a terrible war here. But we already know
too well that this is where we want to live and that we'll never
go anywhere else. We want, however, to live in Jerusalem in
peace and quiet. So divide it—it's already divided.

I think of a meeting held at the Ministry of Education on
"the situation" and "education toward peace," and I ask myself what I need to do so that my children can grow up living
a life of peace. I want them to understand the reality they live
in, but I feel that the reality I depict for them is too complex.
How do I explain to my children why there are no places in
the schools for their friends in East Jerusalem?

When Uri was in kindergarten they were taken to meet
the children from Ein Rafa, the nearby Palestinian-Israeli village. "I don't understand why we have to go there. They
haven't got any toys, and we don't speak the same language
anyway," he said to me. The truth is, when I saw the children
getting on the bus, accompanied by parents, armed escorts,
and a documentary TV crew, I realized this was not the way I
wanted Uri to play with Palestinian children. Some sensitive
soul said it was like a visit to the zoo—under the protection
and good intentions of adults who want them to enjoy playing
with Arab children. The next time they went I told Uri he
didn't have to go and could come with me to work instead. I
took him with me to a meeting at the office of the Palestinian
Women's Center near the A'Ram checkpoint. On the way Uri
asked me a lot of questions: "Why are the street names written in Hebrew if only Arabs live here? Why are there so
many holes in the road?" For three hours he sat in the room

where the meeting was held and played with the Legos he'd brought with him. When we got home he told me he'd had a great day and how much fun it was to be with Mom.

And now, in these terrible times, what do I say to him? What do I say to Gali, who is at an age where she is already pained by the injustice she sees around her? Should I tell her not to see? Not to speak? I love Gali's clear voice and don't want her to stop asking, stop talking. But it pains me to think of the suffering involved in making a voice so different from the dominant voices of our society heard.

The first rains came on Sukkot. My mother says it's a good sign when it rains on Sukkot—a sign of a rainy year. I want a flood. How do you pray for a flood—a terrible flood that will make the helicopters stop flying? Such strong rains that everyone will stay home and do nothing but think. A "days of awe" flood—without CNN or BBC, without stone-throwing youngsters, without policemen who shoot demonstrators and without all the anger. I want there to be such a terrible flood that we'll all say, "Okay, we get it. Something is wrong here. Let's start from the beginning." Instead of the generals we see on the TV every day playing tough, we'll hear mothers discussing how to live together in this place. Discussing hope, and a sense of partnership and self-respect. The commentators speak of a powder keg that the men are tossing matches into—primarily Ariel Sharon, with his reckless stroll around the Temple Mount. Guys, it's the year 2000. Enough already, cut it out. What is this brutal occupation? I don't want to occupy this land. I don't want to conquer the holy of holies, and I don't want any more matches tossed in the midst of this turmoil we're living in.

Enough. For thirty-three years you've been telling us that Jerusalem is united and that it will be the united capital of Israel forever and ever. Tell me, are you crazy? How many Jews visit the Internet cafés in East Jerusalem? What are you thinking? If you say, "This is mine, I was here first," over and over, will the Palestinians disappear?

"That's not a good question," I've been told so many times. What is a good question? It's just like that other sentence they use: "It's more complex than you think." They taught us not to ask what it seems natural to ask. For example, why, in the war on TV, do we only see men? What, isn't this war ours too? Have we nothing to say about how we want to live here? Do we have to raise our children to be what you think they should be?

I want my children to live in a state where the prime minister is not a military man. I know it's not simple. It's not simple because there are very few who think like me, although I think there are many parents who feel the same way.

If only it were possible to send the men home and let the women do the talking. Perhaps then it would be possible to put together something better here. Or maybe I just need to hold on to something. I'm so afraid that everything's going to explode here that this dream of women making peace— which is perhaps an impractical dream—makes me feel a little better anyway. There are too many men involved, too many puffed-up egos, with everyone wanting to be a hero. There's no acknowledgment of the pain and sorrow of both sides. How do they see our future together? What do they wish for our children? What do they wish for Sumaya's children?

April 9, 2002

How many people were killed in the latest attack? What route was the bus traveling? Suad's telephone in Ramallah was still disconnected. One day I drove behind a car that had a red and black bumper sticker saying "War Now!" I wanted to wake up and breathe a sigh of relief, to find out that this was just a bad dream, a nightmare, scary as hell.

More and more ambulances wailed in the night. In the other room Amotz was preparing for the Geological Society conference, writing a lecture on the Soreq cave as a metaphor for the expansion of knowledge, for cooperation in science, for a wider perspective. He was preparing a presentation with pictures of the Sea of Galilee, the Dead Sea, Eilat, and the Crusader fortress at Ateret, places where he researches earthquakes. I remembered when Salim Tamari, who had heard Amotz warning us that the "big one" might happen in the next hundred years, suggested the title "Two Nations—One Earthquake." I was busy with tens of phone calls in an attempt to write the invitation to the demonstration on Friday in preparation for Colin Powell's visit, wondering how to word the request that he help us.

After every demonstration I swear to myself that I'll never do it again. So why was I organizing another one? Perhaps it was because of the e-mails from Dr. Islah Jad in Ramallah. Perhaps because of her description of the first day the curfew was lifted—going with her grown children to donate blood at the hospital and finding the blood bank closed because everyone was busy taking care of the bodies that had waited days for burial. I tried not to watch TV. I heard enough on the radio and read enough in the papers—and I wished I could climb into bed and go to sleep until it was all over. The phone calls hurt my ears. There were so many calls, all of them bringing different voices of horror.

What was this whole Operation Defensive Shield for, anyway? What exactly was the terrorist infrastructure the generals claimed they were attacking? Had anyone seen it? Did they think that blowing up more explosives laboratories and arresting hundreds or thousands more people would stop terror?

In her second e-mail from her home in Ramallah, Islah wrote:

Yesterday, the 5th of April, they lifted the curfew from 1 to 4 p.m. This came after many conflicting reports about the exact hour the curfew would be lifted. It seems that they decided to make it at 1 to avoid having to deal with the Friday prayers and to prevent people from burying their dead. I started the day with a phone call from Siham Barghouthi who spoke to me about her sadness and frustration after the killing of Hisham and Abu Hussein, guards at the office of FIDA [a leftist political party in Ramallah]. There were three of them in that office in the Arizona building, Ahmad Ghanaiem, Abu Hussein and Hisham. They were besieged and locked in the building without food or water and their only contact with the outside world was by mobile phone. Fire was opened on the office and they called Siham to find a way to get them out. Siham went through the same cycle I went through to help my son's friends, calling the Red Cross, the Red Crescent, international organizations, municipalities, but to no avail. Ahmad Ghanaiem realized that no help was coming and threw himself out of the second-floor window, injuring his back. He was arrested immediately and no one has heard from him since. Abu Hussein and Hisham kept calling Siham right up to the last minute when they asked her to take care of their families. The next day, their bodies were found thrown in the street in front of the Rukab building, the famous ice cream shop in downtown Ramallah. Siham collapsed. She told me: I kept screaming and crying and banging my head against the wall, how could I not save their lives, how could I be so helpless.

At 1 o'clock I went out to the street to look for cooking gas and see if there were any fresh vegetables or fruits. Two big tanks blocked my way to the gas shop. They ordered me to go back. I asked if there were any other shops. People said forget about it, there was no gas in town. I decided to go to downtown Ramallah. We wanted to demonstrate against the army presence. On the way, I felt as if I was living in one of those movies showing long lines of arrested Jews and others with their gloomy and tired faces. In the street that passes the Ramallah police station, I saw a long line of detainees, hands over heads, escorted by two tanks in the back and one tank in the front. In the middle two lines of soldiers were pointing their guns at them. I wanted to know where they are taking all these young people. I followed them from another street. I was shocked when I saw that they were taking them into the building of the Ministry of Culture, around which many more tanks were stationed. Why this particular building? Why did they not arrest them when we were under curfew? Why let everybody see them when we could do nothing? During the first uprising in 1987, we women used to attack soldiers and release the arrested young people. Why can't we do it now? Then we would make eye contact with the soldiers, defy them, talk to them. "Don't you have mothers? Don't you have children like we do? Go back home. Why are you here?" But this time they are very distant, they are all inside these big horrible iron tanks. There's no way to approach them. They are also so scared and they shoot to kill.

I went on to El Manarah, the main square with the lion statues, which was another devastating scene—garbage everywhere, the streets were like dirt roads, full of dust, no asphalt left to keep the dust down. There were no women in the square as we had planned. It was full of soldiers, again with their tanks. When they see people approaching they aim their big machine guns mounted on their tanks. What a scary sight. More smashed cars in the square, more destroyed sidewalks, more ruined buildings and broken glass everywhere. Oh, dear Ramallah, what has happened to you? All this destruction. All this ugliness. My eyes filled with tears again.

I left the square and went to see if there were any vegetables in the main market. There was nothing fresh to be found, only some very old bananas and very old green peas. I bought two kilos, better than nothing. Then I went to the bakery to get some bread. Not a chance. There was a long line and no bread left. I'd have to wait for at least an hour to get some. I left the place with my two kilos of green peas. On the way many women asked me, did you see any tomatoes, did you see any cabbage? My answer was no, only old lemons and very old bananas. It seemed as if they were allowing only potatoes into the city and nothing else. Of course, there's no meat to be found, nor chicken or fish—that would really be a joke—but there are some eggs.

My niece Dalia was sick. She had a throat infection and was having some difficulty walking. My sister-in-law and I took her to the nearby hospital. The doctor said she had been given the wrong medication, an antibiotic that was not suitable for her case. We said, this is all we had and we could not get anything else. All the pharmacies are closed and even if they were open we could not leave our houses. He gave her a different medication and we left. On the way back I met Suad Amiry. I had missed her so much. We hugged. Salim, her husband, calls me every day to ask how she is. Her phone line has been disconnected since the beginning of the occupation of the city. His mother's phone is also disconnected because it is her bad luck to live very close to the presidential compound. The entire area has no phone lines. They are all disconnected. He keeps asking me if he can come back from Paris. Yes, you can come back, but how are you going to get into Ramallah? We are under curfew, I said. Suad took me in her car.

She needed to visit Salim's mother, an old lady of 89. Most of her close neighbors have left the building and she is left with Zakeiah, a slightly younger woman, to take care of her. We approached Um Salim's street and the tank stationed there immediately pointed its gun at us. We raised the bread bag to show that we needed to deliver some food. They didn't allow us to use her main door, but only to approach the back of the building. We shouted at Zakeiah to come out and get the things. She came out and called: "we are alone in the building. . . . The shooting is horrible around us; we cannot sleep day or night. Today is better. I just need to move my feet a bit, even when they lift the curfew we cannot go out because we are so close to the president's compound. Um Salim is on her bed. She does not want to see anybody—what for if she cannot talk to you? What for—just to wave to you? She is OK." We left the building, the machine gun moved again. We reached my house and still had half an hour to talk. We heard the news—six Palestinians from Hamas were encircled in a house in Toubas near Jenin. Soldiers opened fire on them, killing four. The other two came out of the house waving white flags and were both shot dead. They don't want to take any prisoners. They have no place in their prisons. In El Bireh, twin city of Ramallah, they arrested 800, released 200, and are still holding 600. All from a small town like El Bireh. They reopened Ansar III prison in the Negev desert. They're going to lock everyone up there. We hear the news all the time. We keep hearing the news.

Suad is in pain—they are destroying the old cities of Bethlehem and Nablus, they are occupying Bethlehem University, a beautiful old building and turning it into a military camp. These are historical places. UNESCO has to save them; the civilized world should not allow their destruction. It would be a loss for civilization and for humanity. Suad is an architect and runs RIWAQ [Centre for Architectural Conservation, a] center for the preservation and renovation of old Palestinian sites and buildings. Now they are attacking them with rockets.[3] They have already destroyed many building in the Casbah of Nablus. Who can stop these barbaric acts? Who can save this miserable people with its buildings and history? Who can save its prisoners, its injured, or its dead? Suad left. I gave her my mobile phone so that we could remain in contact. She phoned me when she arrived home safely, and told me that on the way back she met two people who needed a ride. One was returning from burying his uncle and the other one from burying his father. No funerals are allowed. The dead are not honored on the way to their graves. The usual scene of Palestinians wrapping their dead in their national flag is no longer allowed. Any funeral will show the people and they want this war to be against "terrorists." No people should appear in the picture. That is why the tanks are in the main square of Ramallah—no more demonstrations while their "operation" is taking place.

I keep hearing news from Jenin and Nablus. In

Jenin's public hospital, the morgue refrigerator can take only three corpses. Of the five that managed to reach the hospital, two are left in a room to decompose. They are thinking about burying them the same way they did in Ramallah, by digging a hole in the hospital courtyard. Many injured cannot even dream of getting any medical treatment, they are left to bleed to death.

I heard terrible noise around me and went out to see what was going on. Yes, they've blocked my street with smashed cars and rubble from the old wall of the Beautiful Friend Quaker school playground. It seems that they want to stop the movement of all cars when they lift their curfew next time. This apparently means that they are not leaving soon.

Keep your voices raised my friends. Keep protesting by all means and ways to stop this occupation from growing. You are our only windows to the world. They keep shooting at journalists. They only let them come into the city when the curfew is lifted. They don't want the world to see what a degraded state they've become. Force Israel to come to its senses. They're still giving lots of support to this war criminal Sharon. Yesterday he had 72% support for approving "actions" against the Palestinians, and 65% trust his leadership of the country. But there are still some Israelis with us who are faithful to their humanity. They protest every day and are subjected to very violent treatment from their police. They get death threats for supporting the Palestinians. We have all to join hands to stop this barbarity from growing. My love to you all and I know that all your hearts are with us now.

So what's the story of this war—is this a "we'll show you" kind of war, "we'll humiliate you until you shout for mercy? Hang your heads and say you're beat"? What then?

Two Days Before Yom Ha'zikaron, April 14, 2002

"They say it's going to rain on Independence Day," I said to Dafna, who had come to visit me after we hadn't seen each other for a long while. She was having her Turkish coffee, two sugars and milk, and I was having my tea with milk and honey. In recent years both of us had stopped eating at night because I'm frugal with nighttime calories. On that evening, however, I was enjoying a piece of hot broccoli quiche with cream. Let's eat and drink, for tomorrow we die?

Dafna told me about the lion statues in Jerusalem that she loves so much. Tel Aviv had statues of penguins and then dolphins. Jerusalem has eighty lions scattered throughout the city. Dafna is a ceramicist, and the lion she and her partner Vera made is the best of all, in my opinion. "Our lion," Dafna told me, "is standing in a part of town that was once considered very central—Hillel Street, a little below Gali's school. Right next to Gillie's restaurant. But Gillie's is closed now [because there are no more tourists and Israelis don't go to restaurants for fear of bombings] and no one wanders around there."

"Let's go out and look at the lions," I said to her, and we

both burst out laughing at the idea of going out. Who goes out in Jerusalem these days?

I told Dafna how every morning when I took Gali to school, I felt like I was taking my daughter to a battlefield and leaving her there alone. Abandoning her in the heat of battle. I was scared. The previous day's attack was on a bus on the number six line—a bus that comes by our house. How could we carry on as if everything's normal?

"I'm sure it won't really rain on Independence Day," said Dafna. "Maybe the khamsin will break, but we'll still be able to barbecue."

It looks like my dream of dancing on Independence Day will have to wait many years. If we want to dance and barbecue on our independence day, why shouldn't the Palestinians celebrate their independence?

This is a war for our homes, they tell me. Whose homes? The homes for the homeless that they have neglected to build? Care for the pensioners and the disabled and education? Instead they hollowed out huge tunnel roads beneath Palestinian areas, and built bypass roads around Palestinian villages, and elevated roads that cut Palestinian villages into two; by the side of the roads they built walls and painted empty green fields on them, so that the settlers would not have to see Palestinians from the armored windows of their cars. When the Palestinians began shooting and killing and attacking, the Israelis started to build roads that bypass the bypass roads.

Killing in order to avenge killing, destroying in order to avenge killing, recruiting thousands of soldiers to do wrong— wouldn't it be simpler to try to talk? To tell all the settlers in the Gaza Strip that they have two weeks to pack up because it's the most crowded piece of territory in the world, and we can't let a few thousand settlers embitter the lives of millions? Instead of buying more bullets and explosives and battle rations, wouldn't it be simpler to build homes inside Israel for those settlers? They don't *have* to grow their lettuce in Gaza.

I hope the day will come when I can dance at a huge Independence Day party. Why can't we sit down and talk and think about how to live here together? What do they mean, there's no one to talk to? Before you fight, before you kill, before suicide bombers blow up, before you destroy houses — isn't it worth trying over and over to talk?

When will we stop? When will we say that Zionism has won and that we are here, but that we want a country with clear and friendly borders? Why didn't we jump at the Saudi proposal tabled at the Arab League summit, which offered peace and recognition in exchange for a withdrawal to the 1967 borders?

In the morning I called Sumaya Farhat Naser to ask her how she was doing. "Do you know what it would be like to see the Israeli flag in Mecca? For Saudi Arabia to recognize Israel and want peace with it?" Sumaya asked me on the phone. "How could Israel not have accepted such a proposal? I want peace. You know how much I want peace and how much I believe in our collaborative work, but why is Sharon doing this? And why aren't you doing something to stop him?"

These were the first days after the Israeli army had moved into and reoccupied the cities. She lives in Birzeit, a village adjacent to Ramallah. "The tanks are in the street," she told me, "and I'm more scared than I've ever been in my life. I hear them all the time. There's no electricity. Our phone has been disconnected. I don't know what will happen when the battery runs low on my cellular.

"Come and see," she continues, "you can come through Beit El and Hamza, I'll wait for you with another ten Palestinian women and we'll go to Ramallah together." I promised her that we would try and come to Ramallah.

On the morning we spoke, a group of foreigners from the International Solidarity Movement went into curfew-bound Ramallah — to the hospital and to Arafat's headquarters, which had been surrounded by the Israeli army — but none of the Palestinians dared be seen in the streets. I was scared to go into the embattled city with a small group, and I also didn't know what we'd do with what we saw there. I said I would try to come in with a larger group bringing food and medical supplies through the Qalandia checkpoint on the main road. We spoke for almost an hour on the cellular phone, with Sumaya telling me about her sister-in-law who had given birth in the hospital in Ramallah and been forced to walk home with her baby, afraid of being shot on the way.

Five days later, on the last day of Passover, a group of us — three thousand Jewish and Palestinian Israelis — marched in the direction of the Qalandia checkpoint to deliver food and medical supplies to besieged Ramallah. The policemen at the A'Ram checkpoint, still inside Jerusalem, blocked our passage and showed us an order — the entire area had been declared a closed military zone. "Perhaps you can at least let through the four trucks carrying food and medical supplies," I suggested to a lieutenant colonel, whose unit of soldiers was assisting the armed policemen at the checkpoint.

"It'll calm things down a little and people will disperse feeling that at least the humanitarian aid got through. People are angry, worried, they want to do something."

"I'm not letting anything pass here," he insisted.

"But you know that according to international law you have to permit the passage of humanitarian aid."

"What is this law? Show it to me."

"Don't you know the Geneva Convention?"

"No. What's that?"

At the end of the day the trucks carrying food and medical supplies did reach Ramallah. But before that the policemen fired tear gas at us and beat us with batons. Then they fired more tear gas. I had never been so scared.

I came home and went to bed, and I was shaking for hours. The violence had gotten inside my body. I knew I couldn't take it anymore. I swore to myself that I would not organize another demonstration in my life. Between the phone calls to journalists and the calls to find out the state of the wounded, I lay in bed shaking and crying, feeling like I could not contain the fear and violence and tension any longer. My body hurt from the soldiers' blows, and the sound of tear gas canisters being fired frightened me over and over again. The fear came back—the fear of the soldiers and the mass of men with flags, slogans, and megaphones almost crushing me and Manal Hassan as we argued, trying to persuade dozens of policemen armed with rifles and batons, helmets and shields, to let us pass. I knew it would explode; I knew for as long as I stood there. We tried to calm the anger and the frustration of thousands of Israeli Jews and Palestinians who wanted to get to

Ramallah to tell their Palestinian friends that we were with them, to bring them food and medical supplies, and to tell the Israeli army to get out of the territories and let people live their lives. We couldn't get through. We knew that because there were Jews among the demonstrators the soldiers would not fire live ammunition. Until then our experience had been that the police and army did not shoot at Jews. But we had stood there for hours, cramped and crowded in the rain, Jews and Arabs, Palestinians and Israelis, singing, calling out, demonstrating, with dozens of TV crews and journalists watching thousands of demonstrators and dozens of police from the side. I knew it would end badly. I hoped no one would get killed. And I was terribly afraid.

It had started the previous Saturday evening at dinner. Once the kids left the table to go to their rooms, I told Hagit Gor Ziv about my conversation with Sumaya and that we had to do something, that we couldn't let our army go into cities and houses and lock thousands of people up so that they couldn't go out to buy food. Even when they could leave their houses, there was no food in the stores because the army wasn't letting it through. We sat down to organize a parade of women in white that would go to Ramallah on foot, bringing food and medicines. We thought the army and police wouldn't stop a few hundred women wearing white and carrying food. Within two days we were joined by members of Ta'ayush (an Arab-Jewish partnership that had already taken convoys of food and medicine past checkpoints to Palestinian villages), Palestinian Israeli Knesset members, members of Yesh Gvul, and a great many other people who could no longer bear the shame. Those Palestinians from Jerusalem who could walked with us. On the last day of our freedom holiday, Passover, the dozens of women in white were swallowed up by thousands of angry demonstrators.

When they wouldn't let the trucks through, we offloaded them. Each person took a bottle of oil, or a bag of flour or sugar, or diapers, and we asked the police and soldiers to allow the food and supplies through the checkpoint to be loaded on trucks on the other side. They refused.

For days afterward I wandered around traumatized. I and other Israeli and Palestinian women had previously been invited to Brussels to meet women members of the European Parliament and European ministers who wanted to hear from us what could be done, and so I went, reluctantly. In Amsterdam, while I was waiting to change planes, Simone Susskind, my friend from Brussels, called. She never tires of trying to make the voices of Israeli and Palestinian women who want peace heard; she insists on helping us meet European women and leaders who want to help us make peace. She called and told me to go straight to dinner at the home of one of the European ministers. And I couldn't take it anymore. I didn't want dinner. I wanted them to come and see for themselves how Israeli soldiers prevented Palestinians from leaving their homes to buy food. I got on a plane and flew home.

I should have listened to Rana Nashashibi when I asked her if we should go to Brussels. I had called to find out whether she was planning to join the delegation of Palestinian and Israeli women flying to Belgium. I didn't want to go, and I wanted her to tell me that she was not going.

On the phone Rana sounded exhausted, and yet she still wanted to talk. She had just come back from a visit to the refugee camp in Jenin after the Israeli army invasion of it. There were children there who couldn't find their parents, families separated in the tumult of fleeing. "You know what's hardest for me?" she said. "The hardest thing is that they're refugees who've already been expelled once and now they're living through the trauma of expulsion again."

And no, of course she could not leave now and go to Brussels. "Daphna, we haven't even buried our dead yet," she said. Rana is a child psychologist and director of the Palestinian Counseling Center in East Jerusalem. She told me about the emergency telephone line that they established, and the hundred of calls they received from children or parents whose children are in trauma, and I heard the fatigue in her voice. "I'm tired," she said. How much pain can one person contain?

"No, I won't go to Brussels, but we have to keep saying what we have said for ten years. We have a long way to go, many more years of working together. It's important for us to hear the voices of these Israelis who oppose this horror. And keep working. There's a long way to go yet. This time we have to succeed. There's no other way. We have to talk about the real issues. We didn't really deal with these issues in depth after the Oslo accords. We didn't really touch on all the painful questions. We still need many years of talking."

When I tell her I feel I'm not doing enough, her response is that none of us is doing enough. "You're doing what you can, though. And that's important."

Yigal's son is in Nablus. Dan's grandson is in Jenin. Odeda's son is in Nablus. Amotz got an exemption because of his age.

One morning I was at a conference called "Women Refuse," a meeting of women who refuse to raise children for the army, refuse to be silent, refuse not to know.

I wish we could find ways to refuse together, all the women. Not iron their uniforms, not let our brothers go, not encourage our children to go. In the hallway between one workshop and another at the conference, I shared an embrace with Vered Shomron, who was pregnant for the sixth time and more lovely than ever, and with Hagit Gor Ziv, whose home was host to the establishment of the Movement Against War—an umbrella organization of dozens of peace movements. Fatma Yunis and I tried to remember when last we'd seen each other. "Of course I condemn these awful suicide bombings," she said. "It's terrible to kill people, children, women, like that. But what is a young man like that thinking? One who's willing to give up his life, everything, to kill? What is bringing so many people to think these kinds of thoughts that we can't understand?"

I remember listening to Fatma and thinking that I wished all the Jews in Israel could hear her. I wished they could hear the friendship, the partnership, the pain, the loss, and the hope in her voice—the voice of so many Palestinian Israelis. "In Israel we use the shekel. I pay in shekels, you pay me back in shekels. And what currency does Israel think the Palestinians will use to respond to force? Israel uses force and more force, and wants to dictate to the Palestinians what currency to pay them back in."

Her pain, her desperation, cut through the layer of sleepiness that surrounded my enormous anxiety—the layer of denial that I had been wondering for years how to crack and was trying to hold together around the fear. Not to know. Not to turn on the television if you don't have to. Not to know. Not to know.

Because I had not had the time to prepare an organized lecture for this conference, organized by New Profile, I told them about a conversation I'd had with Uri when he was eight and we talked about how I didn't want him to go into the army. Now he was almost twelve and I was even more adamant that he not go. And my Gali was already fifteen and going with me to demonstrations. I remember once, many years ago, looking at those families with admiration—the ones with two generations going together to demonstrations. I was sure it would never happen to me. It couldn't happen that I would turn gray and still be going to demonstrations, and still shouting, "End the occupation." And surely Gali would not go with me. I had not known how painful the confrontation with denial and knowledge would be.

I spoke to the conference about Stanley Cohen's three phases of denial. In the first phase we refuse to acknowledge the facts; we know but refuse to believe what our army does in the Occupied Territories. After accepting the facts, we say in the second stage that there must be a good reason: Barak offered them everything and they refused, or there's no one to talk to. But after the first two stages of denial—once we acknowledge what is being done in our names, and feel pain, and recognize the moral and economic costs—there is still one more stage of denial: surely we cannot make a difference, there is nothing we can do to change anything.

Usually I believe that this last phase can be overcome, that it is indeed possible to have an impact, to write, demonstrate, convince, and help. But that day it was especially hard.

❊

"We're guilty and so are they," I heard more and more of my Israeli friends saying. It reminded me of the old saying "It takes two to tango," which was often applied to wife-beating men and usually followed by "She shouldn't upset him."

Rema Hammami e-mailed me a report on the destruction of Palestinian nongovernmental organizations. Like hundreds of Israeli organizations active in trying to mend Israeli society, hundreds of organizations have arisen in Palestinian society that work to protect human rights, promote women, promote democracy. Because Palestinians are not allowed to see Jerusalem as their capital, and most Palestinians are not allowed in Jerusalem, a large number of these organizations were established in Ramallah. The long list of organizations that have been damaged is divided into four groups according to the type of damage: intentional attacks on radio and television installations; vandalism at organizations occupied by soldiers; severe and intentional damage to organizations not defined as targets, which did not house soldiers; and organizations where computers and other items were looted or disappeared, which sustained light damage.

I read the list, shuffled through the names, found the Love and Peace FM radio station and an educational television station that was working on a production of *Sesame Street* in Hebrew and Arabic. I read Randa Seniora's description of the destruction at Al-Haq, a human rights organization.

Whom will we talk to when we've destroyed all of Palestinian civil society? Why destroy a cultural center? There's only one computer left at the educational television station in Ramallah, and it lies in parts in the bathroom. On a board in the main office one of the soldiers left instructions: *1. Eat. 2. Drink. 3. Destroy.*

I remember the truck that stopped in our street after the war in 1967. I was ten and the picture is a little fuzzy, but I remember us kids jostling together behind the truck and someone handing out all kinds of things he'd brought from there, from the war. Lots of pens, I remember, and watches. And now I read these organized lists of the damage done, the equipment taken: seventeen computers, two petty-cash boxes, microphones . . .

What now? How do we go on from here? Whom do we talk to? What do we talk about? How do we live here together after we've destroyed the entire infrastructure—not the terror infrastructure, because it is made of despair and we have only created even more of that, but the infrastructure of hope, of trust, of friendship built over the years, of Palestinian civil society that wanted to create an open, democratic, vibrant, egalitarian society, a society that respects its past, feels the pain, and dreams of a better future alongside us?

After all the pictures of terror attacks, the war, and the blood, I don't know why the pictures of the broken computers and smashed copy machines made me despair so.

"Now, when most Israelis feel they've won the war," Jack Persekian asked me at his gallery in the Old City, "is there a plan?"

"There's no plan," I told him. "We are trying to make other voices heard in Israel, without much success. Most Israelis don't know that there are Palestinians who believe in life and are not part of the wave of war that has swept over us. Our two societies are immersed in the craziness of worshiping power, destruction, death. We Israelis needs to hear sane voices like yours—of Palestinians who believe in life, dignity, hope, peace. Perhaps you can invite all the artists who came to Bethlehem for the millennium to come again right now, so that their presence can solve the problem of the Church of the Nativity?" I asked him.

"I don't do things like that," Jack said.

"Like what?"

"Like demonstrations. Like reacting to events."

"Isn't it terrible what's happening? Don't you want to do something to stop this horror?"

"Of course."

"Of course what?"

"I do it here. I keep on living. We have to agree," Jack said, "on our distant future—on equal rights for all, regardless of ethnic origin—on majority rule and protection of minority rights. It's in all our interests. Even if each group has other interests—eventually the best solution for all of us will be to respect the interests of all groups. Eventually we will live in one society, our grandchildren will have to live together, be influenced by one another, respect the different cultures. If this is our vision for fifty years' time, then we can build mechanisms and agreements for each stage of the process. We can build a wall between us in the meantime, and slowly the parts of the wall that are no longer necessary will be removed. The wall will disappear over the years—perhaps the parts of it that are unnecessary will disappear."

But Jack did not mean a wall like the one that is currently being built across from his house—a wall that cuts his street in two, a wall that leaves his mother, wife, and children on one side and his aunts and cousins on the other, a wall that is supposed to bring us security but cannot.

Israel is building a system of cement walls, electric and

barbed wire fences, guard towers and lookout cameras — all of which is called the "defense barrier." The route of the barrier was dictated by extraneous considerations which have little to do with security. Almost no attention was paid to the extensive harm this route will cause Palestinians. The barrier divides neighborhoods and cuts off access to jobs and schools. Thirty-eight percent of the West Bank Palestinian population will be harmed by the barrier, and some 102,000 Palestinians are trapped in enclaves, dependant on the IDF to conduct all aspects of daily life. Jack's vision of a glass wall on the 1967 border could not have been further from the horrible reality the new wall created.[4]

TEN

ON THE ROAD TO RECONCILIATION

May 10, 2003

Everyone was asking me what was wrong, why I had a smile on my face. And I had to explain that I'd just come back from South Africa full of hope and optimism. I tried not to apologize too much for the smile on my face, but I knew that these days, people are suspicious if someone seems to be as happy as I did. I told anyone who cared to listen that if South Africa has changed, maybe we can do it too. I kept repeating the stories I had heard from many South African activists—that in the 1980s, each year they thought the situation could get no worse, while every year it did.

Everyone we met in South Africa was talking about the miracle of the transformation to the new South Africa. People were very critical of the economic policies and the pace of change, but there was much hope in the air.

Things are still difficult, of course. In Langa, we saw terrible poverty and visited three families who live together with their children in a single small room, separated only by curtains, as many are forced to do. In this black township of

250,000 people, 60 percent are unemployed. But it looked very different from the townships I'd seen on my last visit to South Africa, eleven years ago. Now there is electricity and some running water—the clouds of pollution that hung overhead in those days have mostly disappeared. Professor Mark Zwelling, of Stellenbosch University, described to us the many problems in the new South Africa: the lack of housing, the shortage of trained teachers, AIDS, alcoholism, growing income inequality. "It is like fixing an airplane while it's still in the air," he said. "We will do it carefully; we are not there yet, but hopefully we will be."

The Cape Town–based Human and Social Research Council asked Rema Hammani and I to invite twenty Israelis and Palestinians to a conference on the restoration of hope. For three days we sat in a beautiful resort near the ocean and met with past and present South African leaders: former president F. W. de Klerk, ANC leaders who are now government ministers, newspaper editors, and many others. Rema, who coordinated the Palestinian group, told the organizers that we had to dance. And during the two nights we spent there, we did not stop dancing. Palestinians, Israelis, and South Africans of all backgrounds—we all danced.

I came home full of hope because so many people told us of the shock they felt on February 2, 1990, when de Klerk announced abruptly that he was lifting the ban on the ANC and the Communist Party. Because we were Israelis and Palestinians dancing and hoping together. Because I spent wonderful days with Rema. Because visiting the District Six museum in Cape Town, which preserves the memory of an area from which sixty thousand people were forcibly ejected by the apartheid regime, moved me to think that maybe one day we too will have institutions to help us remember.[1]

I was repeatedly asked a number of questions in South Africa: Why are peace activists in Israel so divided? Why is there no Israeli-Palestinian peace movement? We have asked ourselves these questions countless times and considered various answers. But in light of recent history in South Africa, where hundreds of organizations joined forces in the struggle against apartheid, the question takes on new significance. Why do social activists and peace movements in Israel not work together? Why do members of Gush Shalom and Peace Now not work together? Where is the Israeli-Palestinian peace movement?

I can't answer these questions. I can only begin to surmise that the answer lies somewhere in the fundamental difference between the conflict in South Africa and the one that afflicts our region. The difference is that the dream of one state unified anti-apartheid activists in South Africa, enabling the various anti-apartheid factions to overcome differences of opinion. Here, like in every divorce negotiation, we are quibbling over details—over dividing the assets. We're trying to dismantle a package that was never successful to begin with. We have no passion and no faith, and we can see no hopeful solution. Optimism, generosity, and love are elements of marriage but not of divorce. What is our common dream? A wall? What is our common vision? We have none. With no shared vision, the issues that divide us arise immediately. Where will the fence be situated, and what will be done about the settlers and the Right to Return? If we had a clearly defined shared vision with which to begin negotiations over our common future, we could address the details later. For now, the details are all there is to argue over.

Many of the South Africans we met did not understand why we want two states and not one binational state. If the Bantustan solution didn't work for them, why should it work for us? Georg Meiring, the last chief of the South African Defense Forces under apartheid—a man who can by no means be considered a left-winger—asked why we did not consider the option of a single state. For him, and for many South Africans, the map of the future Palestine is too reminiscent of the Bantustans. Because most of us have not chosen this option, which seems the simplest of all to the South Africans, we find it hard to come together behind a clear and simple vision, not even within the peace movement. Because the imminent solution is one of divorce, we are divided over the distribution of assets. After years of peace demonstrations, the one message we can all unite behind is the one even Prime Minister Sharon has been forced to state: end the occupation.

When the process of change began in South Africa, many disputes remained unresolved. How could economic equality be achieved after years of discrimination? Did the redistribution of land include all of the territory that had been expropriated from black South Africans? These and other questions were not resolved to the satisfaction of all concerned, and fierce differences of opinion exist to this day. Nevertheless, since the Freedom Charter of 1995, the vision of a South Africa that belongs to all who live in it, black and white, has made it easier to present a united front. It's a simple, clear, single, absolute vision that unites everyone who opposed apartheid.[2]

Another question that I brought back from my trip to

South Africa was: What can we learn from the South African insistence on maintaining negotiations at all costs? The ship of the future ran aground on many different reefs during the negotiations in South Africa. Often it all seemed about to fall apart. How did they manage to keep the negotiations going despite the attacks, the assassinations, the violence that took the lives of more than ten thousand South Africans? What made it possible to continue the negotiations? That was the principal question I asked at the seminar.

De Klerk explained that it had been clear there were no other options. South Africa was isolated from the rest of the world: students were not accepted for university education abroad, athletes were banned from the Olympic games and international tournaments. This deepening isolation and economic pressure, at least for a time, united the country ideologically—"the whole world is against us" was the prevailing sentiment. But in the long term, it became clear that apartheid was untenable; in order to join the community of nations they had to reverse course. The economy was deteriorating, young people were leaving the country—there was simply no choice. In his presentation to the Israelis and Palestinians, de Klerk said that it was clear that maintaining the apartheid regime would destroy the country economically; the white regime, he said, which had already tried everything to preserve white hegemony and failed, was destined to come to an end.

What de Klerk did not tell us—but his former opponents did—is that when he began the process of reform he believed it would be possible to modify the white regime without ending it, without giving up power. The National Party tried hard to retain its veto authority, not just during the transition

period but permanently. But once the process of demo-
cratization had begun, even if it stumbled a bit, it could not
be stopped.

Which brings me to the most important question I came
back from South Africa with: How do we prepare now for
what will happen here after the talks, after the compromise,
after the struggle? It seems strange to even dream about a
Truth and Reconciliation Commission in Israel, but peace
will never be possible if we do not prepare, beforehand, ways
to heal the pain. The Truth and Reconciliation Commission
began operating after the South Africa's democratic revolu-
tion, but the preparations—the understanding that a public
process of reconciliation would take place—were under way
beforehand. The transition was made possible by the acknowledgment that signing the agreement would mark not
the end of the conflict but rather the beginning of a process of
reconciliation and dialogue.[3] In Israel, the generals are busy
trying to end the conflict with a few signatures on a piece of
paper. Instead we should start to plan the rewriting of the
history books, opening our hearts to the suffering of others,
planning our lives together in peace.

February 2004

Ha'aretz ran an interview with the historian Benny Morris,
the author of *The Birth of the Palestinian Refugee Problem*.[4] Morris was one of the first courageous historians to describe how
the Israeli army forcibly expelled hundreds of thousands of
Palestinians from their homes in 1948, puncturing the myth
that most had left of their own volition. But now, after three

years of awful violence in the new intifada, Morris told *Ha'aretz* that we would be better off today had *all* the Palestinians been expelled: "If [David] Ben-Gurion had carried out a large expulsion and cleansed the whole country . . . he would have stabilized the State of Israel for generations. . . . There are circumstances in history," Morris went on to suggest, "that justify ethnic cleansing."[5]

On the day the interview with Benny Morris was published, Jack came to visit me and we talked about reconciliation; I told him about the District Six Museum in Cape Town. The issue of *Ha'aretz* with the Morris interview inside was lying on the table between us, but Jack doesn't read Hebrew, and I was so horrified by the headline of the interview that I had resolved not to read it. We discussed the process of reconciliation and the need to remember the past while building a shared future.

The next day Jack called from his home in North Jerusalem and asked me what I thought of the interview. He wanted to know how many Israelis think like Benny Morris. I tried, unsuccessfully, to convince him that Morris is just crazy. But he persisted, asking me about every detail of the interview. What did I think Morris thinks about the Mizrahim? Do most Israelis believe the Palestinians are "barbarians" who need a "cage . . . built for them," as Morris said? Finally, at the end of our long conversation, Jack said, "Daphna, I had to talk to someone about this interview. Don't you think that Benny Morris has said what most Israelis believe?"

When I was a girl, in the sixties, we were told that there were no Palestinians. We were told by our teachers, our parents, and our government that there were only Arabs, who did not really have any connection to our land. Later we were told that we should not talk to them, and contact with Palestinians was effectively illegal. But we were never told why the Palestinians were so angry with us. We were never told what it was they wanted. I can't remember when I first understood that there were hundreds of thousands of Palestinians here before the establishment of the State of Israel; that, as Benny Morris said, the Jews "cleansed" this land of its inhabitants in order to establish a state.

Why is it so difficult for us to say we are sorry? We are sorry that we built a state for the Jews, who had been persecuted for so long, on your land, on land that Jews lived on centuries ago, to which we longed to return. We are sorry. Could we gather our courage to say such a thing—to apologize to Um Salim, who is now ninety-two and still remembers the day she left her house in Jaffa, when they told her it would only be for a few days?

After the signing of the Oslo accords in 1993, it was possible to hope that finally both sides in this unending conflict might understand that it was pointless to deny the existence of the other—to pretend that the present situation, in which Palestinians live with no rights under Israeli control, could continue indefinitely.

But that hope is long vanished. In May 1999, when the Labor Party under Ehud Barak came into power, many Israelis believed that he would resume peace talks and perhaps begin the process of reconciliation. But Barak, an army man, did not talk about reconciliation—he talked about ending the conflict, on his terms. In all the peace negotiations—in Washington and Taba and Cairo and Sharm el-Sheikh, all the places whose names we have already forgotten—there was no talk of reconciliation; no one asked how Jews and Arabs might live here together. They were a bunch of generals eager to put an end to the conflict. They did not pursue peace, only a piece of paper with maps and borders and everyone's signature.

In an August 2003 article in the Israeli daily *Yediot Aharanot*, Barak offered his explanation for the failure of the talks: "We don't have a partner. Frustrating or not, that's a fact." Contradicting the prevalent Israeli myth that he "offered everything" to the Palestinians at Camp David, Barak wrote: "Here's the truth: Barak did not give away a thing. I did not give away a thing."[6] There you have it: he did not give away a thing. Like the leaders before and after him, he was searching for victory, not reconciliation.

March 18, 2004

When Uri was eight, he came home from school one day, hungry as usual, and with a mouth full of spaghetti he looked at me with his big blue eyes and asked: "Who was more important in the army, your father or Dad's father?"

"They were both important," I answered him. "I don't know what your dad's father did in the army. My father fought against the British. He was in the Lehi—an underground militia that wanted the British to leave Israel."

"Dad's father told me he was in the Palmach," the commando unit of the Israeli militia prior to statehood.

I was making pesto for Amotz and Gali and myself. Uri doesn't eat pesto. He only eats unambiguously colored foods.

"And Dad, was he a commander in the army?"

"No, but he was in that secret unit that's so famous, the one everyone calls 'the unit,' that Bibi [Binyamin Netanyahu] and Barak were in."

"Who was more important?"

"Barak. But Bibi had a brother, Yoni, who was a hero. He was killed in Africa when the unit went to rescue Israeli hostages whose airplane had been hijacked to Entebbe. It was a really big story then. Everyone loved Yoni because he died like a hero trying to save Israelis. People thought perhaps Bibi was a hero too."

"But Bibi wasn't a hero, right? Maybe he wasn't really Yoni's brother. Maybe he just said he was."

"He was really his brother, but not all brothers are alike. Anyway, Yoni was a good soldier, but that doesn't mean he could have been a good prime minister. We don't need prime ministers who have been good soldiers. You're not going to be a soldier, are you?"

"No, I'm not."

"I'm glad to hear you say that. I'm glad you're not going to be a soldier."

"But what'll I say to them when they tell me to come?"

"Say your mother won't let you."

"But I'll be big. Big people don't say things like that. What if they make me?"

Gali has gotten her first army call-up papers. When I saw the white envelope with the IDF symbol, I was horrified. I'd been dreading this moment since the day she was born. Now it has arrived, and she is the only one who can decide what to do. It is hard for me to write this. Gali is almost seventeen. I

believed that it was important to run around organizing
demonstrations and writing reports and making speeches in
favor of withdrawal from the Occupied Territories in order
to ensure a better future for her, for Uri, and for all the children here. I was convinced that when they grew up there
would be no army at all, just as my grandmother and mother
had promised me when I was small. I thought I could promise my children that they would not have to serve in an occupying army. But I told Gali that I would support whatever
decision she made.

I'm not sure about anything anymore. When I was her
age I had no doubts about having to serve in the army. I look
back at the photographs of my friend Rachel and me looking
funny as we tried on our uniforms at induction. There are
other photos of me holding a rifle in the officers' course. I
pasted them into my childhood album. I remember the pride
I felt the first time I went home wearing the officer's rank on
the shoulders of my new and freshly ironed officer's uniform.
A short while after I was discharged I developed a kind of
blackout, and now I remember virtually nothing and no one
from my army days. It wasn't that I was involved in anything
special or particularly interesting in the army—I spent most
of my service as a staff officer making sure that other officers
in the maintenance division received their salaries on time.
We spent a lot of time counting all the soldiers in the division,
each time arriving at a different tally. There were no computers yet, and we were uncertain as to exactly how many officers in the maintenance division we were responsible for.
Just before I finished my two years of service, I was called
up to a pilot's course—a huge honor, which I shared with
only two other female soldiers in the entire IDF. Although it

meant committing myself for another five years of service, I seriously considered the option. I passed all the tests and very much wanted to prove to myself that I could be like the successful boys in the pilot's course. I even convinced the psychologist who interviewed me and did his best to catch me out with questions like "What if you get pregnant?" In the end, after I was accepted, I decided not to go. Seven years seemed, even then, like a long time to spend in the army. Also, I wasn't sure that I would survive the course along with all the boys; indeed, the two girls who took the exams with me dropped out before finishing.

I think my position regarding the army began to change during the Lebanon war. In April 1982, Ariel Sharon, then minister of defense, led Israel into a war that was known as Shalom Hagalil—Peace for Galilee. It seems to me that the war was as unnecessary and awful as the name was ridiculous. There had been peace and tranquility in the Galilee for months, yet Sharon sent the Israeli army to conquer southern Lebanon, bombing and killing and destroying Lebanese cities, all the way up to Beirut. For eighteen years, during which thousands of people were killed, Israel continued to occupy south Lebanon, which we were told was a necessary measure for our security. "We have no choice," they told us, year in and year out, as the death toll mounted.

This is why I became a supporter of Yesh Gvul—in Hebrew, it means both "there is a limit" and "there is a border." In other words, we are willing to defend borders of the State of Israel but not to serve in Lebanon or to be an army of occupation in south Lebanon or the West Bank and Gaza. It was a challenge to the establishment: enough is enough. When

Gali was a baby, not yet a year old, and we were still in the United States and I was only footnotes away from completing my doctorate, I spent hours organizing support events for Yesh Gvul and aid for reserve soldiers who refused to serve in the Occupied Territories.

Today, the thought of my children being drafted horrifies me. It's not just because everything has gotten even more terrible and the role of the military has become more and more that of an oppressive force, but also because I've learned that what seems illogical sometimes really *is* illogical.

At Gali's school they lit candles in memory of Benayahu Jonathan Zuckerman, who was murdered on the number fourteen bus two days after he told Gali about what he planned to do during the summer. The pictures of him, of a boy filled with joy and hope, brand us with sorrow and pain.

Amotz, who served with Benayahu's father, Moysh Zuckerman, in the elite Sayaret Matkal commando unit, walked with me on the road of refusal. When I first met him, he was still very much a part of the close circle of friends who had served with this elite unit in places he will not tell me even today. But slowly, he refused to serve in the Occupied Territories, and joined Yesh Gvul, and then decided that he could no longer serve as a guard for the prisoners who are held without trial in Ketziot. One recent morning, I asked him about his refusal to serve at the Ansar III prison in 1990. He said:

> When I came back to Israel after studying abroad I
> was already a supporter of Yesh Gvul and a believer
> in refusal to serve in the Occupied Territories. When
> we got to Israel we learned about administrative

detentions, mainly through your work with B'Tselem and your visits to Ketziot. It was clear to me that going to guard Ketziot would not sit with my conscience. My only hesitation was whether I was willing to be put in prison repeatedly, with a three-month-old son and three-year-old daughter, at a time when we were supposed to be moving houses. When I arrived for reserve duty I was determined to refuse to serve. The reserve officer told me that she wouldn't talk to me until everyone had left, and asked me to wait by the bus with my kit bag. That's part of the psychological warfare. When everyone was on the bus with their kits, she approached me and told me that I should get on the bus along with everyone else and stop making a fuss—enough *balagan*. I told her that I refused to get on the bus. Then she said she would meet me in the office.

Once there, she told me that she saw from my file that my objection was indeed a matter of conscience, but that if she let me get away with it, others who just wanted to get out of serving would jump on the bandwagon, claiming conscientious objection. I told her that I understood what she was saying and that she should do whatever she considered best. She told me she'd have to put me in prison, because the only jobs she had open were for noncommissioned officers in Ketziot and officers in Gaza. I told her that I accepted this and that she should go ahead. After a long wait a clerk came up and asked me to serve at a base inside Israel. I said of course.

They stationed me at a base, guarding a company

made up of new immigrants from Romania and Ethiopia along with Israeli-born soldiers. The captain of the watch trained us in preparation for attacks and intrusions and was impressed to find out that he had a combat soldier present. On Yom Kippur he and I met in the shower block, when everyone else was in synagogue or watching blue movies, and he asked me what a combat soldier was doing in this kind of platoon. I told him that I had been stationed in Ketziot but that I had refused to serve.

"Why did you refuse?" he asked.

"Because of the conditions," I replied.

"But the conditions there are not that different from ours," he said. "Here you guard for eight hours and rest for eight hours. There you guard for six and rest for six."

"The conditions of the prisoners—not the guards," I told him.

He looked at me in the way you might look at someone who was not bright enough to grasp very simple concepts, and said: "The prisoners there are Arabs."

I told him they were human beings.

His jaw dropped open and the soap slipped from his hand. "What are you," he said, "a Labor supporter?"

For years Amotz and I supported Yesh Gvul and the soldiers who refused to serve in the Occupied Territories. But the more the bad years drag on, becoming even worse, sadder, the more convinced we become that we have to do more.

As the occupation continues, more and more soldiers join Yesh Gvul and refuse to serve. After the outbreak of the Second Intifada in 2000, hundreds of reserve soldiers declared publicly that they could no longer take part in the occupation, and many more refused quietly to report.

At the concluding event of a conference entitled "Soldiers' Testimony and Human Rights" in March 2004—an evening organized by the Minerva Center for Human Rights at the Hebrew University (where I teach) and the University of Maryland—we screened three films on conscientious objection at the Jerusalem Cinematheque. First we showed the film *Hirbat Hizaa*, based on the story by Samech Yizhar about a soldier in 1948 who participates in the expulsion of Palestinians from a village. Before the next films, about soldiers' testimonies in the First and Second Intifadas, I led a discussion with Rami Levy, the director of *Hirbat Hizaa*, and Jonathan Shapira, an Air Force pilot who, along with twenty-six of his fellow pilots, had written a public letter to the commander of the Air Force announcing that they would refuse to carry out illegal orders. Jonathan corrected me after I presented him to the audience. He said he was no longer a pilot.

> Until a few months ago I was a pilot and operational leader in an air force squadron of Blackhawk helicopters. On the eve of last Yom Kippur I was called in for a discussion with the commander of the Air Force and informed that I had been demoted. I was no longer a pilot in the Israeli Air Force because I had made it known that I would not consent to participate in carrying out orders that were illegal and immoral.

I sat opposite the commander of the Air Force during this discussion and he asked me whether I would withdraw my signature from the letter. I asked him if he would withdraw what he had said and done, and then I heard him repeat that all the actions the air force had performed, including the difficult ones, were deeply rooted in his moral values.

Shapira, a very handsome young man, apologized and said he was not accustomed to speaking in public. Instead he read to the hundreds of people who packed the hall from papers he had prepared.

Now let's go back to the night of July 22, 2002. An air force base. Late at night. Squadron 16, emergency crew including pilot and navigator. Take off for Gaza. Wait for firing orders. Orders received. Bomb released. Direct hit—alpha. Return to base. Landing. Debriefing and return to routine.

In this assassination, a one-ton bomb (equivalent to one hundred suicide bombing belts) was dropped on a house in the El-Daraj neighborhood, one of the most crowded places in Gaza and in the world. Fourteen people were killed and over 150 others injured. Four families, including nine children, two women, and two men, were taken out by the crew of the airplane that performed the mission and hit its target believing with a whole heart that by doing so it was protecting the inhabitants of the State of Israel. With a whole heart.

Dan Halutz, commander of the air force, responded as follows: "I assert that everything that takes place prior to a mission meets my moral standards, and is deeply rooted therein."

To the pilots, he said: "Sleep well tonight . . . you did a perfect job."

We did not sleep well that night, or on other nights:

Not on August 31, 2002, when Dararme was assassinated, along with four children, nor April 8, 2003, when Arbeid and Al Halabi were assassinated along with two children and five other adults.

Not on June 10, 2003, when an attempt to assassinate Rantisi killed a girl, a woman, and five men.

Not on June 10, 2003, when Abu Nahal, two women, and five men were assassinated.

Not on June 12, 2003, when Salah Taha, a one-year-old baby girl, a woman, and five men were assassinated.

The list goes on and on.

Just a few months ago a blitz of five attacks killed two fugitives and another twelve innocent people.

Effi Eitam [the head of the right-wing National Religious Party] and senior IDF officials do not like the expression "innocent Palestinians." They prefer to call them "uninvolved" or "environmental damage."

A total of 221 people have been killed by assassination, almost half of them—90 people—passers-by.

And what kind of security do we have to show for it? Bombings and more attacks, us using Apaches and them suicide bombers, dancing this terrible, senseless dance. So we didn't sleep at night. Instead we wrote this letter:

We, Air Force pilots who were raised on the values of Zionism, sacrifice, and contributing to the state of Israel, have always served on the front lines, willing to carry out any mission, whether small or large, to defend and strengthen the state of Israel.

We, veteran and active pilots alike, who served and still serve the state of Israel for long weeks every year, are opposed to carrying out attack orders that are illegal and immoral of the type the state of Israel has been conducting in the territories.

We, who were raised to love the state of Israel and contribute to the Zionist enterprise, refuse to take part in Air Force attacks on civilian population centers. We, for whom the Israel Defense Forces and the Air Force are an inalienable part of ourselves, refuse to continue to harm innocent civilians.

These actions are illegal and immoral, and are a direct result of the ongoing occupation, which is corrupting all of Israeli society. Perpetuation of the occupation is fatally harming the security of the state of Israel and its moral strength.

We who serve as active pilots—fighters, leaders, and instructors of the next generation of pilots— hereby declare that we shall continue to serve in the Israel Defense Forces and the Air Force for every mission in defense of the state of Israel.

We spoke with over a hundred pilots, including former senior officers in the air force, many of whom were afraid to sign but supported the idea.

When my country is like a plane wildly nose-diving towards the ground, I have three options: I can bail out . . . I can face my death with apathy . . . or I can keep pulling at the stick with all my legal might, to try to stop the crash from taking place.

We are about to crash.

They come and tell us that terror is running wild in the streets. I say that's true; unfortunately I have witnessed it myself. In recent years I've volunteered with Sela, an aid organization for immigrant terror victims. I've accompanied the injured through recovery, led groups for orphans and bereaved family members. Each individual person is a world unto herself, and each bereaved person is surrounded by rings of sorrow and pain, like the infinite concentric ripples a small stone makes when thrown into the water.

Sorrow, pain, distress, anger, desperation and more. So we have to fight against the evil of terror. If I have to kill a suicide bomber on his way to an attack, and even die doing so, knowing that I am saving the lives of other people, I will do it with no hesitation. But not one of the targeted killings was against a suicide bomber on his way to an attack (the IDF confirms this).

So we have to fight terror, but also fight against becoming more and more like the terrorists.

The fact that buses are exploding does not give Sharon, [defense minister Shaul] Mofaz, Bogey [IDF chief of staff Ya'alon] and [Israel Air Force commander] Dan Halutz the justification to "unintentionally" kill nine children while they sleep, and to terrorize a population of millions living under a regime of closure, curfews, and checkpoints—a population under lockdown behind fences and in camps, massacred by a giant and threatening army armed to the teeth with thundering jets and attack helicopters that repeatedly fire missiles into cars and house windows in crowded and derelict cities.

So I said that I would sacrifice my life with a whole heart to stop even one suicide bomber, and perhaps this is the time to talk about that wholehearted belief. After all, what are we actually talking about? We're talking about losing our faith in the system that sends us to enact scandalous and controversial policies. We don't believe in the prime minister, the minister of defense, or our senior commanders when they send us to fire missiles at places that turn out to have women and children in them.

I've seen a lot of blood during my recent service in the squadron. I've had to evacuate dozens of wounded people, soldiers and civilians, children injured in horrific attacks. Sometimes we take the wounded to the hospital, clean the blood off the chopper floor, and head back for more.

I ask myself, why? Are we really so dense and naive that we think we can oppress three million people who have lost their fear of death? Have we also gone crazy? I think we have.

I think we're a society in an advanced stage of psychosis, a kind of split personality, and the only way many of us have to survive is to detach and disappear into ourselves. If there's something worth blowing up here, it's that bubble we've disappeared into. How? Just look at the facts, at what's happened to us in the last three years.

Two thousand three hundred sixty-one Palestinians have been killed by IDF fire, 447 of them minors, and 10 of those children under fourteen. Thirty-two Palestinians have been killed by Israeli citizens.

Six hundred fourteen Israelis and foreigners and 263 members of the armed forces have been killed by Palestinians.

According to IDF figures, 10,000 dunams of groves and agricultural land have been uprooted and razed in Gaza alone. According to the UN, the IDF has demolished 655 houses in Gaza alone.

The IDF confirms that of the 2,361 people that it killed, only some 550 were militants. I ask the question: what about the other 1,811 people?

A few months prior to the evening at the Cinemathéque, a group of reserve soldiers from the Sayaret Matkal, the crème de la crème of the IDF, had announced in an open letter that they would no longer be able to serve the occupation. That same secret military unit that had brought forth Israeli prime ministers and leaders, in which Amotz too had served, was now saying, "Enough."

I respect their courage to draw a line in their readiness to serve, but I have questions about what it means to serve in the army but not in the occupation. The border that they do not want to cross is imaginary. In fact, our state does not have recognized borders because the government wiped the Green Line off the map and did not replace it with a new, clear, and recognized border. I don't understand how anyone could serve in this army and not feel that he or she was serving the occupation. We all serve it: the taxes that we pay are used to build roads for settlers and buy more bombs. How many families could be fed for the price of the bombs that were dropped on Gaza? I respect the pilots who refuse to drop a one-ton bomb in the heart of a crowded city. But who loaded that bomb onto the aircraft at a base inside Israel? We can't keep claiming to be a democracy and believing that our army is a defense force after almost forty years of occupation. Soon Israel will have existed for twice as long with the occupation as it did without.

New Profile was established because we were convinced that it was not necessary to live in a soldiers' state, that we, our children, our partners, need not go on living as warriors, endlessly mobilized. It is hard to express this type of opinion in Israel today. In a soldiers' state there are equal citizens and less equal ones: the social ladder is topped by those who fight. And those are unfailingly men. They are believed to have privileged knowledge, giving them precedence in decision making. Attitudes casting doubts on "security"-related decisions, questioning the state's enormous military budgets, or examining its ongoing policies of military confrontation are branded "naive," "hysterical," "ignorant." Any doubt about the fundamental principle of compulsory enlistment is almost incomprehensible in a soldiers' state. It is rejected as illegitimate.

Yet thousands of young women and men are currently avoiding conscription or combat duty. Presently some 25 percent of recruits annually are exempted for health-related reasons or found "unfit" for service. It is common knowledge that a large proportion of these in fact choose not to serve. They feel unable to identify with the implications and meaning of military service in Israel today. Because there is no legal option for conscientious objection, a discharge on grounds of unfitness or poor health is virtually their only way out. Opting out is even more widespread among reservists. Army spokesmen have stated that only a third of the reserve forces in fact do active service. We all know how pervasive the private but intentional avoidance of duty—"gray refusal"—is among reservists.

At present, Israeli law does not acknowledge the basic human right to conscientious objection—at least not for men. And thus the struggle of a few young men and women who object to military service and ask to serve the country in a civil way seems to me one of the most important under way in Israel. I have tried to be present at the legal proceedings in which young refusers demand that the state accept the legal status of conscientious objection.

While a very, very small number of young men and women are discharged if they can convince a military commission that they are pacifists, the army will not discharge men who declare any other grounds for objection. Five young men—Shimri Zamaret, Noam Bahat, Adam Maor, Matan Kaminer, and Haggai Matar—went on trial in April 2003 because they refused to be drafted into the army, not because they are pacifists (they are not) but because they declared that they could not serve in an occupying army.

Every time I came to the military court in Jaffa where they were being tried, the hall was packed with people—there wasn't space in the tiny courtroom to hold all the parents and siblings and grandparents and friends, along with dozens of photographers and journalists. On the occasions that I did manage to squeeze in, I listened with admiration. These young men stood before uniformed judges in a military court in the middle of an Arab neighborhood in Jaffa and explained with great eloquence and passion why their conscience would not let them serve in a force that oppresses millions of Palestinians. I hope that Gali and Uri will not have to stand before a judge and say the same things; I hope that these brave young men might pave the way for other young Israelis to say, "We want to serve our country. But not in the army." Instead, the military court sent the five young men—who had been held in detention for months—back to jail for another year. Since then, they've also begun to lock up young women who refuse to serve.

When I interviewed Smadar Nahab, whose son Matan Kaminer is one of the five young refuseniks; he had already been in jail for more than five hundred days. Smadar has been a peace activist for many years, and I asked her why, if she served in the army, she supports her son's refusal to do so. She told me:

> In my generation to be an Israeli patriot was to serve in a commando unit like Sayaret Matkal. Today being a patriot means refusing to serve. A moral person cannot serve in this army these days. Matan is preserving our heritage. He and his friends are sacrificing their lives to influence others—if they had not cared so much, they would have found an easier way to avoid service. He is defending the values we grew

up with. He cares so much about his society that he is ready to sacrifice so much of his time for it. If he is really released after two years in jail, he will have spent 10 percent of his life there.

As Matan Kaminer said after the court passed down its guilty verdict in December 2003:

> The most easy thing for an 18-year old in this country is to get an exemption from the army through all kind of backhand[ed] tricks. Anybody can do it, and many do. We chose to go the hard way. We say that the occupation is a moral abomination which moral people cannot tolerate and that this is the reason that we refuse to enlist. If our sincerity means that we will sit many years in prison—then we will sit many years in prison.

Over the course of their trial—which dragged on for more than eight months, during which time they were all held in jail—the five young men spoke beautifully and passionately, again and again, about the need to refuse. Matan Kaminer explained his own decision in this way:

> I did not decide to refuse in one day. I went through the first military tests, believing I would find a way to serve without participating directly in the dirty machine of occupation, and that if I had to refuse an immoral order I would know to do so and face the consequences, all within the framework of the army. But with time, with the worsening of the oppression

in the [Occupied] Territories and the loss of the peace horizon during the intifada, I began to understand that my conscience would never make it possible for me to participate, even indirectly, in the work of occupation.

I do not think there is any serious person in the world who could claim, from a moral standpoint, that one should never refuse an order. It is obvious that there are orders so immoral that one should not fulfill them, regardless of their legality. The only question is: what are these orders? That is a question of conscience. . . . I am well aware that the IDF does not make its own policy, that the occupation is a policy decided upon by the elected government of Israel. I protest any way I can against this government and any government of occupation; but that is not enough. My conscience makes it impossible for me to pledge allegiance to a body that carries out this heinous policy, and to carry out its orders.

My conscience commands me to do all I can for Israeli society—my society. I've done so in the past and shall continue to do so in the future. The occupation is a terrible crime, immoral, malignant, a crime against another society . . . I cannot join the army in such a situation.

Soldiers of an occupying army are in an impossible situation. They are men of war, trained to deal with other men of war. They are not social workers, doctors, lawyers, judges or mayors, but they are often given responsibilities that only such professionals should wield.

As men of war, they use the tools known to them: the command, the emotional distance, the threat, the gun.

Smadar and I have talked about our own refusal and what it means for us—women in the middle of their lives, who were born and raised in Israel, in patriotic families, women who had served in the army, who pay taxes and live here—to refuse. Smadar told me that she refuses to keep going as if everything is normal. That she devotes at least half a day every week to political work. And we agreed that we must continue to look for ways to refuse.

I refuse to carry on believing the soldiers and officers who say, while they are serving in the army, that "we have no choice." And I refuse to believe the officers who say, once they are no longer in the army, that indeed we could have done things differently. I think we hear too many soldiers. And it is a great pity that some of them can only see that something is very wrong once they have left—after so many wrongs have been committed. Consider the following testimonies, from our military men:

The more that the [Palestinians'] distress grows, the more the power of Hamas increases. If the Palestinian public has nothing to lose, we will lose. Rather than go to work, they will prepare explosives and ambushes, and will blow themselves up in Tel-Aviv.

— Major General (Reserves) Ya'akov Or, coordinator
of government activities in the Occupied
Territories from 1997 to 2001,
in *Yediot Aharonot*, July 13, 2001

IDF soldiers face hundreds and thousands of people waiting at checkpoints every day. . . . This reality, the intolerable friction between Palestinians and
IDF soldiers, creates potential suicide bombers
every day.

— Former chief of staff, Lieutenant General (Reserves)
Amnon Lipkin-Shahak, in *Ma'ariv*,
December 21, 2001

I do not like this situation. It encourages large-scale
hatred over the long term. . . . Two weeks ago, I saw
a father walking with two sacks and carrying a five-
year-old boy on his shoulders. Stumbling behind
him was the mother with what may have been a
newborn infant. It was mid-afternoon and they were
walking from the junction to their home. Tell me,
how does this help? What good does it do? I can picture my wife walking like that with our daughter,
shuffling through the mud. I swear, it gives me the
chills.

— Lieutenant Colonel Dov Zadka, head of the
Civil Administration, 1998–2002,
in *B'Mahaneh* (an IDF magazine),
December 28, 2001

I fear that even if we win the war, in the end we will
not be able to look at ourselves in the mirror. We
have a problem. All this fighting is not good for our
health, from the perspective of our moral strength. A
soldier who is ordered to stand at a checkpoint,

where it is easy and tempting to loot does not add to our moral strength.

—Lieutenant General Moshe Ya'alon,
Army chief of staff, in *Yediot Aharanot*,
July 4, 2003

I refuse to go on listening to the testimony of those responsible for the misery of thousands of Palestinians at the checkpoints, who say it's the only way to keep us safe.

I refuse to listen to those who, after they are discharged, say we should ease the pressure on the Palestinian population for our own security.

I refuse. I refuse to believe that it acceptable to imprison an entire nation in the name of our security. I refuse to believe that the imprisonment of an entire nation—or two nations, for we are imprisoned as well—will provide security. I refuse to believe those who only know the ways of war.

I know that we can remember the past and build a better future together. I refuse to believe that the only choice is force.

I refuse, until we choose the path of reconciliation.

REFERENCES

INTRODUCTION: ONLY YESTERDAY

1. S. Y. Agnon, *Only Yesterday*, trans. Barbara Harshav (Princeton: Princeton University Press, 2000), 3.

ONE: THE LAST CLASS AT SUMMER SCHOOL

1. For the different versions of the story of the thirty-five soldiers, see Yitzhak Sadeh, *Bamahaneh*, January 1948; A. Finkerfeld (ed.), *35 Who Fell in the Hebron Hills While Coming to the Aid of Gush Ezion on the Fifth Day of Shvat 5708* (Jerusalem: Rubin Mass Publishers, 1998).
2. The water consumption is 357 cubic meters per Israeli and 84.6 cubic meters per Palestinian. The disparity in industrial use of water is as high as 1,400 percent. On the water problem in the Occupied Territories, see B'Tselem's information paper *The Waters of Conflict: Israel's Responsibility for the Water Shortage in the Territories* (Jerusalem: B'Tselem, September 1998), and also *Thirsty for a Solution: The Water Shortage in the Territories and Its Solution in Terms of the Permanent Settlement* (Jerusalem: B'Tselem, 2000).
3. Maya Rosenfeld, *Confronting the Occupation: Work Education and Political Activism of Palestinian Families in a Refugee Camp* (Stanford, CA: Stanford University Press, 2004).
4. The closure never stopped all Palestinians from entering Israel. Some bypass the checkpoints; others, like Suad, talk to the soldiers until they are let through.

TWO: THE DANCE FOR JERUSALEM

1. Over 80 percent of the land expropriated since 1967 was privately owned by Arabs. Some 45,000 housing units have since been built on these lands for Jewish residents, but not a single one for Palestinians. In all of Jerusalem, since 1967, fewer than six hundred housing units for Palestinians have been built with any government aid. According to Israeli law, Palestinians who move to the suburbs of Jerusalem that are outside the municipal boundaries risk losing their right to an identity document. Only those who can prove that the "center of their lives" is in Jerusalem—that is, those who pay taxes to the municipality of Jerusalem, work there, or have children registered at schools in the city—have the right to live legally in Jerusalem.

   After the annexation, Israel held a population census in the annexed areas and gave permanent citizenship to inhabitants who were present at the time of the census. Permanent residents could, if they wished to and if they met certain criteria, receive Israeli citizenship. These conditions included pledging allegiance to the state, proving that they were not citizens of another country, and having some knowledge of the Hebrew language. The conditions were proposed when it was clear that most Palestinians would not be able to meet them. Only a few thousand chose Israeli citizenship. The determination of the municipal boundary in a particular neighborhood or village hence created a distinction between Palestinians in terms of rights, because those who lived outside the annexed areas fell under military rule. The master plan for Jerusalem was formulated between 1967 and 1968 on the initiative of the municipality of Jerusalem and in cooperation with various government ministries, with a view to ensuring Israeli control over all of Jerusalem by means of massive building for the Jewish population that would change the demographic geography of the city. Attorney Danny Seidman, an expert in municipal policy for the development of Jerusalem, says, "Israeli policy in Jerusalem had achievements on the one hand, and failed on the other. Israeli policy created almost numerical equality between Israelis (some 210,000) and the number of Palestinians (some 190,000) in East Jerusalem. This policy makes political division of the city extremely difficult. However, the fact that political division of the city has been discussed, and that the proportion of Palestinian population has grown from 25.5% to 33% today, indicates that Israeli policy was also a failure. The new neighborhoods interfere with the ability to reach an agreement, but don't preclude it" (interview from March 13, 2002).

For more on building in Jerusalem, see Sarah Kaminker, "Who Really Needs Har Homa? Housing for Palestinians in East Jerusalem," in A. Badran, D. Golan, and J. Persekian (eds.), *Sharing Jerusalem* (Jerusalem: The Jerusalem Link, 1999), reprinted and updated from the *Journal of Palestinian Studies* 26, 4 (1997).

2. For the struggle to free Taysir Aruri, see for example the *New York Review of Books* 36, 13 (August 17, 1989), letter to the editor by Edward Witten and Freeman J. Dyson.

3. Israel's Supreme Court not only hears appeals from the district court but also adjudicates petitions to grant relief against the state or any of its administrative authorities, including the IDF. The Court has been receptive to affording Palestinians the opportunity to challenge the military government actions. This unprecedented phenomenon of allowing the civilian population access to the occupying power's national courts and subjecting the military government's conduct to domestic judicial review has, on some level, shaped and modified policies of the military government, and at the same time legalized or "Judicialized" them. See for example Dan Simon, "The Demolition of Homes in the Israeli Occupied Territories," *The Yale Journal of International Law* 19, 1 (1994), 1–80, or David Kretzmer, *The Occupation of Justice: The Supreme Court of Israel and the Occupied Territories* (New York: State University of New York Press, 2002).

4. On the movement called the 21st Year Against the Occupation, see Reuven Kaminer, *The Politics of Protest: The Israeli Peace Movement and the Palestinian Intifada* (Brighton, UK: Sussex Academic Press, 1996); Daphna Golan, "A Letter to an American Friend," in Deena Hurwitz (ed.), *Walking the Red Line: Israelis in Search of Justice for Palestine* (Philadelphia: New Society Publishers, 1992).

5. For a critical perspective on the study of the Holocaust and the weeks between Passover and Yom Ha'atzmaut in the education system in Israel, see Eyal Sivan's film *Yizkor: Slaves to Memory* (Israel: IMA Production, 1991).

6. All quotes are from Daphna Golan, *Detained Without Trial: Administrative Detention in the Occupied Territories* (Jerusalem: B'Tselem, 1992).

THREE: COMPASSION AND THE LANGUAGE
OF HUMAN RIGHTS

1. Stanley Cohen and Daphna Golan, *Interrogation of Palestinians During the Intifada: Ill-Treatment, "Moderate Physical Pressure," or Torture?* (Bethlehem: B'Tselem, March 1991).

2. Stanley Cohen, *States of Denial: Knowing About Atrocities And Suffering* (London: Polity, 2001).

3. For more on the universality of human rights, see Dennis Driscoll, "The Development of Human Rights in International Law," in Walter Laqueur and Barry Rubin (eds.), *The Human Rights Reader* (New York: New American Library, 1990), pp. 41–56; Hilary Charlesworth, "What Are 'Women's International Human Rights'?" in Rebecca J. Cook (ed.), *Human Rights of Women: National and International Perspectives* (Philadelphia: University of Pennsylvania Press, 1994), pp. 58–84; Rolf Kunneman, "A Coherent Approach to Human Rights," 17 *Human Rights Quarterly* 323 (1995); Peter Baehr, "Controversies in the Current Human Rights Debate," 2 *Human Rights Review* 7, Oct.–Dec. 2000; J. Donnelly, "The Universal Declaration Model of Human Rights: A Liberal Defense," Human Rights Working Papers no. 12, University of Denver, 2001; T. E. Downing, "Human Rights Research: The Challenge for Anthropologists," in T. E. Downing and G. Kushner (eds.), *Human Rights and Anthropology* (Cambridge, MA: Cultural Survival, 1988), pp. 9–19; M. Edwards and D. Hulme, "Introduction: NGO Performance and Accountability," in M. Edwards and D. Hulme (eds.), *Beyond the Magic Bullet: NGO Performance and Accountability in the Post–Cold War World* (West Hartford, CT: Kumarian Press, 1996), pp. 1–19; A. X. Fellmeth, "Feminism and International Law: Theory, Methodology, and Substantive Reform," *Human Rights Quarterly* 22, 3 (2000): 658–733; M. Freeman, *Human Rights: An Interdisciplinary Approach* (Malden, MA: Blackwell, 2002); V. S. Peterson and L. Parisi, "Are Women Human? It's Not an Academic Question," in T. Evans (ed.), *Human Rights Fifty Years On: A Reappraisal* (Manchester: Manchester University Press, 1998), pp. 132–60; P. Schwab and A. Pollis, "Globalization's Impact on Human Rights," in A. Pollis and P. Schwab(eds.), *Human Rights: New Perspectives, New Realities* (Boulder, CO: Lynne Rienner, 2000), pp. 209–23.

4. On human rights in Israel, see:
    Ruth Gavison, *Human Rights in Israel* (Tel Aviv: Ministry of

Defense, 1994) (Hebrew); Daphna Sharfman, *Living Without a Constitution: Civil Rights in Israel* (Armonk, NY: M. E. Sharpe, 1993).

FOUR: A VICTORY AT THE HIGH COURT

1. See H.C. 5100/94, The Public Committee Against Torture in Israel versus the Government of Israel (3)99, 458. See www.court.gov.il/mishpat.

2. Stanley Cohen and Daphna Golan, *Interrogation of Palestinians During the Intifada: Ill-Treatment, "Moderate Physical Pressure," or Torture?* (Jerusalem: B'Tselem, 1991).

3. Allegra Pacheco, *The Case Against Torture in Israel: A Compilation of Petitions, Briefs and Other Documents Submitted to the Israeli High Court of Justice* (Jerusalem: PCATI, 1999).

4. For a vehement position on the international prohibition against torture, see a speech by the chair of the UN Committee Against Torture, Nigel Rodley, "The Prohibition of Torture and How to Make It Effective," in proceedings of the seminar "Israel and Human Rights Law: The Issue of Torture," held on June 9, 1995, by the Center for Human Rights at the Hebrew University of Jerusalem, pp. 6–7.

5. Quotations from Justice M. Cheshin, High Court discussion, January 13, 1999 (personal recording of court hearing); quotations from Shai Nitsan's address to the High Court, May 21, 1998 (personal recording of court hearing).

6. The first part of the Landau Report was published under the title "Report of Commission of Inquiry on the Subject of the General Security Service's Methods of Interrogation Regarding Hostile Terror Activity," Jerusalem, October 1987. For criticism of the Landau Report, see "Symposium on the Report of the Commission of Inquiry into the Methods of Investigation of the General Security Service Regarding Hostile Terrorist Activity," *Israel Law Review* 23, 2–3 (1989).

7. Attorney Avigdor Feldman's arguments were expressed at a conference organized by the Minerva Center for Human Rights of the Hebrew University of Jerusalem to commemorate fifty years since the Global Declaration of Human Rights, and held at the Jerusalem Cinematheque, December 1998.

8. On the continued use of torture, even after the High Court ruling, see the report of the Public Committee Against Torture, "Back to a Routine of Torture: Torture and Ill-treatment of Palestinian Detainees

During Arrest, Detention and Interrogation (September 2001–April 2003)," and also the organization's Web site: www.stoptorture.org.il.

FIVE: AN ARAB HOUSE

1. For current statistics on house demolitions, see the B'Tselem Web site, www.btselem.org.
2. Yigal Zalmona, "To the East?" in *To The East: Orientalism in the Arts in Israel* (Jerusalem: Israel Museum, 1998).
3. Roni Talmor, *Demolition and Sealing of Houses as a Form of Punishment in the West Bank and Gaza Strip During the Intifada* (Jerusalem: B'Tselem, 1989). See also *Demolishing Peace: The Policy of Mass Demolition of Palestinian Houses in the West Bank* (Jerusalem: B'Tselem, 1997).
4. During the Al-Aksa Intifada, hundreds of Palestinian houses have been demolished as acts of punishment, in order to "expose" areas for security purposes, and also on the grounds of illegal building. UN organizations estimate that between September 2000 and September 2004, a total of about 21,142 people have been displaced by house demolitions in the Occupied Palestinian Territories (Global IDP Project, *Occupied Palestinian Territories: Thousands displaced by house demolitions and Separation Barrier: Executive Summary, http://www.db.idpproject.org/Sites/idpSurvey.nsf/wViewSingleEnv/Palestinian + TerritoriesProfile +Summary*). Israeli officials claim that all destruction of houses by the army is necessary for security reasons. For example, the destruction of houses in Rafiah in January 2002 was aimed at achieving security objectives. At first the Minister of Defense, Mr. Ben Eliyahu, claimed, "If there is really someone whose home was demolished, I'm willing to send him a caravan."

   The statistics are as follows:
   - Sixty houses were completely demolished. These houses were occupied by 112 families, i.e., 614 individuals were left homeless. At the time of the demolition 84 families—475 individuals—were living in their homes.
   - Four homes were partially demolished. Eleven families, numbering 24 individuals, lived in these houses. All were in their homes at the time of the demolition.
5. On planning or lack of planning, see Tovi Fenstner, *Gender Planning and Human Rights* (London: Routledge, 1990). See also www.bimkom.org.
6. Gideon Levy, "The Moral of the Story" *Ha'aretz*, September 5, 1999.

7. The names of Hassan's wife and daughter were changed to protect their privacy.

SIX: ON FOOD, FRIENDSHIP, AND NORMALIZATION

1. For more on the difficulties in cooperation between Israeli and Palestinian women, see Daphna Golan, "Separation, Normalization and Occupation: The Challenges of the Jerusalem Link—A Women's Joint Venture for Peace," *Palestine-Israel Journal* 2, 2 (1995). Sumaya Farhat-Naser, *Daughter of the Olive Trees* (Basel: Lenos Verlag, 2003).
2. Jack Persekian, "Excerpts from a Conversation" in A. Badran, D. Golan, and J. Persekian (eds.), *Sharing Jerusalem* (Jerusalem: The Jerusalem Link, 1999), 71–73.
3. Jamaica Kincaid, *A Small Place* (New York: Penguin, 1988).
4. On the relationship between conqueror and conquered and on women's peace activism, see, for example, Cynthia Cockburn, *The Space Between Us: Negotiating Gender and National Identities in Conflict* (London: Zed Books, 1998); Naomi Chazan, "Israeli Women and Peace Activism," in Barbara Swirski and Marilyn Safir (eds.), *Calling the Equality Bluff: Women in Israel* (New York: Pergamon, 1991), pp. 152–61; Galia Golan and Zahira Kamal, "Bridging the Abyss: Palestinian-Israeli Dialogue," in Harold Saunders (ed.), *A Public Peace Process: Sustained Dialogue to Transform Racial and Ethnic Conflicts* (New York: St. Martin's, 1999); Nira Yuval-Davis, *Gender and Nation* (London: Sage Publications, 1997); Tamar Mayer (ed.), *Women and the Israeli Occupation: The Politics of Change* (New York: Routledge, 1994); Simona Sharoni, *Gender and the Israeli-Palestinian Conflict: The Politics of Women's Resistance* (Syracuse: Syracuse University Press, 1995).
5. Albert Memmi, *The Colonizer and the Colonized* (Boston: Beacon Press, 1965). (First published in French in 1958).

SEVEN: SEPARATE BUT NOT EQUAL

1. According to data published by the Central Bureau of Statistics in July 2004. (see www.cbs.gov.il):
   - In 2001, only Jewish towns were classified as being high on the socioeconomic scale, while some 70 percent of the country's poor towns are Arab.
   - In 2002, 46.8 percent of Palestinian Israelis lived below the poverty

line, as opposed to 14.9 percent of Jews. Half of all Palestinian-Israeli children and a fifth of Jewish children lived below the poverty line.

- The infant mortality rate among Jews was 4.1 per 1,000 births, compared to 8.2 among Muslims in 2001.
- Over 90 percent of 17-year-old Jewish males were enrolled in educational frameworks, compared to 68.2 percent of Palestinian Israelis. Between 1990 and 2002, the number of male teenagers who passed matriculation exams rose in both sectors, reaching 45 percent among Jews, compared to 24 percent among Palestinian Israelis in 2002. Palestinian-Israeli girls also lagged behind their Jewish peers in 2002, with 39 percent passing their exams, compared to 61 percent.
- Higher education figures in 2001 show that for every 1,000 people aged 18–29, 65.8 Jews and 27.4 Arabs studied for their Bachelor's degree; 17.8 of every thousand Jews studied for their Master's degree, compared to 3.4 per thousand Arabs.

2. Of 22 billion NIS (some $4.5 billion) — the Ministry of Education's budget for 2001 — the ministry was supposed to invest at least 4.4 billion NIS in Arab students, who represent over 20 percent of children in Israel. How much does the Ministry of Education invest in Arab education? It's hard to say, but the investment definitely falls far short of the above amount. If we examine the payment to teachers for teaching hours (the form of payment that is the major part of the Ministry of Education's budget and is calculated per hour), in elementary education an average of 1.7 hours is invested in a Jewish student and 1.4 in an Arab student; 43.8 hours are invested in an Arab class as opposed to 48.7 in a Jewish class.

In Hebrew elementary and secondary schools in 1997–1998, there were, on average, 12 and 9.4 students per teacher, respectively. In Arab schools, however, there were 16.6 students per teacher in elementary education and 14 students per teacher in secondary education.

In that same year the average number of students per class in Hebrew schools was 27.1. In Arab schools, that number was 30.8.

The average number of student hours was also higher in Hebrew education. While in Arab schools there were 1.5 student hours, in Hebrew schools there were 1.87. See *The Education System from a Numerical Perspective*, published by the Ministry of Education in 2000 (pages 58, 19, 51 and 50, respectively).

The discrimination of Arab schools for special education is especially grave, and although there is a policy of mainstreaming, very little is done in the Arab schools. While in Hebrew schools in 1998–1999 there were 75,819 hours for mainstreaming, in Arab educational settings there were only 6,992 hours. See the Ministry of Education's Budget Proposal for 2001, page 158.

The unequal distribution of support funds that the Ministry of Education gives to associations and nongovernmental organizations acting outside the education system is especially interesting. In 1999 the Ministry of Education gave NIS 1,309,588,679 (some $350 million) to associations, less than 1.5 percent of which went to Arab associations. In other words, every year the Ministry of Education assists in the promotion of associations and bodies working on behalf of education (youth movements, newspapers, museums, and so forth) but gives almost no help to Arab associations.

3. See State of Israel, Central Bureau of Statistics, report on school allocations, August 2004.

4. See, for example, Carol Gilligan, *In a Different Voice: Psychological Theory and Women's Development* (Cambridge, MA: Harvard University Press, 1982).

5. This practice has been challenged by Adalah—The Legal Center for Arab Minority Rights in Israel—in a petition to the High Court of Justice, submitted in September 2004. See Aryeh Dayan, "Teacher's Pests," *Ha'aretz*, October 1, 2004.

6. See, for example, Khaled Abu Assba, "The Establishment of an Independent and Autonomous Administration for the Arab Education System in Israel," in Daphna Golan-Agnon (ed.), *Inequality in Education* (Tel Aviv: Babel Publications, 2004). (Hebrew) See also Human Rights Watch, "Second Class Discrimination Against Palestinian Arab Children in Israel's Schools," September 2001.

7. Samie Sharkawi, "You Can't Hide the Sun with a Net" (unpublished).

EIGHT: LETTER TO SUSAN SONTAG

1. In the municipality budget for 2001, of NIS 2,071,139,000, about 14 percent (NIS 288,426,515) was directed at East Jerusalem.

I thank Jerusalem City Council member Meir Margalit for publishing a number of statistics that characterize the budget allocation in the city:

- There are 680 kilometers of roads in West Jerusalem as opposed to 87 kilometers in East Jerusalem; 650 kilometers of sidewalks in West Jerusalem and 76 in East Jerusalem; 1132 public parks in West Jerusalem and 45 parks in East Jerusalem; and a sewage system stretching 650 kilometers in West Jerusalem as opposed to 76 kilometers in East Jerusalem.
- There are 36 libraries in West Jerusalem as opposed to 4 in East Jerusalem; 21 community workers in West Jerusalem and 1 in East Jerusalem; 83 clubs for the elderly in West Jerusalem and 9 in East Jerusalem; 75 educational psychologists in West Jerusalem as opposed to 5 in East Jerusalem; 37 mother and child stations in West Jerusalem and 5 in East Jerusalem; 43 community centers in West Jerusalem and 5 in East Jerusalem; and 20 social service bureaus in West Jerusalem as opposed to 3 in East Jerusalem.
- Out of the 405 social welfare personnel paid by the municipality, only 41 work in East Jerusalem, which receives 12.5 percent of the total social welfare budget.
- Out of the 2,560 education personnel paid by the municipality, only 622 work in East Jerusalem, which receives 16.6 percent of the total education budget.
- Out of the 183 health personnel paid by the municipality, only 16.5 work in East Jerusalem, which receives 6.2 percent of the total social welfare budget.
- Out of the 185 social services personnel paid by the municipality, only 7.5 work in East Jerusalem, which receives 3.5 percent of the total social welfare budget.
- Out of the 156 culture personnel paid by the municipality, only 7 work in East Jerusalem, which receives 2.6 percent of the total social welfare budget.
- Out of the 69 sport personnel paid by the municipality, only 6 work in East Jerusalem, which receives 8.1 percent of the total social welfare budget.
- None of the 56 art personnel paid by the municipality work in East Jerusalem, which receives 2.2 percent of the total social welfare budget.
- Out of the 45 youth advancement personnel paid by the municipality, only 6 work in East Jerusalem, which receives 5.9 percent of the total social welfare budget.

- None of the religious services budget of NIS 23,747,000 (some $5,277,111) is allocated to East Jerusalem.
- In total, out of the 3,659 social services personnel paid by the municipality, only 706 work in East Jerusalem, which receives 12.4 percent of the overall social services budget.
- In total, NIS 133,528,079 is allocated to East Jerusalem for all social service divisions, 12.4 percent of the total social services budget of NIS 1,079,803,154; 706 of the total 3,659 social services personnel work in East Jerusalem, 19.3 percent overall.

2. On the subject of failure to register Palestinians students in the municipal education system in Jerusalem because of a shortage of classroom space, see High Court—5125/00 and also 5125/01: *Students Eligible for Compulsory Education v. The Municipality of Jerusalem and the Ministry of Education.*

3. Jack Persekian (ed.), *Exposure Jerusalem* (Jerusalem: Al Ma'mal Foundation for Contemporary Art, 2001).

NINE: IN SEARCH OF AN OPTIMISTIC ENDING

1. See Richard Abel. *Politics by Other Means: Law in the Struggle Against Apartheid, 1980–1994* (New York: Routledge, 1995).

2. F. A. Johnstone, *Class, Race and Gold: A Study of Class Relations and Racial Discrimination in South Africa* (London: Routledge, Kegan Paul, 1976).

3. See Suad Amiry, *Sharon and My Mother in Law* (New York: Granta, 2004).

4. For information on the separation wall, see www.btselem.org or www.gader.org.

TEN: ON THE ROAD TO RECONCILIATION

1. See Ciraj Rassool and Sandra Prosalendis, *Recalling Community in Cape Town: Creating and Curating the District Six Museum* (Cape Town: District Six Museum, 2001).

2. For a summary of the seminar in South Africa, "Restoring Hope: Building Peace in Divided Societies," see Aviva Lori "Now, It's Your Turn," Ha'aretz, May 15, 2003 and Yuli Tamir, "Living Outside History," Ha'aretz, May 23, 2003. Daphna Golan-Agnon, "Like Fixing an Airplane while in the Air," Walla, July 16, 2003. See Shaun Johnson,

Strange Days Indeed: South Africa from Insurrection to Post-Election, with foreword by Nelson Mandela (London: Bantam Books, 1994). For the coalition of anti-apartheid movements, see Jeremy Seekings, *The UDF: A History of the United Democratic Front in South Africa 1983–1991* (Cape Town: David Philip, 2000).

3. *Truth and Reconciliation Commission of South Africa Report,* 5 volumes (London: Macmillan, 1998, 1999). Antjie Krog, *Country of My Skull* (Johannesburg; Random House, 1998). Desmond Tutu, *No Future Without Forgiveness* (London: Rider, 1999).

4. Benny Morris, *The Birth of the Palestinian Refugee Problem 1947–1949* (London: Cambridge University Press, 1987).

5. Arie Shavit, Interview with Benny Morris, "Survival of the Fittest," *Ha'aretz,* January 8, 2004.

6. Ehud Barak, "What Now?" *Yedioth Ahronoth,* Aug. 29, 2003.

BIBLIOGRAPHY

ABEL, RICHARD. *Politics by Other Means: Law in the Struggle Against Apartheid, 1980–1994.* New York: Routledge, 1995.

ALHAIRI, BASHIR. *Letters to the Lemon Tree.* Jerusalem: Center for Alternative Information, 1997.

AMIRY, SUAD. *Sharon and My Mother-in-Law.* London: Granta, 2004.

AMNESTY INTERNATIONAL. *Israel/South Lebanon, Israel's Forgotten Hostages: Lebanese Detainees in Israel and Khiam Detention Center.* London: Amnesty International, 1997.

B'TSELEM. *Routine Torture.* Jerusalem: B'Tselem, 1998.

B'TSELEM. *The Waters of Conflict: Israel's Responsibility for the Water Shortage in the Territories.* Jerusalem: B'Tselem, 1998.

B'TSELEM. *Thirsty for a Solution: The Water Shortage in the Territories and Its Solution in Terms of the Permanent Settlement.* Jerusalem: B'Tselem, 2000.

B'TSELEM. *Water Shortage in the Occupied Territories.* Jerusalem: B'Tselem, 1998.

B'TSELEM. *Without Bounds: Damage to Human Rights as a Result of the Closure.* Jerusalem: B'Tselem, 1996.

BADRAN, A., D. GOLAN, AND J. PERSEKIAN (eds.). *Sharing Jerusalem.* Jerusalem: Jerusalem Link, 1999.

BAEHR, PETER. "Controversies in the Current Human Rights Debate." 2 *Human Rights Review* 7, Oct.-Dec. 2000.

BARNAVI, ELI. "Civil Rights—An Historical Perspective." In Association for Civil Rights in Israel, *Without Distinction: Human Rights In Israel*. Jerusalem: Idanim, 1998, pp. 11–12.

BARRELL, HOWARD. *MK: The ANC's Armed Struggle*. London: Penguin Books, 1990.

BARRY, K. "Deconstructing Deconstructionism (Or, Whatever Happened to Feminist Studies?)." In Diane Bell and Renate Klein (eds.), *Radically Speaking: Feminism Reclaimed*. Melbourne: Spinifex Press, 1996.

BEN MEIR, YEHUDA. *Civil-Military Relations in Israel*. New York: Columbia University Press, 1995.

BENCOMO, CLARISA. "Human Rights Watch Public Comments in a Briefing About the High Court Case." Jerusalem: Beit Shalom, 1999.

BENVENISTI, EYAL. "The Applicability of Human Rights Conventions to Israel and the Occupied Territories." *Israel Law Review* 26, 1 (1992).

BENVENISTI, MERON. *Conflicts and Contradictions*. New York: Villard Books, 1986.

BENVENISTI, MERON. *Sacred Landscape: The Buried History of the Holy Land Since 1948*. Berkeley: University of California Press, 2000.

BENVENISTI, MERON. *The Dance of Fear*. Jerusalem: Keter, 1992.

BENZIMAN, UZI, AND ATALLAH MANZUR. *Secondary Resident: Israeli Arabs, Their Status and Policy Towards Them*. Jerusalem: Keter, 1992.

BISHARAT, GEORGE E. "Courting Justice? Legitimization in Lawyering Under Israeli Occupation." 20 *Law and Social Inquiry* 359 (1995).

BORAINE, ALEX, JANET LEVY, AND RONEL SCHEFFER (eds.). *Dealing with the Past: Truth and Reconciliation in South Africa*. Cape Town: IDASA, 1994.

CHARLSWORTH, HILARY. "What Are 'Women's International Human Rights'?" In Rebecca J. Cook (ed.), *Human Rights of Women: National and International Perspectives*. Philadelphia: University of Pennsylvania Press, 1994.

CHAZAN, NAOMI. "Israeli Women and Peace Activism." In Barbara Swisrki and Marilyn Safir (eds.), *Calling the Equality Bluff: Women in Israel*. New York: Pergamon, 1991, pp. 152–61.

CIXOUS, HÉLÈNE. *Three Steps on the Ladder of Writing*. New York: Columbia University Press, 1993.

COCKBURN, CYNTHIA. *The Space Between Us: Negotiating Gender and National Identities in Conflict*. London: Zed Books, 1998.

COHEN, STANLEY. *Denial and Acknowledgment: The Impact of Information About Human Rights Violations*. Jerusalem: Hebrew University, Center for Human Rights, 1995.

COHEN, STANLEY. "The Human Rights Movement in Israel and South Africa: Some Paradoxical Comparisons." The Harry S. Truman Institute, Occasional Papers no. 1. Jerusalem: Hebrew University, 1991.

COHEN, STANLEY. *States of Denial: Knowing About Atrocities and Suffering*. London: Polity, 2001.

COHEN, STANLEY. "Talking About Torture in Israel." *Tikkun*, November-December 1991.

COHEN, STANLEY, AND DAPHNA GOLAN. *Interrogation of Palestinians During the Intifada: Ill-Treatment, "Moderate Physical Pressure," or Torture?* Jerusalem: B'Tselem, 1991.

COURSEN-NEFF, ZAMA. *Second Class: Discrimination Against Palestinian Arab Children in Israel's Schools*. New York: Human Rights Watch, 2001.

DALAL, MARWAN. "The Guest, The House and the Judge: A Reading in the Unread in the Qa'adan Decision." *Adalah's Review* 2 (2000): 40–45.

DE KLERK, F. W. *Last Trek: A New Beginning: The Autobiography*. London: Macmillan, 1998.

DERSHOWITZ, ALAN. "Is It Necessary to Apply Physical Pressure to Terrorists—And to Lie About It?" *Israel Law Review* 23, 2–3 (1989).

DONNELLY, J. "The Universal Declaration Model of Human Rights: A Liberal Defense," Human Rights Working Papers no. 12, University of Denver, 2001.

DOWNING, T. E. "Human Rights Research: The Challenge for Anthropologists." In T. E. Downing and G. Kushner (eds.), *Human Rights and Anthropology*. Cambridge, MA: Cultural Survival, 1988, pp. 9–19.

DRISCOLL, DENNIS. "The Development of Human Rights in International

Law." In Walter Lacquer and Barry Rubin (eds.), *The Human Rights Reader*. New York: New American Library, 1990, pp. 41–56.

EDWARDS, M., AND D. HULME. "Introduction: NGO Performance and Accountability." In M. Edwards and D. Hulme (eds.), *Beyond the Magic Bullet: NGO Performance and Accountability in the Post–Cold War World*. West Hartford, CT: Kumarian Press, 1996, pp. 1–19.

ESMEIR, SAMERA. "On Legal Space, Political Forces and Social Justice." *Adalah's Review* 2 (2000): 52–57.

EZRAHI, YARON. *Rubber Bullets: Power and Conscience in Modern Israel*. New York: Farrar, Straus and Giroux, 1997.

FARHAT-NASER, SUMAYA. *Daughter of the Olive Trees: A Palestinian Woman's Struggle for Peace*. Basel: Lenos Verlag, 2003.

FELDMAN, AVIGDOR. "The Democratic State Versus the Jewish State: A Space Without Places, Time Without Continuity." *Iyunei Mishpat* 17 (1995): 717–25.

FELLMETH, A. X. "Feminism and International Law: Theory, Methodology, and Substantive Reform." *Human Rights Quarterly* 22, 3 (2000): 658–733.

FELNER, EITAN. "Quand Israël justifie l'injustifiable." *Le Monde*, December 11, 1998.

FELNER, EITAN. *A Policy of Discrimination: Expropriation of Lands, Planning and Building in East Jerusalem*. Jerusalem: B'Tselem, 1997.

FENSTER, TOVI (ed.). *Gender, Planning and Human Rights*. London and New York: Routledge, 1999.

FINKERFELD, A. (ed.). *36 Who Fell in the Hebron Hills While Coming to the Aid of Gush Ezion on the Fifth Day of Shvat 5708*. Jerusalem: Rubin Mass Publishers, 1998.

FREEMAN, M. *Human Rights: An Interdisciplinary Approach*. Malden, MA: Blackwell, 2002.

FREEMAN, M. A. "Fifty Years of Development of the Concept and Contents of Human Rights." In P. Baehr, C. Flinterman, and M. Senders (eds.), *Innovation and Inspiration: Fifty Years of the Universal Declaration of Human Rights*. Amsterdam: Royal Netherlands Academy of Arts and Sciences, 1999, pp. 27–47.

GAVISON, RUTH, AND HAGAI SHANIDOR (eds.). *Human and Civil Rights in Israel: A Reader*. Jerusalem: Association for Civil Rights in Israel, 1991.

GAVISON, RUTH. *Human Rights in Israel*. Tel Aviv: Ministry of Defense, 1994.

GILLIGAN, CAROL. *In a Different Voice: Psychological Theory and Women's Development*. Cambridge, MA: Harvard University Press, 1982.

GOLAN, DAPHNA. *Detained Without Trial: Administrative Detention in the Occupied Territories Since the Beginning of the Intifada*. Jerusalem: B'Tselem, 1992.

GOLAN, DAPHNA. "A Letter to an American Friend." In Deena Hurwitz (ed.), *Walking the Red Line: Israelis in Search of Justice for Palestine*. Philadelphia: New Society Publishers, 1992.

GOLAN, DAPHNA. "Between Universalism and Particularism: The 'Border' in Israeli Discourse." In V. Y. Mudimbe (ed.), *Nations, Identities, Cultures*. Durham: Duke University Press, 1996.

GOLAN, DAPHNA. "Next Year in Jerusalem." In V. Y. Mudimbe (ed.), *Diaspora and Immigration*. Durham: Duke University Press, 1999.

GOLAN, DAPHNA. "Separation, Normalization and Occupation: The Challenges of the Jerusalem Link—A Women's Joint Venture for Peace." *Palestine-Israel Journal* 2, 2 (1995).

GOLAN, DAPHNA. "What Is a Feminist Agenda?" *Palestine-Israel Journal* 2, 3 (1995).

GOLAN, DAPHNA. *Banned Books and Authors*. Jerusalem: B'Tselem, 1989.

GOLAN, DAPHNA. *Inequality and Arab Education*. Jerusalem: Ministry of Education, 2001.

GOLAN, DAPHNA. *Detained Without Trial: Administrative Detention in the Occupied Territories*. Jerusalem: B'Tselem, 1992.

GOLAN, DAPHNA. *Inventing Shaka: Construction and Reconstruction of Zulu History*. Boulder: Lynne Rienner Press, 1995.

GOLAN, GALIA, AND ZAHIRA KAMAL. "Bridging the Abyss: A Palestinian-Israeli Women's Dialogue." In Harold Saunders (ed.), *A Public Peace Process: Sustained Dialogue to Transform Racial and Ethnic Conflicts*. New York: St. Martin's, 1999.

GOLAN-AGNON, DAPHNA. *Inequality in Education*. Tel Aviv: Babel, 2004.

GORDON, NEVE, AND RUCHAMA MARTON. *Torture: Human Rights, Medical Ethics and the Case of Israel*. London: Zed Press, 1995.

HADLAND, ADRIAN, AND JOVIAL RANTAO. *The Life and Times of Thabo Mbeki*. Rivonia: Zebra Press, 1999.

HARDING, SANDRA (ed.). *Feminism and Methodology*. Bloomington: Indiana University Press, 1987.

HAREUVENI, EYAL. "Welcome to the Third World." *Kol Hair*, April 16, 1999.

HASS, AMIRA. *Drinking the Seas of Gaza*. Tel Aviv: Kibbutz Hameuhad, Hasifriya Hahadasha, 1996.

HODGKIN, ELIZABETH. "Middle East Program, Public Comments in a Briefing About The High Court Case." Amnesty International, 1999.

HOFFMAN, ANAT. "Monologue of a Jerusalem Councilor." *Palestine-Israel Journal* 2, 2 (1995).

HURWITZ, DEENA (ed.). *Walking the Red Line: Israelis in Search of Justice for Palestine*. Philadelphia: New Society Publishers, 1992.

JABAREEN, YUSUF. "On the Oppression of Identities in the Name of Civil Equality," *Adalah's Review* 1 (1999): 26–28.

JOHNSON, SHAUN. *Strange Days Indeed: South Africa from Insurrection to Post-Election*. Foreword by Nelson Mandela. London: Bantam Books, 1994.

JOHNSTONE F. A. *Class, Race and Gold: A Study of Class Relations and Racial Discrimination in South Africa*. London: Routledge, Kegan Paul, 1976.

JUDICIAL AUTHORITY, STATE OF ISRAEL. "Abstract of the Judgment Concerning the Interrogations Methods Implied by the GSS." Available at http://www. court.gov.il/mishpat/html/en/system/index.html.

KAHN, SORREL, AND YAAKOV YELINEK. "Discrimination Against the Non-Jewish Sector in the Allocation of Educational Resources: A Quantitative Estimate and the Implications of Its Rectification." Ministry of Education, 2000.

KAMINER, REUVEN. *The Politics of Protest: The Israeli Peace Movement and the Palestinian Intifada*. Brighton, UK: Sussex Academic Press, 1996.

KAMINKER, SARA. "Who Really Needs Har Homa? Housing for Palestinians in East Jerusalem." *Journal of Palestine Studies* 26, 4 (1997). Reprinted in A. Badran, D. Golan, and J. Persekian (eds.), *Sharing Jerusalem*. Jerusalem: Jerusalem Link, 1999.

KHALIDI, WALID. *All That Remains: The Palestinian Villages Occupied and Depopulated by Israel in 1948*. Beirut: Institute for Palestine Studies, 1992.

KINCAID, JAMAICA. *A Small Place*. New York: Penguin, 1988.

KREMNITZER, M. "The Landau Commission Report—Was the Security Service Subordinated to the Law, or the Law to the 'Needs' of the Security Service?" *Israel Law Review* 23, 2–3 (1989).

KRETZMER, DAVID. *The Occupation of Justice: The Supreme Court of Israel and the Occupied Territories*. Albany: State University of New York Press, 2002.

KRETZMER, DAVID. "High Court Criticism of the Demolition and Sealing of Houses in the Territories." *The Klinghoffer Book on Public Law*. Jerusalem: Faculty of Law at the Hebrew University of Jerusalem, 1993.

KROG, ANTJIE. *Country of My Skull*. Johannesburg: Random House, 1998.

KUNNEMANN, ROLF. "A Coherent Approach to Human Rights." *17 Human Rights Quarterly* 323 (1995).

LANDAU REPORT. *Report of the Commission of Inquiry into the Interrogation Methods of the General Security Services Regarding Hostile Terror Activity*. Jerusalem: October 1987.

LAPIDOT, RUTH. "The Right of Return in International Law with Special Reference to the Palestinian Refugees." *Dapei Reka* 10 (1993).

LAVI, AVIV. "The Terror of the GSS." *Ha'aretz*, August 20, 1999.

LESSING, DORIS. *The Golden Notebook*. London: Flamingo, 1993.

LEVY, GIDEON. "The Shackled Child." *Ha'aretz*, October 18, 1996.

MALAN, R. *My Traitor's Heart*. London: Vintage, 1991.

MAYER, TAMAR (ed.). *Women and the Israeli Occupation: The Politics of Change*. New York: Routledge, 1994.

MEMMI, A. *The Colonizer and the Colonized*. Boston: Beacon Press, 1965.

MORRIS, BENNY. "On Ethnic Cleansing." *New Left Review* 26 (2004). First published as "Survival of the Fittest," *Ha'aretz*, January 8, 2004.

MUDIMBE, V. Y. (ed.). *Diaspora and Immigration*. Durham: Duke University Press, 1999.

MUSSALLAM, SAMI. "The Attack on Orient House and Other Palestinian Institutions in Jerusalem." In *The Struggle for Jerusalem*. Jerusalem: PASSIA, 1996.

O'MEARA, DAN. *Forty Lost Years: The Apartheid State and the Politics of the National Party 1948–1999*. Randburg: Ravan Press, 1996.

PACHECO, ALLEGRA. "Response on High Court and Torture." *News from Within* 13 (1998).

PACHECO, ALLEGRA. *The Case Against Torture in Israel: A Compilation of Petitions, Briefs and Other Documents Submitted to the Israeli High Court of Justice*. Jerusalem: The Public Committee Against Torture in Israel, 1999.

PASSIA. *Jerusalem Documents*. Jerusalem: Palestinian Academic Society for the Study of International Affairs, 1996.

PERSEKIAN, JACK (ed.). *Exposure Jerusalem*. Jerusalem: Al-Ma'mal 2001.

PETERSON, V. S., AND L. PARISI. "Are Women Human? It's Not an Academic Question." In T. Evans (ed.). *Human Rights Fifty Years On: A Reappraisal*. Manchester: Manchester University Press, 1998, pp. 132–60.

PUBLIC COMMITTEE AGAINST TORTURE. Emergency Project, September-October 2000 riots.

RIEFF, DAVID. "The Precarious Triumph of Human Rights." *The New York Times Magazine*, August 8, 1999.

RODLEY, NIGEL. "The Prohibition of Torture and How to Make It Effective." *Proceedings of Israel and International Human Rights Law: The Issue of Torture*. Jerusalem: Magna Press, 1998.

ROSENBLUM, DORON. *The Tragedy of Israeliness*. Tel Aviv: Am Oved, 1996.

RUBINSTEIN, DANNY. *The Embrace of the Fig: The Palestinian "Right of Return."* Jerusalem: Keter, 1990.

SAID, EDWARD W. *Out of Place: A Memoir*. New York: Alfred A. Knopf, 1999.

SAID, EDWARD W. *Peace and Its Discontents: Essays on Palestine in the Middle East Peace Process*. New York: Vintage Books, 1996.

SAMPSON, ANTHONY. *Mandela: The Authorized Biography*. New York: Alfred A. Knopf, 1999.

SASON-LEVY, ORNA. *Consciousness of Revolutionaries, Identity of Conformists: The 21st Year Protest Movement*. Theoretical Studies no. 1. Jerusalem: Schein Center, Hebrew University, 1995.

SCHWAB, P., AND A. POLLIS. "Globalization's Impact on Human Rights." In A. Pollis and P. Schwab (eds.), *Human Rights: New Perspectives, New Realities*. Boulder, CO: Lynne Rienner, 2000, pp. 209–23.

SEEKINGS, JEREMY. *The UDF: A History of the United Democratic Front in South Africa 1983–1991*. Cape Town: David Philip, 2000.

SEGEV, TOM. *Elvis in Jerusalem: Post-Zionism and the Americanization of Israel*. New York: Metropolitan Books, 2001.

SHAMGAR, MEIR. "The Observance of International Law in the Administrative Territories." *Israeli Yearbook of Human Rights* 1 (1971): 262–77.

SHAMIR, RONEN. "Landmark Cases and the Reproduction of Legitimacy: The Case of Israel's High Court of Justice." *Law and Society Review* 24 (1990).

SHARFMAN, DAPHNA. *Living Without a Constitution: Civil Rights in Israel*. Armonk, NY: M. E. Sharpe, 1993.

SHARONI, SIMONA. *Gender and the Israeli-Palestinian Conflict: The Politics of Women's Resistance*. Syracuse: Syracuse University Press, 1995.

SHAVIT, ARI. "12 Days on the Coast of Gaza." *Ha'aretz*, May 3, 1991.

SHEHADEH, RAJA. *Strangers in the House: Coming of Age in Occupied Palestine*. London: Profile Books, 2002.

SIVAN, EYAL (director). *Yizkor: Slaves to Memory* (1992).

SPARKS, ALLISTER. *The Mind of South Africa: The Story of the Rise and Fall of Apartheid*. London: Mandarin Paperbacks, 1990.

"Symposium on the Report of the Commission of Inquiry into the Methods of the Investigation of the General Security Service Regarding Hostile Terrorist Activity." *Israel Law Review* 23, 2–3 (1989).

TAMARI, SALIM. *Jerusalem 1948: The Arab Neighborhoods and Their Fate in the War*. Jerusalem: Institute of Jerusalem Studies, 1999.

VAN ROOYEN. JOHANN. *Hard Right: The New White Power in South Africa*. London and New York: I. B. Tauris, 1994.

WALDMEIR, PATTI. *Anatomy of a Miracle: The End of Apartheid and the Birth of a New South Africa*. New Brunswick, NJ: Rutgers University Press, 1998.

YIFTACHEL, OREN. *Ethnic Frontiers and Peripheries: Landscapes of Development and Inequality in Israel*. Boulder, CO: Westview Press, 1996.

YIFTACHEL, OREN. *On Geography and the Nation-State*. Beer Sheva: Ben-Gurion University of the Negev Press, 1999.

YUVAL-DAVIS, NIRA. *Gender and Nation*. London: Sage Publications, 1997.

ZALMONA, YIGAL. "East! East? On the East in Israeli Art." In *Eastwards: Orientalism in the State of Israel*. Jerusalem: Israel Museum, 1998.

ZIV, NETA. "Communities Lawyers, and Legal Strategies for Social Change." *Adalah's Review* 2 (2000): 34–38.

ZREIK, RAEF. "The Unbearable Lightness of Enlightenment." *Adalah's Review* 1 (1999): 30–33.

ORGANIZATIONS MENTIONED IN THE BOOK

Adalah—The Legal Center for Arab Minority Rights in Israel
P.O. Box 510
Shafa'amr 20200
www.adalah.org

Al-Ma'mal Foundation for Contemporary Art
The New Gate, Old City
P.O. Box 14644
Jerusalem 91145
www.almamalfoundation.org

The Alternative Information Center
P.O. Box 31417
Jerusalem 91313
www.alternativenews.org

The Association for Civil Rights in Israel
P.O. Box 35401
Jerusalem 91352
www.acri.org.il

Bat Shalom
43 Emek Refaim Street
P.O. Box 8083
Jerusalem 91080
www.batshalom.org

BIMKOM—Planners for Planning Rights
36 Azza Street
Jerusalem 92382
www.bimkom.org

B'Tselem—The Israeli Information Center for Human Rights in the Occupied Territories
8 Hataasiya Street
Jerusalem 93420
www.btselem.org

Courage to Refuse
P.O. Box 16238
Tel Aviv 61161
www.seruv.org

HaMoked — Center for the Defence of the Individual
4 Abu Ubeida Street
Jerusalem 97200
www.hamoked.org.il

The Israeli Coalition Against House Demolition
P.O. Box 2030
Jerusalem 91020
www.icahd.org

The Jerusalem Center for Women
Beit Hanina, Dahiet Al-Barid
Al Hirbawi Building, 4th floor
P.O. Box 51630
East Jerusalem
www.j-c-w.org

Kav La'Oved — The Workers' Hotline
P.O. Box 2319
Tel Aviv 61022
www.kavlaoved.org.il

Machsom Watch — Women for Human Rights
c/o Bat Shalom
P.O. Box 8083
Jerusalem 91080
www.machsomwatch.org

New Profile
P.O. Box 48005
Tel Aviv 61480
www.newprofile.org

The Palestinian Human Rights Monitoring Group
P.O. Box 19918
East Jerusalem 91198
www.phrmg.org

Physicians for Human Rights — Israel
52 Golomb Street
Tel Aviv 66171
www.phr.org.il

The Public Committee Against Torture in Israel
P.O. Box 4634
Jerusalem 91046
www.stoptorture.org.il

Rabbis for Human Rights
42 Aza Street
Jerusalem 92384
www.rhr.israel.net

Refusers Parents' Forum
P.O. Box 9013
Jerusalem 91090
www.refuz.org.il

Taayush — Arab-Jewish Partnership
33 Bernstein-Cohen Street
Ramat Hasharon 47213
www.taayush.org

Yesh Gvul
P.O. Box 6953
Jerusalem 91068
www.yeshgvul.org